brazil

a cook's tour **christopher idone**

brazil

a cook's tour **christopher idone**

O Passarinho Voa Para Comer

(Little Birds Fly to Eat)
—A saying mentioned in passing to
friends when one has discovered a little
restaurant or country inn that prepares an
especially good table

First published in Great Britain in 1995 by
PAVILION BOOKS LIMITED
26 Upper Ground, London SE1 9PD

Originally published in 1995 by
Clarkson N. Potter, Inc.
201 East 50th Street
New York, New York 10022

Copyright © 1995 by Christopher Idone
Photographs copyright © 1995 by Christopher Idone

Cosmopolitan South America Map © 1995 by Rand McNally,
R.L. 95-S-57, jacket and pages 2, 54, 90, 142, 170

Design by Elizabeth Van Itallie
Jacket designed by The Bridgewater Book Company Limited/Terry Jeavons

A CIP catalogue record for this book is available from the British Library.

ISBN 1 85793 728 7

Printed and bound in China

2 4 6 8 10 9 7 5 3 1

This book may be ordered by post direct from the publisher.
Please contact the Marketing Department.
But try your bookshop first.

This book is for Libba

contents

acknowledgments

During my visits and travels throughout Brazil I met a host of people who helped me in both plain and grand ways in preparing this book. This generous bunch included friends, home cooks, and restaurant cooks. Some were brilliant and some were simple, but all gave something, and gave with an open hand and honest spirit.

My first thanks are to my Brazilian friends, old and new, who opened their doors and hearts to this project.

In particular I am grateful for the time given and spent with Libba Esteve, Kim Esteve, Cesarina Riso, Dona Lucila Teixera de Barros, and Caito Lanhoso Martins. Without them this book would not have happened. And to a slew of wonderful people I met along this culinary journey who gave encouragement and support, a big thanks and abraço to Hilaria Hedler, Beanie Esteve, Kiminho Esteve, Gillian Fuller, Anita, Hermes, Augusta, Bruno and Jeanete Musatti, Augusto Livio Malzoni, Lynne and Domingos Logulo, Frey Zaragosa, Luiza Strina, Barbara Gancia, Lana Pih Jokel, George and Lulli Esteve, Penny Stewart Granger, Mitzuko and Paulo Bittencourt, Giada and Luiz Misasi, Massimo Ferrari at Masimo, Alexandre Dórea Ribeiro, Robert Blocker, Antonio Peticov, Wesley Duke Lee, Silvana Tinelli, David Zingg, Sig Bergamin, Mariza Calil, Josimar Melo, Ana Elisa Sestini, Nesia Pope, Luis Paulo Barbosa, Edinho at Manaca, Stella Mattoso, Lucilla Assunçao and John Wood, Clifford Ming-Teh Li, Thomas Souto Correa, Chagas at Rodeio, Jupira Angela de Jesus, Laura Bucovich, Fatima Canto, Yara Pedrosa, Daniela and Ze Lourenco, Jonas Felipe de Souza, Luiz Rosa, Marize, José Deusimar at Villa Riso, Leonel Kaz, Marcio Montarroyos, Luiz Correa de Araujo, Sergio, Carmen and Bernarda Bernardes, Nalita and Gerard Le Clerie, Renata de Champs, João Celso de Toledo, Don João de Orleans e Bragança, Eduardo and Carmen Alvarez, Luiz Alfredo Abreu Filho, Gian and Lucila Calvi, Sergio Bernardes Filho, Celina Cortes, Lauretta Marie Joseph, Denise Pinto, Carmen Sampaio at Candido, Carlos Alberto de Moraes, Marcos Antonio de Oliveira Serpa, Negao, Mario, Francisco Lima, João Eugenio and Estela Pacheco e Chaves, Godje and Ronaldo Camargo at Arco, Iris, Guara Rodriques, Sandra Marques Leite, Luiz Carlos Brum de Paula, Louis Carlos Zart, Pedro Correa de Araujo at Solar das Lajes, Sylvana, José Alberto and Anna Neumen, John and Anna Maria

Parsons, Cida Zurlo, Angela Gutierrez, Caito and Angela Martins, José
Luiz Lanhoso Martins Filho, Anna Maria Martin at La em Casa, Altamira,
Chiquinha, Bruno and Lucia Gibson, Ismailino Pinto, Silva, Sra. Palulo
Migueldo Lihano, and Carlos de Saboya, Jr.

I particularly want to thank Nalita Le Clerie for reading my text and
chastising me when my Brazilian/Portuguese translations went haywire.
And to my New York friends who kept tracking my course and made sure
I returned home, a big hug to Linda and Barry Donahue, Rico Puhlmann,
Cheryl Merser, Robert Reynolds, Christine Biddle, Katie Shields, Lee
Schrager, Eugenie Voorhees, Perry Hagopian, Brooks Ogden, James
Steinmeyer, David Easton, Helen McEachrane, Geraldine Stutz, and
Glenn Garelik.

And thanks to Varig, Brazil Airlines for their help and consideration.

At Clarkson Potter I especially wish to thank my editor Katie
Workman for her enthusiasm and loyalty in seeing this book through to
the end, and to Elizabeth Van Itallie for her designs and to Howard
Klein, Jane Treuhaft, Allison Hanes, Maggie Hinders, Camille Smith, Joy
Sikorski, and the rest of the staff, a big thank you.

introduction

I first visited Brazil about a decade ago—a trip I took by accident. It was Christmas and I was to meet some Brazilian friends in France for a holiday of eating and skiing. Europe was always the destination that first came to mind when I planned a major holiday. In spite of a long-standing invitation, visiting Brazil had never really entered my mind. At the last minute, however, plans changed—my friends could not join me in Europe, and I found myself on a plane to Brazil.

Sensitive to my foreignness and inability to speak the Portuguese language, my friends were the best guides and teachers one could hope for. Starting in São Paulo, Brazil's largest city, they entertained me in a style that can best be described as quiet, unpretentious luxury. I was coddled and coaxed at first and then one day pushed out the door to explore Brazil, sometimes with them and sometimes on my own. I visited the beaches along the Atlantic coast between São Paulo and Bahia, where I stayed in an old fisherman's cottage and slept in a hammock under netting that offered some protection

OPPOSITE:
Cold crustaceans with Molho Campanha (Country Sauce)
ABOVE:
Fisherman's Beach at Copacabana

from the bugs, bats, and spiders and bathed in a waterfall up in the sierra. I sipped the nourishing juice of big fat green coconuts for breakfast, discovered the ubiquitous and irresistible bean fritter known as *acarajé,* and dined on grilled fish cooked over the glowing embers of dried-up coconut shells— all of it accompanied by hot malagueta pepper sauce. I drank quantities of juices made from exotic fruits, as well as my share of *cachaça,* a spirit made from distilled sugarcane that could blow your head off, except when weakened with the juice of passion fruit, guava, or limes. I sailed with fishermen on colorful wooden boats with sails made of patched cotton canvas; watched young teenage boys nimbly climb the tall slender trunks of the coconut palm to pluck clusters of nuts drooping like flowers and send them hurtling to the ground. A journey to a cattle ranch in the jungle of the Mato Grosso in the northern part of the country was an all-day trip requiring three planes—each one getting smaller—to cross that great green expanse. The memory of landing on a dirt runway through a cloud of blue butterflies was magic. I was kept on edge by a book on venomous snakes placed next to my bed that featured information on how to treat bites, and instructions from my host as to where to find the refrigerated serum should such an event occur and a request, by the way, to inject it myself so as not to wake the household.

The enormity of the country and the vast green jungle was both invading and consuming. It was like living the films and books I'd seen and read—*Fitzcarraldo, Brazil, One Hundred Years of Solitude*—and eighteen for dinner, every night! Things happen in Brazil that don't happen elsewhere. I'd been told by a Brazilian writer that when a traveler says he has seen some fantastic dream or vision in the wilderness, one does not laugh and make a fool of him.

Brazil is an amalgam of races: native Indian, African, and European. The native Indian culture is still very much alive, its rituals intact, while those of African heritage have blended into the larger cultural scheme. The European influence is predominantly Portuguese and dates back to the "discovery" of Brazil in 1500. The Dutch came and left during the great colonial period, while other immigrants didn't arrive until nearly the end of the nineteenth century, mostly to replace the slave labor force. Germans settled in the colder south; Japanese and Arabs settled in São Paulo, along with a million and a half Italians who migrated to Rio and São Paulo by 1880. Some worked on the sugar, coffee, and cocoa plantations, some labored on farms and ranches, and others moved into commerce; only a few amassed enormous properties and great wealth. United States citizens came too. In a thriving colony called Americana, a couple of hours from São Paulo, one can see pink-freckled, blue-eyed, blond children—descendants of North American Southerners who migrated near the end of the Civil War.

Pockets of foreign influences are apparent all over the place. It isn't odd to visit ranches or small villages scattered along the coast populated with people of any nationality—Japanese, Lebanese, Arab, Chinese. One might encounter a German priest or a red-haired Greek who sells sweets along the roadside—both of them contented in their adopted country. But it is the dominant Portuguese and West African people, their heritage interwoven with that of the native Indians, that keeps this multiethnic fabric together.

Brazil is a paradise whose natural resources are almost boundless. Its rain forests are the lungs of the world—they give its inhabitants the oxygen necessary for the air we breathe; and the country possesses a bounty of food that feeds a nation. If properly organized Brazil could outstrip even the United States agriculturally. Despite the threat of deforestation, it is still a frontier to be compared to the untamed West of the United States more than a century ago.

Once you pass over the equator, that magical line that turns the world upside down so the stars are under your feet and the earth is above your head, you are immediately drawn into an ebullient society of sensuous people. There is great poverty to be sure, but if one is to be poor, far better to have the shelter of a covering of palm leaves and to be in reach of a coconut or banana tree and a tangling of passion fruit vines.

In tropical countries man can live off the abundance of nature with little effort. The Brazilian Indian was basically nomadic, and the idea of farming anything more than a few starch crops was of little interest to him. He hunted and fished, and the river's edge supplied him with edible vegetation and fruits that were nature's spontaneous gifts. The native banana, cashew, papaya, and pineapple, as well as the many palm fruits, supplied him with food and drink. His idea of cultivating the land was to burn a patch of forest, in a process known as *coivara,* and plant the few roots and squashes needed to augment his diet. For millennia he planted mandioca (what we usually call cassava), a glutinous root used as we would the potato. From it he derived tapioca and *farofa de mandioca*—a finely ground meal, toasted dry. Today it is still used as the Brazilians' basic "flour," or toasted in oil or butter and sprinkled as a condiment over rice, beans, meat, and fish. It is the starch replacement for bread. No Brazilian table is without it.

The Portuguese knowledge of seeds and roots and agricultural lore came from the Indian women who cooked, cleaned, and labored in these burned patches. The Indian male hunted and made war with neighboring tribes. But there is a fraternity between animals and these native peoples that is

almost lyrical. Even today the Amazonian Indian makes no distinction between man and animal; intellectually and spiritually they are on the same level. They share their homes with parrots, toucans, and songbirds, monkeys and even snakes, kept for their own pleasure, and that pleasure has infected many urban Brazilians, too. In the jungle I watched a little child share his evening supper with his monkey—allowing the pet to lick his fingers and the dribble that fell onto his chin.

From the beginning of Brazil's discovery by Europeans the native Indian refused to adapt to the new ways. In no time the Portuguese were transporting boatloads of West Africans, virtual villages and small nations at a time, to labor in the cocoa, coffee, and sugar plantations that were rapidly flourishing.

The Portuguese and the West Africans gradually assimilated each other's customs, styles, and values, and the Portuguese have been able, better than any other people of predominantly European origin, to adapt their civilization to the tropics. There is an almost free blending of different cultures that can be seen in predilections as diverse as the European craze for soccer, the taste for French pastry, the love of rice from China, the displays of fireworks from the Orient, terra-cotta roofs and glazed tiles from the Mediterranean, and the toothpick, which is pure Portuguese.

If the Portuguese were the dominant force in the development of Brazil, the Africans also had great influence. The majestic and aristocratic West

Africans brought their native *dendê* palm to produce palm oil, a rich and flavorful oil that dominates cooking in the state of Bahia. In addition, they brought the malagueta pepper, the tiniest and hottest of all cultivated peppers, that would become a common seasoning and condiment on every table in Brazil. They planted their native okra, rice, pumpkin, watermelon, and tamarind, which added another dimension to modern Brazilian cooking. And they brought a taste for sweets. In Bahia the proud elegant mulata still dress in turban, shawl, layers of filmy cotton skirts, ornaments, and heeled slippers, displaying a local grace unrivaled by modern fashion. They rest their trays on wooden stands about the streets of Salvador and spread fresh banana leaves or fringed linen towels as white as altar cloths on top. Neatly displayed are the luscious *cocadas* made of sweetened coconut, *paçoca* (a creamy brittle of cashew or peanuts), tapioca sticks, cakes, and tarts. Every few blocks one falls upon the *doce* (sweets) vendor, and these confections are hard to resist.

That first trip was a discovery of foods both foreign and familiar. What I ate on the beaches was in many ways a reminder of the pleasure I have when cooking a meal in the country when the fish is so fresh and all the fruits and vegetables that come from the local farm markets are picked that day. Like all great ingredients, these foods needed little embellishment.

Brazilian women love to cook, and, in fact, many have pursued it as a career since the days of the great plantation houses of the eighteenth century. Often it is a woman at the stove in the many small restaurants in the big cities, as well as country inns and little beach town eateries. Brazilian home food is still based on recipes that have been handed down from generation to generation. Some ingredients may seem strange, some blissfully familiar to the American palate, resulting in lusty food that appeals to all the senses.

The dishes I present here were picked not just because they were there or new to me but rather because they excite me and best exemplify what Brazilians prepare for themselves and their guests at home.

Each time I return to Brazil my visits become longer. This book is a journal of those trips, with recipes and vignettes about the people I met along the way. It is meant to echo the spontaneity and joy of the Brazilian people, who go about their daily chores to the inner beat of a samba—the women who sway through the streets, the soccer players who dance with the ball, the waiter who sambas through a crowded restaurant with a tray for a partner, and the cook who sings and loves to please.

glossary

Abacate (AVOCADO)

Fruit of an American tree of tropical and subtropical regions. Pear shaped, it can weigh as much as two pounds. Its skin can be smooth or rough and range from light or dark green to deep blackish-purple. It is easily peeled by quartering the fruit with a paring knife and pulling the skin off. The flesh of the ripe fruit is dull creamy yellow, smooth but firm. Pick one that yields without feeling mushy. A hard, unripe avocado will ripen at room temperature in a tightly closed paper bag in two or three days. If it's not used immediately, refrigerate it for up to two days. Brazilians steep the leaves of the avocado plant in boiling water and drink the liquid as a diuretic.

Abacaxi (PINEAPPLE)

Brazilian Tupi Indian name for pineapple, of which there are many varieties, both wild and cultivated, that vary in size from standard to miniature. Exceptionally sweet and flavorful, the pineapple is indigenous to Brazil. It is to Brazil what the apple is to the United States.

Abóbara (PUMPKIN)

Brazilian pumpkin is less dense and fibrous than our jack-o'-lantern types. Substitute West Indian or Hubbard squash for the closest approximation. The French Rouge d'Étampes, called the Cinderella pumpkin, flat on top and bottom with deep pronounced lobes, makes an excellent substitute, too.

Acarajé

A fritter made from a batter of mashed beans called fradinho, which are similar to black-eyed peas, surrounding whole dried shrimp. Fried in dendê oil, these puffed-up fritters are drained, cut open, and filled with a spicy sauce of hot malagueta chili peppers, ground dried shrimp, onions, ginger, and dendê oil. The same dish is known as *abara* when wrapped in banana leaves and steamed.

Avocado

(*See* Abacate)

Bacalhau

Salted air-dried cod preserved with skin and bones. This Portuguese import has been popular in Brazil for four centuries. The recent high cost has put it in the luxury category. Popular dishes containing bacalhão include tomato- and pepper-based stews, soufflés, puddings, egg dishes, and fried codfish balls.

Banana

The fruit of a large tree-shaped tropical herb most likely indigenous to India. Ripe bananas have yellow skins, which are mottled with black when fully ripe, and sweet pulp. They are eaten uncooked when ripe, but in their unripe green stage they can be cooked as a vegetable.

Banana de agua, ladyfinger bananas, are grown throughout the West Indies and South America. They are about five inches long, with pale, thin skin. They are eaten raw but are the banana of choice when fried to accompany various meat and fish dishes.

A couple of other popular varieties include red bananas and apple bananas with pale yellow skin, which are very sweet with a slight acid taste and are excellent for cooking when green. These cook up lighter and crispier than plantains.

Banana leaves

The leaves from a banana plant grow up to ten feet long and two feet wide. They are wilted over a stove (preferably a gas flame) by swishing them back and forth quickly until the oils begin to surface and the leaf turns from vibrant green to dark green. The central rib is cut out, and the leaf is cut into square or rectangular pieces to hold various stuffings of vegetable, meat, and fish purees or wrapped around fish or fowl for steaming or grilling. They are sold in packets at ethnic food emporiums or bought at flower markets. Parchment paper will work as a substitute, though it will give neither the same flavor nor the aroma.

Batidas

Cocktails of fresh fruit juices served over ice with the optional addition of cachaça, vodka, or rum.

Beans (FEIJÃO)

Most Brazilian bean recipes are made with black beans, brown beans, or dark beans. Black beans—feijão negro—are preferred in the states of Rio de Janeiro, Bahia, and Pernambuco. Paler beans are preferred in the south and the southern states, including São Paulo. Minas Gerais has a preference for medium-dark brown beans, known as feijão mulatinha, or mulatto beans, though any of these beans could appear anywhere in the country. Black-eyed peas are used in recipes of Afro-Brazilian influence. Use turtle beans when a recipe calls for black beans. When brown beans are required, cranberry beans, navy beans, or white beans may be used. Kidney beans are virtually never used. Lentils are popular in salads and Middle Eastern dishes that have become part of the Brazilian repertoire.

The cooking time for dry beans can vary. Packaged beans, though they do have a shelf life of a year or more, are not always fresh. It is best to buy beans at ethnic markets or markets specializing in fresh dry beans. Just squeeze them between your fingers, and you will notice a slight resiliency.

- **Black beans (turtle beans)**—small, slightly flat with a tiny white dot

- **Black-eyed peas (cowpeas)**—small to medium, flat with a black spot

- **Navy beans**—small, round, white

- **Pinto beans (cranberry beans)**—medium, oval, light mottled pink to cranberry color, the best substitution for brown beans

Breadfruit

(*See* Fruta de pão)

Cachaça

Sometimes called aguardente de cana or pinga, this is a distilled white alcohol made from sugarcane. Its distinctive flavor ranges from harsh and bitter to mellow and creamy. It is sometimes produced in backyard stills, the equivalent of our moonshine, and on the flip side "estate-bottled" aged cachaça is the counterpart of aged brandies. The liquor can be served neat, mixed with fruit juices in drinks called batidas, and made into caipirinha cocktails. It is also used in marinades and stews, as we would use wine or beer.

Caipirinha

The literal translation is "little country hick," and it is the fond nickname for Brazil's national drink, made with mulled lime sections, sugar, ice, and cachaça. Made with vodka instead of cachaça, it is called a caipiroska.

Caju (CASHEW APPLE)

This bright yellow-and-red-flushed kidney-shaped fruit grows about three to four inches long, with a gray-brown kernel attached to the base. The kernel, known as the cashew nut, or castanha-de-caju, is poisonous when raw and only edible after roasting. The flesh of the fruit is tart-sweet, exotic, and perfumy. It is usually pureed and used for drinks, ices, and fruit puddings. The roasted nut appears throughout Brazil, and it is used especially in many Bahian dishes.

Camarão seco (DRIED SHRIMP)

Along the coast of Bahia, fishermen mix their shrimp catch with a little dendê oil and dry them in the scorching sun. They are usually ground and used especially in Bahian cooking to add flavor and as a thickening agent. Some excellent dried shrimp are available to us here at West Indian, African, and Asian markets. Small packaged varieties tend to be hard as stone and more salty than the large loose varieties. If using the packaged variety it's best to soak them in warm water for about a half hour, or until they give slightly, before preparing the dish. See page 97 for making your own.

Canja

A plain chicken soup. A richer variation includes chicken, rice, vegetables, and sausages.

Carambola (STAR FRUIT)

This fruit usually ranges from four to six inches in diameter and is pale green to sunny yellow. The ovoid-shaped fruit has waxy skin with four to six pronounced longitudinal ribs. When cut across, the fruit is star shaped, hence its name. The flesh is crisp, juicy, aromatic, and can be very acidic. When the fruit is yellow and the ribs are tinged brown, it is at its best. It is used in drinks, jams, ices, and fruit salads, as well as some savory dishes.

Caranguejo

(*See* Crab)

Carne seca

Also carne de sol, charque (pronounced "sharky"). Salted jerked beef that is air or sun dried. Sold in small slabs about an inch and a half thick, it comes in several varieties and must be reconstituted and desalted before cooking. It retains its agreeable chewy texture and salty flavor. It is available in ethnic markets specializing in Latin American foods. Chipped beef or corned beef can be substituted in some recipes.

Caruru (OKRA)

In Bahia this is also the term for a dish of prawns, okra, and cilantro. Throughout the rest of the country okra is usually referred to as *quiabo*.

Churrasco (BARBECUE)

Popular throughout all of Brazil, the authentic churrasco is indigenous to the state of Rio Grande do Sul (in the southern part of the country, south of São Paulo), where the gaucho prepares his evening meal on an open fire in the field. At the popular churrascarias (restaurants serving grilled meats) of São Paulo and Rio, roasted hunks of beef on a spit are served and sliced by a battery of waiters touring the room. Then skewers of ribs, steaks of every cut, kabobs of every part of the chicken, are presented one after the other. To accompany the meats, mammoth help-yourself salad bars offer a wide variety of cold vegetables and greens. The meal ends with quantities of fresh fruit that, they say, cancels out the fat.

Ciriguela

A fruit similar in size and color to the kumquat, but with a pit the size of a lychee nut. Thin, slightly citric skin encases aromatic juicy pulp surrounding a shiny dark seed. It ripens in December before the rains.

Côco (COCONUT)

Fruit of a species of palm that thrives in the tropics. It can be found green (côco verde) or mature (côco seco). The green coconut is usually found at roadside stands, and first its refreshing sweet water is drunk, then it is hacked open, and the white tender pulp is eaten.

The côco seco, or ripe coconut, is the familiar brown husked, hairy, matted nut found in most markets. It should be shaken before purchasing to make sure the interior is filled with water. The transparent liquid is drained out after piercing the eyes of the nut with a sharp pick or nail. It is then cracked open, which is easiest to do with the back of a large chopping knife, holding the handle firmly in one hand and the coconut in the palm of the other. Forcefully hit the middle of the coconut with the knife three times—ta-ta-TA—in one place and continue rhythmically hitting and turning the coconut until you have hit the entire circumference. The shell should open up easily. The white, slightly sweet, firm meat is removed from the outer shell and grated. Most recipes call for coconut milk, which is extracted by adding hot, but not boiling, water to the grated coconut and squeezing the liquid out through a clean kitchen cloth. The process is repeated twice more, and the buttery cream will float to the top just like cream will float to the top of milk. The milk is used extensively in Afro-Brazilian cooking.

Coentro (CILANTRO)

Also called coriander and Chinese parsley. A parsleylike leafed herb with a piquant, citrusy flavor. This delicate herb keeps only a day or two under refrigeration. Coriander seeds are rarely used in Brazilian cooking, and fresh cilantro is used *only* to season fish dishes, nothing else.

Conjiquinha (DRIED CORN)

Corn preserved by an Indian process similar to the American Indian samp. The grains are hard and gritty but are ground as fine as couscous.

Couve (KALE)

Considered one of the most nutritious greens, rich in potassium, calcium, and iron, vitamins A and C, and high in fiber. Early spring crops are milder and preferable. The vegetable is tougher and stronger tasting when harvested in fall and winter. A direct influence from the Portuguese, the Brazilian variety is more tender and slightly sweet. If large, fibrous tough leaves are all that is available, substitute chard, large-leaf spinach, or collard greens. The leaf is usually cut into fine ribbons and briefly sautéed, and is a traditional accompaniment to feijoada, tutu à Mineira, roasts, and grilled meats.

Cozido

A stew using many kinds of meat, marrow bones, and vegetables poached in broth and served with a piquant sauce of herbs and peppers. This Portuguese-based dish is similar to the French pot-au-feu and bollito misto of Italy.

Crab

There are two types of crabs used in Brazilian cookery: siri, a salt-water hard-shell crab similar to but smaller than our eastern shore blue crab, and caranguejo, or land crab. Both are considered delicacies. The caranguejo is a white crab usually found on the muddy banks of rivers and in the wetlands of Florida, Texas, parts of the Caribbean, and Brazil. The bulbous carapace measures about four inches across, and the crab stands high on its pincers and is almost always camouflaged in mud. Highly prized for its sweet meat, it is not unlike the blue sea crab. Substitutes are blue crab and canned pasteurized crabmeat.

Cuscuz

The Brazilian variation of the Moorish-Portuguese couscous made with shrimp or chicken and vegetables, or simply with vegetables, and always with hearts of palm. In place of the traditional semolina, this cuscuz is based on farinha de mandioca (manioc flour). All the ingredients in the dish are mixed together, then steamed.

Dendê oil

Oil from the dendê palm tree. Brought to Bahia by West African slaves, this palm tree is perhaps the only species of palm not indigenous to Brazil. The oil is made from the nuts of the tree and used to flavor dishes and to fry certain foods in Afro-Bahian cooking. Dendê has a high saturated-fat content, which has resulted in a fair amount of controversy in nutritional circles in the United States. The flavor of dendê comes out when heated, and it is essential for reproducing authentic Afro-Brazilian dishes. The recipes in this book call for small amounts of the oil, or a combination of dendê and another polyunsaturated oil. West Indian annatto-seed oil can be substituted, or annatto seeds can be steeped in polyunsaturated oil for twelve hours or more to make your own annatto-seed oil. The result, however, will be a different flavor. This substitute is given basically to achieve the crimson color so typical of Afro-Bahian dishes. Brazilian dendê is lighter and more delicate than its West Indian and African counterpart. Dendê oil is available at Brazilian and some Latin American markets or by mail order. (*See* Sources)

Doce

The word most often used to refer to a sweet or dessert.

Empada, pastel

Small pastries made with any combination of shrimp, chicken, ground meats, vegetables, hearts of palm, cheese, and olives. These hors d'oeuvres are the prelude to all festive meals and are sold as snacks from street stands and along the beaches of Brazil. Empadas are baked and pastels are fried.

Farofa

The name of the dish made from finely ground meal of the manioc root (cassava), similar to a crude flour, but not as fine as cornmeal or semolina, that has been toasted in a dry skillet or with olive oil, dendê oil, or butter. It is sprinkled over rice, beans, meat, chicken, and fish dishes. Other additives include raisins, nuts, olives, carrots, and parsley. (*See also* Mandioca)

Feijão

Dry and fresh beans. (*See* Beans)

Feijoada

Feijoada is the child of Brazilian slavery. The dish evolved from a pot of black beans boiled up with all the lesser bits of the pig. It eventually developed into an elaborate stew built around the beans cooked with assorted meats, smoked pork, sausages, and so on. The meal is served in courses, commencing with the bean liquid, or soup, followed by separate platters of beans, meats, rice, shredded kale, and accompanied by citric fruits, hot peppers, and toasted farofa, which are mixed as the diner wishes at the table. The dish is as sophisticated as a good French cassoulet.

Fruta de conde

The "count's fruit," a relative of the cherimoya and the sweetsop, or sugar apple. This large pinecone-like fruit is considered one of the luxury fruits of Brazil. Usually sold at the peak of ripeness, the fruit is pulled open to reveal a custard-like filling of creamy, ivory-colored, rich sweet pulp surrounding lacquered, dark watermelon-sized seeds. Because of the many seeds, the fruit is best eaten straight, scooped out with a spoon. However, the pulp can be used for purees, ices, and puddings once the seeds are removed.

Fruta de pão (BREADFRUIT)

A magnificent tall tree reaching seventy-five feet in height produces a white gummy latex from trunk to branches and large lime-green globes, weighing up to eight pounds. The fruit must be picked just as it turns from bright green to a slightly lime-yellow hue. The pulp is thick, yellow, perfumy, and slightly sweet. Breadfruit must first be peeled, and it can then be fried, baked, or boiled. Boiled breadfruit is a favorite breakfast food throughout Brazil. The unpeeled fruit is plunged into boiling water for twenty minutes or so, then opened, and the pulp mashed with butter and salt and a little sugar. Introduced in the early nineteenth century from Cayenne (in French Guiana), it has always been looked down on as the "poor man's bread."

Guarana

The name, pronounced "wa-RAN-na," comes from the Amazonian Tupi Indians. The fresh fruit is made into sparkling or flat bottled juice that hints of apple juice or sometimes cream soda, depending on the manufacturer. The seeds are ground into powder and sold in powder or brick form to be grated into water or juice for its vitamin, medicinal, and energizing values.

Guava

(*See* Goiaba)

Goiaba (GUAVA)

This fruit can be eaten raw when ripe or made into ice cream, pastry creams, mousse, jellies, and concentrated paste. The round to oval fruit grows about two to four inches long. The skin can be yellow or green, depending on the variety, sometimes tinged with pink-yellow, white, or deep pink tones. The best varieties have few seeds and a pleasant distinct aroma, and the flavor is sweet with a slightly acidic tang. When ripe the fruit yields to pressure without feeling mushy. It keeps refrigerated for several days.

Heart of palm

(*See* Palmito)

Jabuticaba

The grapelike berries with thick dark blue to black skins adhere in small clusters on the barks of oak-sized jabuticaba trees. The whitish gelatinous pulp contains one to four small seeds and has a pleasant flavor that hints of concord grape and huckleberry. It is used for jams, jellies, juice, and liquors. The jam is available in specialty markets, and may be labeled "Brazilian grape jelly."

Jackfruit

Giant oblong fruits that range in weight from ten to forty pounds. The acidic lime-colored rind is made up of hexagonal spines, and the flesh is a slippery, whitish, juicy pulp that surrounds one large seed, which is encased by a covering of smaller seeds. The odor is like heady perfume, and the sweet flavor so intense it is almost alarming. The fruit is good eaten raw or used in ice creams. The larger seeds are boiled, then roasted and peeled and eaten like chestnuts.

Kale

(*See* Couve)

Limão (LIMES)

Lime juice is the most typical seasoning in all Brazil, used as frequently as we would use salt. It appears in drinks, sauces, salad dressings, marinades, desserts, and wedges are served with all grilled meat and fish dishes, as well as melons and tropical fruits. There are no lemons in Brazil.

The particular variety of Brazilian lime produces a juice that stains the skin when exposed to the sun. Cooks are careful to wash their hands thoroughly after using it. And tourists who take to drinking caipirinhas at the beach and chew or play with the chopped limes are alarmed at first when they notice their hands and mouth have turned a muddy mustard color. The stain lasts for months.

Keep limes at room temperature for one hour before squeezing to get the most juice. One medium lime contains approximately one-fourth cup juice. Sprinkle avocados, bananas, mangoes, and pears with fresh lime juice to prevent discoloring. Strips of peel and grated zest can be frozen to use in various recipes, desserts, and preserves. When using the zest, freeze the juice for future use.

Lingüiça

Portuguese pork sausage made plain or with hot chilies. Variations include smoked lingüiça, called calabreze, and the level of spiciness depends on the butcher or manufacturer. These sausages are available at some Brazilian and Latin American markets and specialty butchers. Substitute sweet or hot Italian sausages or chorizo, depending on the recipe.

Mandioca (MANIOC)

This starchy root, referred to in the States as "cassava" or "yuca," is called aipim in Rio and the northeastern states of Pernambuco and Bahia, macaxeira in the northeast (the Amazonian states), and mandioca in São Paulo and the southern states. There are several varieties, including one that is toxic. The latter is soaked and cooked to rid it of its poisons. Manioc has been the staff of life among the Brazilian Indians for millennia. The fresh pulp is used for fermented drinks and the making of tapioca. The grain, called farinha de mandioca, is sold both toasted and untoasted and is used in place of flour for Indian-type breads, cuscuz (couscous), stews, purees (pirão), and poultry stuffing. Most often it is warmed and toasted again in a skillet with a little butter or oil, becoming a dish called farofa, to be sprinkled over rice, beans, meat, and fish dishes. Farofa is often enlivened with chopped vegetables and other additives like nuts, olives, and raisins, and appears on every Brazilian table as a side dish in one form or another.

For consistency's sake, recipes in this book call for "manioc flour (farinha de mandioca)."

Manga (MANGO)

This fruit has been cultivated in India for more than four thousand years. Avenues of mangoes brought over from India a century ago line the streets of one of the Amazon's largest cities, Belém. Vibrant red-yellow leathery skin covers thick, luxurious yellow flesh enclosing a large, woody-husked seed. Vendors peel the fruit and attach it to a stick, and it is eaten like a lollipop. Natives massage the pulp through the skin, breaking down the fiber, then cut a small hole in the stem end and suck on it as if it were a baby bottle. It is excellent for the digestion. It is used fresh in salads, grilled, as the base for chutney, and in sauces and desserts.

Maracujá (PASSION FRUIT)

This fruit comes from one of the many species of the *Passiflora* genus that produce edible fruit. The sizes vary from a two-inch oval to giant granadilla, which reach twelve inches in length and weigh up to six pounds. The small, dark, wrinkled oval variety and the tennis ball–sized ivory-colored variety are available at specialty fruit purveyors and Brazilian and Latin American markets. The aromatic juice and seeds are eaten directly from the shell with a spoon or used in drinks and desserts. The pulp is available frozen and in juice form.

Mariscada

A Brazilian-style bouillabaisse that includes fish, shellfish, broth, and vegetables. It is not to be confused with the moquecas of the northeast that always include dendê oil.

Molho

Sauces similar to salsas, made with lime juice or vinegar, tomatoes, onions, sweet and hot peppers, olive oil, and seasonings.

Moqueca

A type of ragout or fish stew made with firm-fleshed fish, shrimp, or crab, or any combination of fish and shellfish. The fish is poached in a rich broth seasoned with onions, sweet peppers, coconut milk, lime juice, malagueta pepper, tomatoes, dendê oil, marjoram, and parsley.

Okra

(*See* Caruru, Quiabo)

Paçoca

In Bahia, paçoca is a confection similar to soft nut brittle made with peanuts or cashews and sugar. In the states of Minas Gerais and São Paulo the same word is used to describe a savory dish made with beef jerky.

Palmito (HEART OF PALM)

Fresh heart of palm is harvested from the palmito palm. A seven-year-old palmito will produce a palm heart of an inch and a half to two inches in diameter. The heart is harvested from the inside of the uppermost part of the trunk once the tree is felled. The luxurious three- to four-inch-diameter hearts are produced only after twelve years of growth. Grown principally in Brazil, they are also available from other Latin American countries, the Caribbean, and Florida. Fresh palm hearts are sometimes available at specialty food stores in the States. The best canned varieties are imported from Brazil. Two good brands are Roland and Ivai.

Papaya

(*See* Paw paw)

Passion fruit

(*See* Maracujá)

Pastel

(*See* Empada, pastel)

Pato no tucupi

A dish popular throughout the Amazon made of roasted duck (pato), similar to our Muscovy duck, simmered in broth. The broth is made with tucupi, the extracted juice from the manioc root (cassava), a milky-white liquid hinting of chicory, and flavored with the yellow pimenta-de-cheiro. Jambu leaves, which are related to the coca (cocaine) leaf and leave the tongue and lips tingling, are added to the dish. The original recipe is given on page 149, but tucupi is not available as yet in the United States.

Paw paw (PAPAYA)

A large, yellow- to orange-skinned fruit, the papaya has silken pulp that is similar to sweet melon in flavor, and the color can be mild orange to intense crimson. Both the pulp and seeds are edible. The fruit is enhanced with a little lime juice and is used in drinks, preserves, ice cream, mousses, and desserts.

Pimenta-de-cheiro

A wild, cherry-sized pepper that is colored yellow and red when ripe. It grows in profusion in the Amazon and is made into a condiment, much as the pimenta malagueta is. The heat of the cheiro pepper is less intense and more fruity than that of the malagueta. Habañero or other hot chili peppers can be substituted, but again will produce another flavor.

Pimenta malagueta

This chili is the smallest and hottest member of the *Capsicum* genus. The green variety is less intense than the riper red, but both are very hot. This fiery pepper is made into the standard condiment on all Brazilian tables. The pepper is preserved in oil, vinegar, or cachaça. A little of the liquid is used to add fire to a dish. Tabasco and Scotch bonnet peppers are substitutes, but produce another flavor. The timid usually add a few drops of the liquid to beans, rice, and stews. The heroic use the liquid and the pepper itself with abandon.

Pineapple

(*See* Abacaxi)

Pirão

A mulled, creamy paste of cooked fish, manioc flour (farinha de mandioca), broth, hot chili pepper oil, and dendê oil served as an accompaniment to moqueca and other fish and meat dishes.

Pumpkin

(*See* Abóbara)

Pupunha

The small fruit of the pupunha palm grows in datelike clusters. The orange-mahogany skin encases dry pulpy meat surrounding a large nut. The taste is sweetly bready. Whole clusters are cooked in boiling water, and when they fall off the central stem, they are done. They are usually sold in markets already cooked, and the skin's natural oil gives them a shiny lacquered look. The pulp is usually served as a vegetable, hot with butter and salt, pureed and made into soup, or served in cold shrimp salads.

Quiabo (OKRA)

The name most often used throughout Brazil. In Bahia, "caruru" means okra as well as a dish of prawns, okra, and cilantro.

Rabada

A stew of oxtail made with red wine, vegetables, and spices.

Siri

(*See* Crab)

Star fruit

(*See* Carambola)

Suco misto

Fresh or bottled fruit juices. Sometimes they are sweetened and usually served over ice.

Tacacá

A soup made with a broth based on the juice of the manioc root (cassava), river shrimp, and jambu leaves (a relative of the coca leaf), which is usually served in a gourd. The soup is served from carts and stands in the Amazon, from the populated port city of Belém to the shores of the Negro.

Tamarind

A pod about six inches in length. When ripe, the brittle fruit is brown. The ripe pod contains several large seeds surrounded by a pasty, date-like, tart pulp that is used to flavor fish, meats, fruit desserts, and drinks. It is used mostly in the area of Bahia. When green it is very acidic and can be used judiciously to flavor fish. It is available canned and fresh at Latin American and African markets. When preparing fresh tamarind, cover the seeds and pulp with water and leave them to stand overnight. Once the tamarind is drained, the pulp is easy to remove from the seeds.

Tutu à Mineira

Creamed or pureed beans thickened with manioc flour (farinha de mandioca) and seasoned with onions, garlic, tomato, sweet peppers, parsley, scallions, and chili pepper. This popular bean dish made in the state of Minas Gerais is its variation of feijoada. The puree is served with some sort of pork, such as grilled or roasted marinated loin, chops, or sausages and sometimes accompanied by chunks of fried fatback. Another version of this dish is feijão tropeiro, but in this dish the beans are cooked and served whole.

Vatapá

A spicy cream of fish, bread, ground shrimp, dendê oil, crushed chili peppers, ground cashews, and peanuts. Served as an accompaniment to grilled fish and prawns, it is an essential side dish to xinxim.

Xinxim

A quick sauté of chicken combined with shrimp, onions, garlic, tomatoes, green pepper, coconut milk, and spiked with fresh cilantro. There are many variations of this dish that may also include fish, chicken, or pork.

Xuxu (CHAYOTE)

From the French Antillean word for the same plant, chou-chou, it is also called chayote, christophine, and merliton. White to pale celery-green skin, with smooth to rough bumps, this pear-shaped squash grows from about four to eight inches long. The white flesh is dense but watery and surrounds a single seed. It can be boiled in vegetable dishes and served raw in salads like cucumbers or jicama. It should feel firm to the touch and keeps in the refrigerator for up to a week.

the journey begins...

são paulo

I land at São Paulo's airport, an hour's drive from the city of some fifteen million inhabitants, on a breezy summer morning in early December. It is my third visit to this immense city, and this time I've come to write a cookbook: a daunting task. My friends have sent Guilherme, their trusted jack-of-all-household-chores, to help with my luggage and take me to their home.

A harvest of pineapples for sale at the Mercado Central will be gone by closing time at 4:00 P.M.

Cases loaded, bags piled in, we are on the highway. Guilherme grips the wheel, chuckling as he passes trailer trucks and buses belching out great clouds of soot and exhaust and clipping along at eighty miles an hour themselves. Brazilian drivers are not fainthearted.

We skirt the edge of downtown, passing blackened creamy-toned Beaux Arts buildings, and I catch a distant glimpse of the ornate municipal market. The beef-blood-red Victorian train station nearby is packed with the rabble of pedestrian traffic—mostly hesitant arrivals from the north migrating southward in hopes of a better life.

We head west through a web of highways, avenues of palms and acacia so huge they seem to challenge the very skyscrapers they encircle. Inching our way through traffic we pass displays of fantasy modern architecture, some cantilevered or shooting off the sides of hills in defiance of gravity and taste. As we approach the outer limits of the city the air becomes sweeter: a haze of trees blossoming in pink, lavender, magenta, and vermilion line the quiet streets that lead to houses protected by gates, walls, whitewashed guardhouses, and an occasional unfriendly barking dog.

I am greeted first by a pair of shrieking arraras, blue parrots, flaunting saffron-yellow heads in a cloud of fluttering sapphire feathers, followed by Joachim and his children. There is time for a quick swim in the icy-cool pool before an unhurried lunch—pasta and salad prepared by my host, Joachim, crisp white wine from Rio Grande do Sul, and a bowl of cool tropical fruits served with a cake glazed with fresh pineapple, honey, and nuts, prepared by his cook, Augusta.

Here in the Chacara Flora, a residential part of the city, is where I will plot out my trek through Brazil with the help of Joachim and his friends. Joachim's former wife, Libba, also offers her suggestions. Her house is minutes away from his, and because the two operate separate households, I find myself benefiting from two styles of Brazilian cooking. Joachim's cook, Augusta, is of Portuguese ancestry, and her style of cooking is Luso-Brazilian; Libba's cook, Anita, is native to the state of Bahia, the heart of Afro-Luso-Brazilian delights. Both styles are indigenous of regional Brazilian cooking.

During our chats plans for the next days and weeks unfold: people I must meet, dinners to attend, dinners to give, trips to the country, New Year's in Rio. . . . Most pressing are the plans for next week's dinner for two hundred to honor a friend whose first retrospective is being mounted at the Museu de Arte de São Paulo.

The next few days are for settling in—most important are my crash-course Portuguese lessons. Outside of this household barely anyone speaks any English. The sounds and pronunciations of the Brazilian language are difficult for me, and though most of Joachim's family shifts from Portuguese to English with ease, my mastery of the language can best be described as kitchen Portuguese. My idle hours are spent reading, having lunch with friends, planning logistics for the fete, poking around the kitchen, chatting up Augusta, and making trips to the neighborhood markets and the local *feira,* or outdoor markets. Every day of the week, somewhere in every city or large town, clusters of neighborhood streets are closed to host morning markets—some are a couple of blocks long, while others take over entire commercial neighborhoods.

The big Saturday market is held outside the soccer stadium at Pacaembu, a neighborhood in the heart of the city. Vendors set up their tented stalls to display a visual spectacle of fruits, vegetables, cheeses, meats, fish, chicken, and flowers. To get acquainted with the produce at hand I make early morning forays to shop, admiring and tasting the pineapple sliced by the vendor to seduce the shopper into a purchase. There's also carambola, known to us as star fruit; *fruta de conde,* a relative of the *cherimoya,* a bulbous, slate-green pinecone-shaped fruit split open to reveal the creamy coated seeds that taste like a blend of mango, bananas, and slightly gritty Anjou pears; the *caju,* a beautiful crimson-and-gold kidney-shaped fruit with its cashew nut still attached at the base. And, always, varieties of mango and papaya, along with *ciriguela,* tiny orange fruits that look like small kumquats. I greedily grab one and bite into it, tasting its slightly citric skin surrounding the sweet, translucent white-orange pulp, and spit out a mahogany pit the size of a lychee. It's a delicious and erotic surprise, and I buy a kilo to take back to the house. By the time I've tasted the miniature banana, the avocado, and the seedy pink guavas, as well as the more familiar strawberries, which are as good as any farm-fresh berry I eat at home, and muscat grapes, it is time to pause for a *café com leite* at one of the many small coffee stands that pop up all over the city. I've had my breakfast for thirty-five cents! Produce is a bargain: four pineapples for a dollar, luscious mangoes a quarter each, a bunch of cilantro twenty cents, limes sold by the sack of six for thirty cents. Only the plums and pears from Argentina are pricey. Everything is fresh and as ripe as if the fruits had just fallen from the tree. A half-dozen cooking spoons hewn from bamboo will cost another dollar; a small metal contraption to grate coconut is a fifty-cent investment. Eventually these bargain prices will escalate, and we must check the banks for the dollar rate every day. The cruzeiro currency mounts seemingly by the minute, and the entire country spends its mornings adjusting the daily prices to reflect inflation. When you're buying a pencil, filling a tank with gas, or

The olive stall

buying a bathing suit, the salesperson or attendant rushes off to check some complicated price list. No advertised item is priced or marked. By the time I leave, Brazil will have a new currency called the *real.*

Some of the vendors are of Japanese lineage, descendants from the original eight hundred who immigrated in 1908 to work the coffee plantations. The Japanese living in Brazil compose the largest Japanese population in any country outside of their home islands, and, though they continue to resist integration, their contribution to agriculture and aquaculture in Brazil is impressive. The efficient Japanese trawlers that fish for shrimp, squid, lobsters, snapper, and tuna have all but replaced the picturesque seagoing rafts of the famous *jangadeiros,* whose sails would sparkle in the sun along the Atlantic shore.

In the Liberdade district, São Paulo boasts one of the largest Japanese towns outside of Japan. And so for a change of diet we often stop at one of the 1,500-plus sushi bars and restaurants, usually favoring establishments where the head sushi maker had been Tokyo trained. Unlike us, the Brazilian is not squeamish, and most of the fish is cut live, left almost quivering on the plate; even the shrimp are still wriggling. The quality of fish in some of these places is beyond perfection.

Joachim has his list of the few regional restaurants in the city that I must visit—a small list indeed, since the Paulistas, as people who live in the city of São Paulo are called, prefer dining at the stylish French and Italian restaurants, especially the Italian, which proliferate in the city. They have been so influenced by tourism and the *(continued on page 10)*

By 6:00 A.M. 331 stalls selling a variety of foods opens to the public.

7

Caipirinha

1 lime	8 ice cubes
2 tablespoons sugar	4 ounces cachaça

Cut the lime in half from stem end to bottom. Slice away the stringy pith that runs down the center of each half. Slice each lime piece in half crosswise, and then into small slices. Place half of the sliced lime in each of two rocks glasses, add a tablespoon of sugar to each glass, stir, and mull until the sugar dissolves.

Crack 8 ice cubes and add half to each glass.

Pour 2 ounces of cachaça in each glass, stir vigorously, and serve.

MAKES 2 DRINKS

Feijoada

The Cariocas, natives of Rio, prepare feijoada with black beans, onion, and garlic. The Paulistas, on the other hand, make this dish with brown beans and the addition of orange juice, parsley, scallions, and cachaça. Both are equally good, but the classic black bean version that follows is what most Brazilians expect.

Preparation is best begun three days ahead, beginning with shopping, though it can be done in two. The cuts of meat and odd parts of the pig can be purchased from a good butcher or specialty Brazilian or Latin American meat market.

THE MEATS
- 1 pound carne seca (available at Brazilian specialty shops) or salted corned beef
- 1 smoked beef tongue (about 1¾ pounds) or cured beef tongue
- 1 salted pork butt (about 1¾ pounds)
- 1 pound salted pork ribs (all attached)
- ½ pound salted slab bacon
- ½ pound fresh pigs' ears
- 3 fresh pigs' tails
- 1 pound (about 3) fresh pigs' feet, split in half lengthwise
- ½ pound paio (a fatty blood pork sausage, available at Brazilian specialty shops; optional)
- ½ pound lingüiça sausage (or other sweet Italian pork sausage)
- ½ pound smoked calabrese-type sausage (or other smoked spicy sausage)

THE BEANS
- 2 pounds dried black beans, washed and picked clean
- 1 medium onion, peeled
- 4 bay leaves
- 1 tablespoon vegetable oil
- 3 large garlic cloves, chopped
  Salt and freshly ground pepper to taste

  Simple Boiled White Rice (see page 12), sliced or whole peeled oranges, Kale (see page 13), Simple Farofa (see page 109), and preserved malagueta peppers, for serving

THE DAY BEFORE
In a very large stockpot, add the carne seca, beef tongue, pork butt, and ribs. Add enough water to cover generously and refrigerate for 24 hours, changing the water once or twice. At the same time, in a separate stockpot, add the salted bacon, pigs' ears, and pigs' feet. Add enough water to cover generously and refrigerate for 24 hours, changing the water once or twice.

In a large kettle, combine the beans and cold water to cover and set aside. Allow to soak for at least 6 hours, or refrigerate overnight.

Day Two

Remove the meats and beans from the refrigerator. Wash out the meat kettles and add the carne seca, beef tongue, ribs, pigs' ears, tails, and feet to one. In a separate kettle add the pork butt. Fill the kettles with cold water to generously cover and bring to a boil for 5 minutes. Remove the meats, drain the water, and repeat the process 4 times more with fresh water.

Add the bacon to a saucepan of cold water, bring to a boil over high heat, and boil for 5 minutes. Drain and set aside.

Prick the sausages with a fork in 4 or 5 places and set aside. In 3 separate saucepans place the paio, lingüiça, and smoked sausage, cover each with cold water, and bring to a boil. Reduce the heat and simmer the paio for 15 minutes, the lingüiça for 10 minutes, and the calabrese for 5 minutes. Remove the sausage from the saucepans and drain the water. Return the largest pan to the heat, add all the sausage, and lightly brown on all sides. Remove the sausages from the pan and set aside. When the boiled meats are cool enough to handle, remove the soft bones from the pigs' ears and discard.

Drain the beans, combine them with the onion and bay leaves in a large kettle, and cover with cold water by 8 inches. Place the beans over high heat, bring to a boil, reduce the heat, and simmer, covered, for 30 minutes. Add the bacon and continue to simmer the beans, covered, for 1½ hours (see Note).

In a small skillet, heat the oil over medium heat. Add the garlic and cook for 5 minutes, or until golden. Add the garlic mixture, salt, and pepper to the beans.

Add all the meats and sausages to the beans, bring to a boil, reduce the heat, and simmer, partially covered, for 1 to 1½ hours, or until the beans are tender but not thoroughly cooked. Stir from time to time so the beans do not stick to the bottom of the pan. Check the liquid level from time to time, adding boiling water as needed to keep the level at 8 inches. Remove the meats from the beans and cool. Cover the meats and beans separately and refrigerate. This should be done a day ahead to ensure greater flavor.

Serving Day

Remove the beans and meats from the refrigerator. In a large heavy-bottomed kettle, add the beans and meats and enough cold water to cover by 8 inches. Cover and bring the mixture to a simmer over low heat for 1 hour.

Preheat the oven to 200° F.

Remove the ears and slice in julienne, the tails in 1-inch pieces, the bacon in thin strips, and the feet in 1-inch pieces. Slide off the tongue casing and slice the tongue in ¼-inch slices, cut the sausages in 1-inch pieces, and cut the carne seca or corned beef in small flaked pieces and arrange them in heatproof serving dishes (you may place them in individual dishes or pair 2 or 3 meats together on heatproof platters). Remove a cup or more of bean liquor from the pot and moisten the meats. Cover with foil and keep warm in the oven if not serving immediately.

Place the beans in a large, warmed, glazed ceramic bowl or whatever large oven-proof bowl you have and serve with the meats and rice, oranges, kale, farofa, and preserved malagueta peppers.

Serves 15

Note: Cooking time for dried beans varies according to the freshness of the beans. Most beans will cook in 2½ to 3 hours. The good Brazilian cook removes one bean from the pot and presses it with his thumb on a board, then rubs it in a long brush stroke line. If it is smooth and pasty the beans are cooked.

Warm Pão de Queijo, cheese breads, served with butter or dipped in Molho Campanha, accompany a meal.

tastes of the wealthy that to learn anything about the national foods of Brazil, one has got to do more than just scratch the surface. Upscale markets and the few existing fancy food shops cater to an Italian population that began migrating to São Paulo during the early twentieth century. Imported Gorgonzola, chunks of Parmesan from huge wheels imported from Parma, tubs of olives, and bottles of olive oil from Portugal are sold, along with local farm-produced mozzarella, salami, mortadella, macaroni, and fresh pasta at reasonable albeit ever-escalating prices.

On my first Saturday our major outing is joining the throngs of Brazilians who would not think of missing their traditional plateful of feijoada (page 8). After a short stroll down the Avenida Paulista we head for Massimo's. Massimo's is one of São Paulo's finest restaurants, offering what I think is the city's best *feijoada completa*.

Caipirinhas (page 8; the word is a diminutive of *caipira,* meaning "little country hick"), those painkilling cocktails crammed with limes zealously mulled with sugar, cracked ice, and a generous pouring of cachaça are the traditional drink of choice. Made from distilled sugarcane, they taste more herbal and rougher than rum and take most gringos by surprise. A particularly lethal green variety is known colloquially as *pinga*—a name that harks back to one of the bandits, nicknamed Pinga Fogo, or Fire

Caipirinhas, the national drink

Drop, who roamed the country. A bottle of this—what I call white lightning—is the price of a pack of cigarettes, and bars and lean-tos in towns and along the beaches are more apt to make your cocktail with this stuff.

The feast begins with appetizers: small plates of olives, sliced grilled sausages, crisp fried pork skins, and *pão de queijo* (page 13; literally "cheese bread"—a popover-like puff of a roll that rivals any of the world's great breads, accented with the faint taste of the sweet-tart cheese from Minas Gerais).

A tiny cup of bean soup—no more than three or four sips—introduces the feijoada, accompanied by a small glass of cachaça served neat. The cachaça is also added to the soup as we would add a little sherry to a true Southern black bean soup.

Feijoada is at first glance a baronial feast. The Southern Hemisphere's answer to a French cassoulet, it comes from humble origins. The dish evolved in the slave quarters of the cocoa and sugar plantations in the northeast of Brazil, where the West African cooks concocted simple dishes for their families and farm workers, similar to those devised by our southern cooks in the eighteenth and nineteenth centuries. The lesser bits and scraps of the pig, like the tail, ears, snout, feet, *(continued on page 19)*

11

Arroz

SIMPLE BOILED WHITE RICE

When cooking white rice, use a ratio of 2 cups water to every cup of rice. When boiling large amounts of rice, make sure not to cover the rice with more than 1 inch of water. Brazilian rice always requires rinsing and draining before cooking, unlike most rice available in the United States, which has been prewashed. Check package directions. An Asian rice cooker will ensure perfect cooked rice every time.

2 cups cold water
½ teaspoon salt
1 cup long-grain rice, rinsed in cold running water until water runs clear, if necessary, and drained thoroughly

1 tablespoon unsalted butter (optional)

In a medium saucepan, bring the water to a boil over high heat. Add the salt, rice, and butter if desired and stir. Cover, reduce the heat, and cook for 20 minutes, or until the rice has absorbed the water. Remove the rice from the heat and allow it to stand 5 minutes, or until all the remaining moisture is absorbed.

SERVES 4 OR 5

Arroz Brasileiro

SAUTÉED WHITE RICE

3 tablespoons extra-virgin olive oil or unsalted butter
1 small onion, chopped
1 garlic clove, chopped
2 cups uncooked long-grain white rice, rinsed if necessary

1 whole clove
5 cups hot water
Salt and freshly ground white pepper to taste

In a medium saucepan, heat the oil or butter over medium heat. Add the onion and garlic and sauté until the onion is translucent, about 5 minutes.

Add the rice, stirring constantly until the rice has absorbed the oil or butter and the grains are translucent. Add the whole clove and the hot water and bring to a boil over high heat. Reduce the heat, season the rice with salt and pepper, cover, and simmer for 20 minutes, or until the rice is tender. Remove from the heat, cover, and allow to stand 5 minutes until all the moisture is absorbed.

SERVES 6

Pão de Queijo
CHEESE ROLLS

These chewy little rolls, similar to our popovers, are popular throughout São Paulo, Rio, and Minas Gerais. They are made with polvilho azedo, a sour and slightly gritty flour, processed from the manioc root.

OVERLEAF:
Feijoada Completa, an elaborate stew of beans (top right) and every part of the pig, accompanied by sausages, carne seca (bottom right), rice, kale (bottom left), farofa, and citrus fruit

- **1 cup polvilho azedo flour (see Note)**
- **½ cup plus 2 tablespoons all-purpose flour**
- **1 teaspoon salt**
- **½ teaspoon rapid-rise dry yeast**
- **¼ cup plus 2 tablespoons grated Parmesan cheese**
- **½ cup milk**
- **3 tablespoons unsalted butter, melted**
- **1 large egg, beaten**

In a large bowl combine the polvilho flour, flour, salt, yeast, and Parmesan cheese. In a small saucepan, warm the milk over low heat, then remove and add the butter. When the butter is melted, pour the liquid mixture over the dry ingredients.

Combine the ingredients with a wooden spoon, then add the egg and stir until combined. Cover and set aside for ½ hour.

Preheat the oven to 350° F. Using a teaspoon, spoon the dough in small rounds onto an ungreased baking sheet. Bake for 15 to 20 minutes, or until lightly golden. Serve hot.

MAKES 24 ROLLS

NOTE: Polvilho flour is available at Brazilian and Latin American markets. The rolls may be made ahead, then cooled and frozen. Warm them through in a 325° F oven.

Couve
KALE

The Brazilian cook rolls the *couve* leaves like a long tight cigar. She holds them from the top in one fist, carefully slicing over her thumb and forefinger with a sharp knife in the other. The needlelike ribbons are perfectly shaped as she moves down the rolled greens.

- **1½ pounds young kale, washed and dried**
- **1 tablespoon extra-virgin olive oil**
- **Salt and freshly ground pepper to taste**

Fold the kale leaves in half lengthwise and cut away the stems and inner ribs. Pile about 5 or 6 leaves on top of one another, folded in half lengthwise. Starting at the top and cutting across the leaves, julienne the leaves in needle-thin strips.

In a large skillet, heat the oil over medium heat. Add the kale, season with salt and pepper, and toss. Cook just short of the wilting point. It should retain its color and remain slightly crisp.

SERVES 10

Empada, Empadinha

BAKED PASTRIES, LITTLE PASTRIES

Empada and empadinha fillings include fish, cheese, chicken, and vegetable versions.

PASTRY

- 2 cups all-purpose flour, sifted
- ½ teaspoon salt
- 5 tablespoons unsalted butter
- 1 tablespoon lard
- 1 large egg
- 2 tablespoons water
- 1 large egg yolk

FILLING

- 1 tablespoon extra-virgin olive oil
- 1 medium onion, grated
- 1 medium tomato, peeled, seeded, and chopped
- ¼ cup homemade or canned low-sodium chicken stock
- ⅛ teaspoon ground nutmeg
- 1 cup chopped hearts of palm
- ½ cup small green or Niçoise-type black olives, pitted and chopped
- 1 tablespoon finely chopped fresh parsley
- Salt and freshly ground pepper to taste

In the bowl of an electric mixer, combine the flour, salt, butter, and lard at low speed until the mixture is the consistency of cornmeal. Add the whole egg and 1 tablespoon of the water and mix until the pastry pulls away from the sides of the bowl and forms a soft ball. Form a ball, cover, and set aside to rest.

Beat the egg yolk with the remaining 1 tablespoon water to brush the tops of the pastries. Set the egg wash aside.

Preheat the oven to 375° F.

For the filling, in a medium nonreactive skillet, heat the oil over medium heat. Add the onion and sauté for 1 minute. Add the tomato, stock, nutmeg, hearts of palm, olives, parsley, and salt and pepper. Bring the mixture to a simmer and cook for 2 minutes. Remove from the heat.

On a lightly floured board, roll out the pastry to a thickness of about ⅛ inch, working with half the dough at a time, if necessary. Using a 1½-inch pastry cutter, cut out 32 circles. Press each of the pastry circles into individual 1-inch tin pastry shells. Fill the shells with 1 heaping tablespoonful of the filling, or enough to almost fill. Cover with the remaining pastry circles, pressing down around the edges.

If you like, roll out the remaining pastry scraps and form into little leaves or diamond shapes and place in the center of each mold, pressing lightly.

Brush the tops of the pastry with the egg wash. Place the tins on a baking sheet and bake for 20 minutes, or until lightly golden.

MAKES 16 PASTRIES

VARIATIONS: Peeled and chopped raw shrimp or cooked and shredded chicken can be substituted for the hearts of palm.

Croquetes de Queijo

CHEESE CROQUETTES

Croquettes, along with *pastel* (fried pastries) and empadinhas (little baked pastries), are the snack foods of Brazil. Brought by Portuguese cooks in the early seventeenth century, these little nibbles are served small and large at breakfast, with tea and cocktails.

1½ cups all-purpose flour, sifted
1 cup freshly grated Parmesan cheese
6 tablespoons unsalted butter, at room temperature and cut into small pieces

1 large egg, separated
Salt and freshly ground white pepper to taste
1 cup fine dry bread crumbs

Preheat the oven to 350° F.

Lightly butter a large cookie sheet.

In the bowl of an electric mixer, add the flour, cheese, butter, and egg yolk and season with salt and pepper. Mix at low speed. Do not overbeat—the dough should be grainy and not pasty.

With your hands, form the mixture into balls about the size of a walnut.

In a medium bowl, whisk the egg white until frothy. Dip each cheese ball in the egg white and roll lightly in the bread crumbs, shaking off any excess. Place on the buttered cookie sheet and bake for 25 minutes, or until golden. Serve hot.

MAKES ABOUT 16 CROQUETTES

Tomate com Quiabo

STEWED TOMATO AND OKRA

1 tablespoon extra-virgin olive oil
1 small onion, chopped
1 garlic clove, chopped
1 small malagueta pepper, seeded, deveined, and diced, or 1 teaspoon seeded, deveined, and diced hot chili pepper

2 large ripe tomatoes, peeled, seeded, and chopped
¼ teaspoon chopped fresh oregano
1 pound okra, trimmed and cut into ½-inch rounds
Salt and freshly ground pepper to taste

In a medium sauté pan, heat half the oil over medium heat. Add the onion and sauté for 1 minute. Add the garlic and malagueta or chili pepper and sauté another minute. Add the tomatoes and oregano and cook, stirring occasionally, for 10 minutes.

Meanwhile, in a nonstick pan, add the remaining oil and heat over high heat. Add the okra and cook 10 minutes, or until the okra is tender, stirring constantly. Add to the tomato mixture and season with salt and pepper.

SERVES 4 OR MORE

OPPOSITE:
*Picadinho served
in a baked
pumpkin*

LEFT: *Gringo
Moqueca, my
version of the
classic Bahian
fish stew*

and so on, were blended with black beans and kale by these slaves. Their
masters dined on the choicer cuts. Today feijoada is an elaborate stew of
creamy beans slowly cooked with choice pork and salted meats,
Portuguese sausages, smoked tongue, and *carne seca* (a classic salt-cured
meat similar to our jerky). The stew is served divided into courses, starting
with the bean liquid, followed by separate bowls of beans, meats, barely
wilted sautéed shredded kale (page 13), and boiled white rice. The meal is
accompanied by bowls of sliced tart oranges that cut the heaviness and add
extra piquancy. A bowl of finely ground meal made from the root of the
manioc (cassava) is served as a condiment to be sprinkled over the rice and
beans. When the meal is toasted, the dish is called *farofa* (page 109).
Miniature pots of *pimenta malagueta,* tiny fiery peppers that are hotter than
the cayenne or habanera, which have been preserved in oil, vinegar, or
cachaça, are set on the table. The preserving liquid is sprinkled over the
meats and beans, and the peppers eaten at the discretion of the diner.

Tall glasses of delicious cold draft beer are served, and nothing is better to
wash down this meal. Brazilians call it *chope,* and its refreshing goodness is
no surprise considering after the Franciscans and Jesuits arrived to convert
the natives, the Germans followed, spreading their gospel of hops and malt.

At 5:00 A.M. the day before the party, Baros, the gardener, and I climb into the van and head for the Ciasa—São Paulo's main terminal market almost an hour away in the outskirts of the city.

The Ciasa is an enormous corrugated-roofed, hangarlike construction
that on designated days displays fish, meats, *(continued on page 26)*

Picadinho com Abóbora
CHOPPED BEEF IN BAKED PUMPKIN

Most picadinho served in restaurants is made with ground beef. Home cooks, however, will make it with thinly sliced beef, or with leftover roasts of beef, which have been chopped.

PUMPKIN

1 4- to 5-pound pumpkin, as round as possible
Salt and freshly ground white pepper to taste
A few gratings of mace
1 cup homemade or canned low-sodium chicken stock
⅛ cup cachaça or dry white rum
Vegetable oil

PICADINHO

2 pounds sirloin or top round, trimmed of all fat
2 tablespoons red wine vinegar
⅛ teaspoon ground cinnamon
Pinch of ground cloves
¾ cup extra-virgin olive oil
1 yellow bell pepper, cored, seeded, ribs removed, and diced
1 red bell pepper, cored, seeded, ribs removed, and diced

2 medium onions, chopped
2 garlic cloves, chopped
3 tablespoons tomato paste
2 large tomatoes, peeled, seeded, and chopped
1 cup homemade or canned low-sodium beef stock
1 small malagueta or hot chili pepper, seeded, ribs removed, and diced
Salt and freshly ground pepper to taste
1 tablespoon Brazilian Jimmy sauce or Worcestershire sauce (Jimmy's is better)
3 tablespoons chopped fresh parsley
¼ cup chopped pitted green olives
2 tablespoons large capers, washed, drained, and dried

Simple Boiled White Rice (see page 12) and preserved malagueta peppers or hot pepper sauce, for serving

Preheat the oven to 375° F.

Cut a circle about 3 inches from the stem of the pumpkin to form a "lid." Scoop out the seeds and clean away the fibers. Lightly salt and pepper the inside and add a pinch or two of mace. Add the stock and cachaça or rum. Replace the lid to fit, rub the exterior of the pumpkin with vegetable oil, and place on a well-oiled baking pan. Bake for 50 minutes, or until the interior flesh is tender and the exterior still firm.

Remove the pumpkin from the oven and cool 5 minutes. Slide a spatula under the pumpkin and carefully transfer it to a warm serving platter.

Remove the lid and, using a bulb baster, extract the liquid from the pumpkin. Replace the lid, cover the pumpkin with foil, and keep warm until ready to fill with the picadinho.

Meanwhile, to make the picadinho, as the pumpkin is baking, slice the meat into ¼-inch-thick slices. Put the slices on a flat pan, cover with plastic wrap, and place in the freezer for 30 minutes.

Cut the slices into small dice, place in a large bowl, and toss with the vinegar, cinnamon, and cloves. Set aside for 20 minutes.

In a large skillet, heat ¼ cup of the olive oil over medium-high heat. When it begins to smoke, add the diced meat and brown quickly, stirring. Remove the meat from the heat and strain the juice into a bowl. Reserve the meat and juice separately.

In a large skillet, heat another ¼ cup of the olive oil and sauté the yellow and red peppers until they are limp, about 5 minutes. Remove with a slotted spoon and add to the meat mixture.

Add the remaining ¼ cup olive oil to the skillet and sauté the onions and garlic until golden brown. Add the tomato paste and stir occasionally for about 5 minutes until the mixture darkens and thickens. Add the tomatoes, the reserved meat juice, and stock and bring to a boil. Reduce the heat and simmer for 10 minutes.

Add the onion mixture to the meat mixture, along with the chopped malagueta or chili pepper, and season with salt and pepper. Return the picadinho to the skillet and cook over medium heat at a slow simmer for 20 to 30 minutes, or until all the ingredients are tender and most of the liquid is absorbed. Add the Jimmy or Worcestershire sauce, parsley, olives, and capers and cook another 5 minutes.

Using a thin-bladed paring knife, remove the pumpkin lid and extract any remaining liquid from the well of the pumpkin with the bulb baster. Fill the pumpkin with the picadinho and set the lid on top. Serve, scooping out a little of the pumpkin meat with some of the picadinho.

Serve with boiled white rice and preserved malagueta peppers or hot pepper sauce.

SERVES 6 TO 8

Beijos de Côco com Chocolate
CHOCOLATE COCONUT KISSES

2 cups grated fresh coconut (about 1 coconut)	**⅓ cup seedless raisins**
½ cup sugar	**1 cup semisweet chocolate chips, melted**

In a medium heavy-bottomed saucepan, combine the coconut, sugar, and raisins and cook over medium-low heat, stirring until the sugar is melted. Remove from the heat and cool.

When the mixture is cool enough to handle, form it into balls about the size of a whole walnut and place them on a lightly oiled cookie sheet.

Place the chocolate in the top part of a double boiler and melt the chocolate over medium heat. Using a teaspoon, cover the coconut balls with the melted chocolate. Cool and serve.

MAKES ABOUT 24 KISSES

Gringo Moqueca com Pirão

GRINGO FISH STEW

About ¾ cup extra-virgin olive oil

3 garlic cloves, chopped

2 medium onions, chopped

3 large ripe tomatoes, peeled, seeded, and chopped

1 yellow bell pepper, cored, seeded, deveined, and cut into thin strips

1 red bell pepper, cored, seeded, deveined, and cut into thin strips

1 green bell pepper, cored, seeded, deveined, and cut into thin strips

1 pound robalo (a southern Atlantic fish) or other firm, white fillets, such as grouper, sea bass, or snapper, with skin (heads and trimmings reserved, ask your fishmonger)

Salt and freshly ground pepper to taste

1 pound squid, cleaned and cut into 1-inch rings and tentacles

1 pound medium shrimp, in their shells

1 pound small sea scallops

About 8 cups fish stock

1½ pounds small littlenecks or New Zealand clams

PIRÃO

1 cup manioc flour (farinha de mandioca)

2 tablespoons dendê oil

1 tablespoon preserved malagueta pepper oil or hot pepper sauce, or more to taste

3 cups fresh or canned unsweetened coconut milk

1 tablespoon chopped fresh oregano, or 1 teaspoon dried oregano

¼ cup chopped fresh cilantro, or more to taste

½ cup chopped fresh parsley

Simple Boiled White Rice (see page 12), Simple Farofa (see page 109), and malagueta pepper oil, for serving

In a large, deep nonreactive sauté pan, heat ¼ cup of the olive oil over medium-high heat. Sauté the garlic for about 1 minute, add the onions, and cook just until wilted, stirring frequently, about 5 minutes. Add the tomatoes, simmer another 5 minutes, and set aside.

Meanwhile, in a separate skillet, heat ¼ cup of the olive oil over medium heat and sauté the yellow pepper for 8 minutes, or until limp. Remove the pepper strips from the pan with a slotted spoon and add them to the tomato mixture. Sauté the red pepper for 8 minutes, or until limp. Remove strips with a slotted spoon and add them to the tomato mixture. Repeat with the green pepper strips and add them to the tomato mixture. (The peppers are cooked separately to prevent the distinct flavors and colors from fusing.) Bring the tomato-pepper mixture to a boil, reduce the heat, and simmer for 10 minutes. Reserve.

Cut the fish fillets into 2-inch chunks, checking for stray bones. Season the fish with salt and pepper and reserve. Season the squid, shrimp, and scallops and reserve. In a large nonreactive saucepan, bring the fish stock to a simmer. Add the fish heads and trimmings to the stock and simmer for 15 minutes. Strain, reserving the solids, and keep the stock warm over very low heat.

Heat the remaining ¼ cup olive oil in a nonreactive sauté pan over medium-high heat. Add the cubed fish and sauté, skin side down, until golden but not cooked through. Remove the fish with a slotted spoon and reserve. Add the shrimp and sauté briefly, until they are just pink. Remove the shrimp with a slotted spoon and reserve (see Note). Add the squid rings and tentacles and sauté for 1 minute, or until they are lightly glazed. Remove the squid with a slotted spoon and reserve. Add the scallops and sauté briefly just until golden outside, then remove with a slotted spoon and reserve. Place the clams in the freezer for no more than 10 minutes before cooking (this enables them to open faster).

Drain the pan of any excess oil and deglaze it with a half cup of unseasoned warm fish stock. Add the deglazing liquid to the tomato-pepper mixture.

To make the pirão, pick off the cheeks and excess meat from the heads and trimmings. Combine 1 cup of the fish meat, trimmings plus some cubes, with a quarter cup of the infused fish stock and puree in a food processor or blender.

In a medium saucepan, add the manioc flour and whisk in the heated stock a half cup at a time, adding about 4 cups or enough to make the pirão the consistency of thin, cooked Cream of Wheat. Whisk in the fish puree, 1 tablespoon of dendê oil, and 1 teaspoon of malagueta oil (or more to taste) and season with salt and pepper. Cover the pirão and keep it warm while you finish the moqueca.

Over medium-high heat, bring the tomato-pepper mixture to a simmer. Add 2 cups stock and 3 cups coconut milk and the chopped oregano, cilantro, and parsley, bring to a simmer, cover, and cook 10 minutes. Add the clams and cook 4 minutes, or until they begin to open. Add the reserved fish and shellfish and their juices and continue simmering until the clams are completely open. Add the remaining tablespoon of dendê and 1 teaspoon of malagueta oil. Transfer the mixture to a heated tureen. Accompany with the pirão, boiled white rice, farofa, and malagueta pepper oil.

SERVES 10

NOTE: Shrimp are usually served in their shells and eaten shell and all. If they are peeled, do so after the brief sauté, just before adding them to the moqueca.

Ovos Mexidos com Bacalhau e Batata
SALTED COD WITH SCRAMBLED EGGS AND MATCHSTICK POTATOES

- **1 pound salted codfish**
- **1 tablespoon white cider vinegar**
- **2 large russet potatoes, peeled and halved, or canned fried matchstick potatoes**
- **3 cups vegetable oil, for frying**

- **4 tablespoons olive oil**
- **4 large eggs, lightly beaten**
  Freshly ground white pepper to taste
- **4 or more dashes malagueta pepper oil or hot pepper sauce to taste**
- **1 tablespoon chopped fresh parsley**

Place the cod in a large bowl and cover with cold water. Refrigerate for 48 hours, changing the water 4 or 5 times. Drain. In a large kettle, add the cod, vinegar, and enough water to cover. Bring it to a boil and cook for 15 minutes. Cool. Remove the skin and bones and shred the cod into needle-sized pieces with a fork, to yield about 2 cups shredded cod.

Shred the fresh potatoes, if using, into matchstick pieces on a mandoline, or use the grater attachment of a food processor. Wash in cold running water to remove the starch. Place the potatoes in a large bowl, cover with cold water, and refrigerate for 20 minutes. Drain the potatoes thoroughly and dry them in a clean kitchen towel.

In a deep fryer or heavy saucepan, heat the oil until smoky (350° to 375° F.) and fry the potatoes in batches until golden. Drain on paper towels and reserve.

In a medium nonstick skillet, heat the olive oil over low heat. Add the eggs and stir for about 2 minutes, or until lightly scrambled. Add the cod and the fried or canned potatoes, season with pepper, a few dashes of malagueta oil, and cook for another minute. The eggs should be creamy and light. Sprinkle with parsley and serve.

SERVES 4

BELOW: *The Portuguese salted cod is incorporated into many Brazilian dishes, such as this egg dish called Ovos Mexidos com Bacalhau e Batata.*

OPPOSITE: *A vase of tropical flowers from the garden*

vegetables, and fruits for sale, and this Tuesday is also given over to flowers. Growers in spattered vans sell roses, phlox, delphiniums, lilies, tuberoses, calla lilies they aptly call *copa de leite* (cup of milk), and orchids. Phalaenopsis, cymbidiums, and orchid varieties I've never seen before in pinks, white, purples, blues, and blacks are priced at ten dollars to twenty dollars a pot. We find one of the porters with a flatbed cart to load our purchases into the parked van. After a quick *cafezinho*—a little cup of strong rich foamy coffee with the sugar already added—and a *bombocado,* a sweet cheese and coconut muffin, we head downtown to the Mercado Central. We give the high sign to a barefoot waif who will watch our car for a few cruzeiros (an inexpensive precaution: São Paulo car thefts reach a staggering 1,500 a day!).

This limestone Beaux Arts palace is a temple to the pleasures that will reach the table. The cast-iron interior structure frames stained-glass windows depicting scenes of laborers, farmers, ranchers, and fishermen gathering the fruits of their harvest; bursts of red, blue, green, and golden shattered light reflect upon stalls and stands piled high with melons, sugarcane, coconuts, bags of spices, heaps of beans and meal, barrels of olives, basins of fish, yards of dried cod, and snakelike coils of tobacco. White-coated butchers, knife in hand, stand ready to cut any part of the pig or cow.

We need enough fruit to decorate twenty tables, and function as dessert as well, plus fifteen big waxy pumpkins that will be baked and then filled with *picadinho* (page 20), a dish that rivals the chili of Texas. I quickly learn the art of bargaining.

Purchases complete, we signal one of the men in a *(continued on page 30)*

Pudim de Leite da Augusta

AUGUSTA'S FLAN

CARAMEL
1¼ cups sugar
2 tablespoons water

CUSTARD
1 vanilla bean, or 1 teaspoon vanilla extract
1 3-inch strip orange zest

3 cups milk
¾ cup sugar
3 large eggs
6 large egg yolks

Fresh berries or diced fruit, for serving

To make the caramel, combine the sugar and 2 tablespoons water in a heavy saucepan and place over medium heat. Stir constantly with a wooden spoon until the sugar dissolves. Swirl the pan continuously until the syrup becomes a medium-dark-amber color. Pour the caramel into the bottom of a 1½- to 2-quart charlotte mold or shallow ring mold. Hold the top of the tin and tilt it, covering the bottom and sides with the liquid, working quickly so the caramel does not harden. Set aside.

To make the custard, preheat the oven to 325° F. and heat a teakettle or saucepan full of water to a boil.

Cut the vanilla bean, if using, in half lengthwise and scrape out as many of the tiny black seeds as possible. In a heavy saucepan, combine the seeds, pod, orange zest, milk, and ¾ cup sugar and bring just to a simmer over high heat.

Remove the mixture from the heat and allow it to steep for 15 minutes. In a large mixing bowl, whisk the eggs and egg yolks until thick and lemon-colored.

Gradually add the warm milk while whisking. Add the vanilla extract if not using the bean.

Strain the milk mixture and discard the orange zest and vanilla pod. Pour it into the mold.

Place the mold in a roasting pan and add enough nearly boiling water to come halfway up the sides of the mold. Place the pan in the center of the oven and bake for 50 minutes, or until the custard is firm but shaky; if you insert a paring knife in the center of the custard, it should come out clean but slightly wet.

Remove the mold from the water bath and allow it to cool for 20 minutes. Cover the flan and refrigerate for 3 hours or overnight.

To serve, run the blade of a paring knife around the edge of the pan and tube section. Dip the mold in a bath of hot water for a minute or two. Set a large, deep serving platter that can hold the caramel sauce over the pan, invert the flan, and unmold.

Serve with fresh berries or fruit.

SERVES 8 TO 10

Mariscada de Bacalhau
SALTED CODFISH STEW

This is another recipe that needs to be begun 48 hours ahead, as the salted cod must be soaked.

2½ pounds salted codfish
2 tablespoons white cider vinegar
6 medium potatoes, peeled
  About 4 tablespoons extra-virgin olive oil
1 large onion, chopped
3 garlic cloves, crushed
2 yellow bell peppers, cored, seeded, deveined, and cut into 2-inch strips
2 red bell peppers, cored, seeded, deveined, and cut into 2-inch strips
1 small hot chili pepper, cored, seeded, deveined, and cut into thin strips
3 medium leeks, washed, trimmed of most of the green, and cut into 2-inch strips

3 carrots, trimmed, peeled, and cut into 2-inch pieces
2 medium fennel bulbs, trimmed and thinly sliced (fronds reserved to embellish the dish)
6 medium tomatoes, peeled, seeded, and chopped
½ cup pitted green olives, chopped
1 tablespoon chopped fresh thyme
3 cups light unsalted fish stock
1 cup dry white wine
¼ cup chopped fresh parsley

Prepare the cod 2 days ahead. Place the cod in a large bowl and cover with cold water. Refrigerate for 48 hours, changing the water 4 or 5 times.

Drain the cod and place it in a large saucepan, and add the vinegar and enough fresh cold water to cover. Bring to a boil and cook for 15 minutes. Drain the fish and cool. Remove the skin and bones and cut into 2-inch cubes. In a medium saucepan, add the potatoes and enough cold water to cover. Cover the pan and bring to a boil over high heat and cook until the potatoes are almost tender.

Drain and cool the potatoes and slice into ½-inch rounds.

In a large skillet, heat 2 tablespoons of olive oil over medium heat and sauté the onions and garlic for 5 minutes, or until limp and translucent. Place the onion mixture in a large nonreactive saucepan and set aside.

Add the remaining oil to the skillet and sauté the yellow peppers until slightly limp, about 5 minutes. Remove the peppers with a slotted spoon and reserve. Add the red peppers and chili peppers to the skillet, adding more oil if necessary, and sauté until slightly limp, about 5 minutes. Remove with a slotted spoon and reserve.

Add the peppers and chili pepper to the saucepan along with the potatoes, leeks, carrots, fennel, tomatoes, olives, thyme, stock, and wine. Bring to a boil, reduce the heat, and simmer for 10 minutes, or until the vegetables are almost tender. Add the cubed cod and parsley and cook for another 10 minutes, or until the cod is flaky. Ladle onto warm plates and sprinkle with fennel fronds.

SERVES 6

tan cotton smock and an apron who follows us with his pushcart as we retrace our footsteps, picking up the goods and then loading the van. This service makes shopping on such a large scale a breeze!

We return by noon to a lunch Augusta has prepared—a corn chowder, then a delicious odd mix of shredded salted cod with scrambled eggs and matchstick potatoes (page 25) and a compote of stewed tomatoes and okra (page 17). We eat a wonderful flan and fruit for dessert.

The Portuguese have an obsession for salted cod, which they call *bacalhau.* For centuries their fishermen brought it from the Newfoundland Banks to all of Portugal, and the dried fish staved off the hunger of the sailors who sailed to these Brazilian shores. Their love of this preserved fish is still an influence in the Brazilian kitchens. Except for the coastal towns and cities close to the sea, where spectacular fresh fish dishes are prepared, cod is fish. The nineteenth-century explorer Richard Burton recorded on the subject: "While the river flowing before their doors produces the best of fish, the townspeople eat the hard dry bacalhau brought in dribblets from Newfoundland." In the north, farm workers pack a chunk of bacalhau in their hip pocket much as the cowboy from Rio Grande do Sul would pack his dried beef jerky. Today it remains popular, but expensive.

The party preparation continues. Fruits are washed and stored; piles of onions and peppers chopped; the meat, slightly frozen, is finely diced; plates, glasses, and silver are washed and polished; clothes and napkins checked for pressing. It's time for a swim, a piece of fruit, and a siesta.

Joachim is a social animal. He loves to entertain, surrounding himself with friends, family, painters whose art he buys, *(continued on page 34)*

Palmito Assado

BAKED FRESH HEART OF PALM

Dining on fresh hearts of palms is one of the true culinary delights of visiting the fazendas in the farm regions of São Paulo. If a guest is lucky, at one point during a weekend stay a freshly baked palm heart is served as a first course. The palm arrives on a platter atop a banana leaf, accompanied by melted butter, salt and pepper, and honey. I can only attribute the addition of honey to the Brazilian sweet tooth—it is equally delicious without. Fresh hearts of palm do appear on the shelves of specialty greengrocers in the United States, especially in Florida, where they are grown or imported from the Caribbean.

1 cup (2 sticks) unsalted butter	Salt and freshly ground pepper to
2 large fresh hearts of palm	taste
(about 1½ pounds)	¼ cup good-quality mild honey (optional)

Preheat the oven to 325° F.

To clarify the butter, in a small saucepan, melt the butter over medium heat. When it begins to foam, remove the pan from the heat and skim off the foam. Set aside for a minute or two, then carefully pour the clear butter into a small bowl and discard the milky liquid that settles in the bottom of the pan. Set aside.

Run a sharp paring knife down the length of the first layer of outer bark surrounding the palm heart. It should easily be removed with your fingers. The second layer is more tender but still slightly hard. Leave this intact. Place the palm hearts on a double layer of foil and generously brush with the butter. Wrap the palm hearts fairly tightly and place them in a large baking pan. Bake for 1½ hours, or until they can be easily pierced with a paring knife. The consistency will be soft and buttery. Remove the hearts from the foil and serve immediately. Accompany with salt, pepper, and honey if desired.

SERVES 4

Sopa de Palmito

HEART OF PALM SOUP

½ cup (1 stick) unsalted butter	4 cups homemade or canned low-sodium
1 medium onion, chopped	chicken stock
1 garlic clove, minced	1 medium potato, peeled and sliced
1 medium leek, washed, trimmed, and	Salt and freshly ground white pepper
chopped	to taste
1 celery rib, chopped	2 cups heavy cream
2 large fresh hearts of palm (about 1¼	3 tablespoons snipped chives or
pounds), or 2 10-ounce cans large	chopped scallions, including some of
hearts of palm, drained and halved	the green
lengthwise	

In a large saucepan, melt the butter over medium heat. Add the onion and garlic and sauté for 5 minutes, or until translucent. Add the leek and celery and cook another 3 minutes, or until wilted. If using fresh hearts, add them now and sauté for 15 to 20 minutes.

Add the stock and sliced potato, season with salt and pepper, and bring to a boil. Reduce the heat and simmer for 20 minutes, or until the potato and hearts of palm are soft and tender. If using canned hearts of palm, add them just when the potatoes become tender, and heat through for 4 to 5 minutes.

Strain the mixture, reserving the stock, and puree the vegetables with a little stock in a food processor or blender. Add the remaining stock and cool.

Stir in the cream and chill 2 hours or more.

Serve in chilled bowls and sprinkle with the chopped chives or scallions.

SERVES 8

Arroz de Rodeio
SOCCER PLAYER RICE

The famous soccer player Biro Biro dined frequently at São Paulo's Rodeio, one of the town's formidable churrasco restaurants. This is a robust dish that makes a great foil to simply prepared grilled or roasted beef dishes.

3 russet potatoes, peeled (or substitute 3 to 4 cups canned or frozen matchstick potatoes)	1 large onion, finely chopped
	2 large eggs, lightly beaten
	1 cup fresh parsley leaves, minced
3 tablespoons extra-virgin olive oil	¼ cup chopped scallions, including the green part
2 cups uncooked rice	
Salt to taste	4 slices cooked smoked bacon,
About 3 cups vegetable oil for frying	chopped

Cut the potatoes into matchstick slices on a mandoline or using the grater attachment of a food processor. Rinse the potatoes under cold running water to remove the starch. Place them in a mixing bowl, cover with fresh cold water, and refrigerate for 20 minutes.

In a large saucepan, heat 1 tablespoon olive oil over medium heat and add the rice. Stir for 3 minutes or until the rice has absorbed the oil. Add 4 cups cold water, bring to a boil, season with salt, and cover and simmer over medium-low heat for 20 minutes, or until tender.

While the rice is cooking, drain the potatoes and dry thoroughly on a clean kitchen towel. Heat the vegetable oil in a deep heavy saucepan or deep-fryer until it begins to smoke, or reaches a temperature of 350° F. Fry the potatoes in small batches until golden, then drain on paper towels and reserve.

In a medium skillet, heat the remaining 2 tablespoons olive oil over medium heat and sauté the onion until golden, about 5 minutes. Reduce the heat, add the eggs, and stir with a fork until lightly scrambled. Stir in the rice (there should be no liquid left in the pot, but drain if necessary). Add the parsley, scallions, and bacon and stir for another minute. Stir in the fried potatoes and serve.

SERVES 6

writers whose books he reads, architects whom he employs to add yet another addition or expand a gallery. . . . I know few people who derive such enjoyment from orchestrating a party.

He has organized a battalion of helpers setting up tables and chairs, bars, serving tables, a pantry in one of the sheds. The flower arrangements are in place, and candles are placed in lanterns to line the paths.

In the kitchen, thin slices of a delicate smoked transparent whitefish are arranged on thin slices of dark grain bread and cut into triangles by a couple of young girls, croquettes are breaded and prepared for frying, and *empadinhas* (page 16), little pastries filled with crab, chicken, or vegetables, are arranged on baking sheets. Onions, garlic, and sweet and hot peppers are sautéing in olive oil, tomatoes are peeled and chopped, herbs gathered from the garden, the beef is slowly cooking, and the pumpkins have been scooped clean and prepared for the oven. Pyramids of tiny sweets flavored with chocolate, coconut, guava, and nuts are arranged on little plates protected by a covering of gauze and sent to the garage.

Brazilian parties are neighborhood affairs; everyone is invited, numbers swell, and no one cares. The party goes off without a hitch, with plenty to eat and drink. Typically, dinner is served around midnight, dancing follows, and the night flies into dawn.

The picadinho is a hit. This beloved peasant dish was made chic throughout Rio in the fifties, when journalists and critics gathered at a local eatery late at night so they could eat the dish traditionally served to the restaurant help. Their praise made it acceptable party fare. Ours drew many surprised compliments: "You've taken a humble dish and served it in a pumpkin! You've glorified it!" Well, I did. Chunks of stewed pumpkin often accompany this dish—why not serve the picadinho in the vegetable itself?

The next morning Joachim says we must dress and have lunch at Rodeio. "A hangover lunch," he says cheerfully to no one in particular, but we are all in need of this remedy.

Rodeio is a sophisticated version of the popular *churrascaria,* or steak joint, located in the elegant shopping area of the city called the Jardins. This one is a carnivore's dream of heaven. Our daily menus at the house are mostly pasta, salads, fish, rice, and beans, but I am also eating a lot of beef—every time someone gives a party, it seems.

Rodeio has the feeling of an old-fashioned clubby businessmen's restaurant. Joachim orders cups of beef tea for us all. Each little cup is a reduction of one kilo of lean beef simmered until it shrivels and gives off its juices. No seasonings, no water, no salt. Accompanied *(continued on page 42)*

Roasted Chicken with Mustard Greens, Farofa, Sautéed Bananas, and Pão de Queijo al fresco

Galinha Assado com Mostarda

ROASTED CHICKEN WITH MUSTARD GREENS

2 3½- to 4-pound roasting chickens
6 sprigs marjoram or oregano
  Kosher salt and freshly ground
  pepper to taste
2 small tart oranges
2 to 3 tablespoons olive oil
1 medium onion, quartered

STOCK AND GRAVY
1 celery rib, chopped
1 small bay leaf
4 whole peppercorns
2 sprigs parsley
1 tablespoon all-purpose flour (optional)
1 tablespoon Dijon-type mustard

½ cup jabuticaba jam or preserve
  (see Note)

GREENS
1 pound young mustard greens or
  2 bunches watercress
1 tablespoon olive oil
½ cup chopped fresh parsley
  Salt and freshly ground pepper
  to taste

Toasted Farofa (see opposite), Fried
Bananas (see opposite), and Simple
Boiled White Rice (see page 12),
for serving

Cut the wing tips from the chickens at the second joint and discard the interior fat. Reserve wings, neck, and giblets for stock. Wash the chickens and pat them dry.

Place a small sprig of marjoram or oregano between the skin and flesh of each breast. Season the cavities with salt and pepper and add a sprig of the remaining marjoram to each cavity. Prick the exterior skin of the oranges with a fork and insert one into each cavity. Truss the birds and refrigerate uncovered for 1 hour or more.

Preheat the oven to 425° F. Place the chickens on the rack of a roasting pan, rub with olive oil, and liberally season with salt and pepper. Add the onion to the pan and roast for 1 hour and 20 minutes, basting from time to time.

To prepare the stock, in a medium saucepan, place the wing tips, neck, gizzard, and heart, celery, bay leaf, peppercorns, parsley, and enough water to just cover. Bring to a boil for 5 minutes, skim, reduce to a simmer, and cook for 30 minutes, or until the wings are fork tender. Strain and reserve.

After it's cooked for about 1 hour and 20 minutes, pierce the chicken at the leg and thigh joint. If the juices run clear, remove the chicken from the oven. If they are still pink, roast the chicken another 5 to 10 minutes.

Place the chicken on a warm platter, cover with foil, and set aside. Skim off most of the fat from the roasting pan and place over medium-high heat. Sprinkle the pan with flour, if using, and scrape up the brown bits with a fork. When it begins to bubble, add the stock and bring to a boil. Swirl in the mustard, reduce heat, and simmer for 10 minutes, or until the gravy begins to thicken. Add the *jabuticaba* jam or preserves and cook another minute or two. Strain the gravy into a warmed gravy boat.

To prepare the greens, remove the stems and, if using mustard greens, cut into fine julienne strips. Heat the olive oil in a large heavy skillet over medium-high heat. Swirl in the parsley and add the mustard greens or watercress and salt and pepper. Toss and warm through for about 1 minute, or until hot and steamy.

Place the greens, farofa, and bananas around the chicken. Serve with the gravy and boiled white rice.

SERVES 6

NOTE: *Jabuticaba* jam and preserves are sold in specialty markets as Brazilian grape jam. As a substitute, use half huckleberry or tart blueberry jam and half grape jam.

Farofa Peri Peri
TOASTED FAROFA

OVERLEAF:
*Lunch in the
garden*

- **2 tablespoons extra-virgin olive oil**
- **1 medium onion, chopped**
- **1 garlic clove, chopped**
- **½ red bell pepper, cored, seeded, deveined, and chopped**
- **1 medium carrot, peeled and grated**
- **4 scallions, white part only, trimmed and thinly sliced**
- **¼ cup blanched sliced almonds**
- **¼ cup chopped pitted black or green olives**
- **⅓ cup sultana raisins, soaked in ½ cup cachaça or dry white wine**
- **1 cup flaky corn farofa or manioc flour (farinha de mandioca)**
- **2 tablespoons chopped fresh parsley**

- **Chicken, or beef or pork roast, for serving**

In a large skillet, heat the oil over medium heat and add the onion and garlic. Sauté for 5 minutes, or until translucent. Add the bell pepper and sauté for 5 minutes, or until limp. Add the carrot, sauté another minute, then add the scallions and sauté another minute or two. Add the almonds and olives, reduce the heat, and keep the mixture warm.

Drain the raisins and discard the cachaça or wine. Add the raisins to the mixture.

Heat a separate pan over medium heat for 1 minute. Add the farofa and toast for 1 minute, stirring with a wooden spoon. Stir this into the vegetable mixture, add the parsley, and place the farofa in a warm bowl.

Serve with chicken as you would stuffing, or with beef or pork roasts.

MAKES ABOUT 2½ CUPS

Banana Frita
FRIED BANANAS

The sweetness of the banana complements chicken. In Brazil, however, cooks also serve these bananas as an accompaniment to fish.

For this recipe, use ripe but firm small bananas, such as *manica,* or finger, or apple bananas. If using larger bananas, cut them on the diagonal into 1-inch-thick slices.

- **6 small bananas, peeled**
- **1 large egg, beaten**
- **1 cup fine bread crumbs**
- **½ cup (1 stick) unsalted butter**
- **Salt to taste**

In a mixing bowl, gently toss the bananas with the egg to moisten, then lightly roll the bananas in the bread crumbs.

In a large skillet, melt the butter over medium heat.

When the foam subsides, add the bananas and fry on all sides until golden. Season with salt and serve hot.

SERVES 6

Cuscuz Paulista

COUSCOUS FROM SÃO PAULO

Just as we would refer to someone from New York City as a New Yorker, the term "Paulista" is a reference to a person who lives in the city of São Paulo. This dish is a favorite among the Paulistas, and though the recipe has its roots in North Africa, this version's ingredients are particular to Brazil. The dish is more a pudding than a stew, and the grain used is made from manioc flour rather than semolina and a flaky corn flour. Knowing we do not have flaky corn flour available to us in the States, a smart Brazilian cook said why don't you substitute cornflakes. It's almost the same thing. This dish is usually served as part of a buffet or first course.

1½ **pounds medium shrimp, peeled and deveined (heads and shells reserved if making homemade stock)**

3 to 4 **cups light homemade fish stock or stock made from fish bouillon cubes**

4 **cups Brazilian flaky corn flour or plain cornflakes**

1 **cup untoasted manioc flour (farinha de mandioca)**

5 **medium tomatoes, peeled, seeded, chopped, and drained (juice reserved)**

1 **tablespoon salt or to taste**

¼ **cup dried shrimp (either homemade, see page 97, or store-bought, soaked)**

½ **cup fresh or frozen green peas**

¼ **cup vegetable oil**

2 **medium onions, grated**

¼ **cup black Moroccan or Niçoise-type olives, pitted and roughly chopped**

1 **cup 1-inch rounds large heart of palm**

3 **fresh or canned sardines, filleted, tails intact**

¼ **cup chopped fresh parsley**

2 **scallions, trimmed and chopped Freshly ground pepper to taste About 5 kale leaves, stemmed and center ribs removed**

Rinse the fresh shrimp, set aside 6 shrimp, then roughly chop the rest. If making homemade stock, rinse the shells and heads and place them in a medium saucepan with water to cover by 1 inch. Bring to a boil over medium heat, reduce the heat, and simmer for 10 minutes. Strain and discard the shells. Combine the shrimp stock with enough fish stock to make 4 cups. Cool and reserve the extra stock.

In a large bowl, combine the corn flour or cornflakes and manioc flour. Add the reserved tomato liquid and gradually add the stock, working with your fingers until the mixture is smooth and slightly damp. If too dry, add a little more stock. Set the *cuscuz* mixture aside.

In the bowl of a food processor, grind the dried shrimp, pulsing on and off until they are finely ground, and reserve.

Bring a small saucepan of water to boil over medium-high heat and cook the peas for 2 minutes. Drain.

In a medium skillet, heat the oil over medium heat, add the onions, and sauté until translucent. Add the tomatoes and ground dried shrimp and cook for 5 minutes. Remove from the heat. Reserve 1 tablespoon each of the olives and peas and add the remainder to the tomato mixture. Reserve 6 heart-of-palm slices, roughly chop the remainder, and add them to the tomato mixture.

Lightly oil a *couscousière* (not a Moroccan type) or small rounded colander, then sprinkle it lightly with water. Decorate the bottom and lower half of the mold with the sardines, skin side down, and some reserved whole shrimp, olives, and peas, and set aside.

Fold the tomato mixture, chopped fresh shrimp, parsley, and scallions into the cuscuz mixture. Season with black pepper. It should be damp but not wet. Add more stock if necessary. Spoon the mixture into the couscousière or colander, packing it down gently, decorating the upper sides with the remaining peas, olives, heart of palm, and shrimp as you fill the mold. Cover the surface with the kale leaves, then seal with aluminum foil and place over a pot of simmering water, making sure the water does not touch the bottom of the mold. Cover with a tight-fitting lid and steam for 20 minutes.

Remove the cuscuz from the heat and let it rest for 10 minutes. Run the blade of a thin, sharp knife around the couscousière or colander and invert it onto a serving platter. Serve immediately.

SERVES 8

Rabada da Anita
ANITA'S OXTAIL STEW

4 **pounds oxtail, cut into 2½-inch-thick rounds**
2 **tablespoons vegetable oil**
1 **large onion, chopped**
1 **garlic clove, chopped**
4 **tomatoes, peeled, seeded, and chopped**
1 **sprig oregano, or ¼ teaspoon dried oregano**
¼ **cup chopped fresh parsley**
3 **cups homemade or canned low-sodium beef or chicken stock**

Salt and freshly ground pepper to taste
2 **teaspoons arrowroot, for thickening the sauce (optional)**
1 **bunch watercress, washed and trimmed**
1 **tablespoon fresh lime juice**

Polenta (see page 176), and Malagueta Pepper Sauce (see page 96), for serving

Rinse the oxtail pieces under cold water, place them in a large nonreactive saucepan, and add cold water to cover. Bring to a boil, cover, reduce the heat, and simmer for 20 minutes. Drain and set aside.

In another large nonreactive saucepan, heat the oil over medium heat and sauté the onion until it is lightly browned. Add the garlic and sauté another 3 minutes. Add the tomatoes, oregano, parsley, and stock and bring the mixture to a boil. Submerge the reserved oxtail in the mixture. If necessary, add more stock or water to cover the oxtail by 1 inch. Season with salt and pepper, reduce the heat, cover, and simmer for 1 to 1½ hours, or until the oxtail is fork tender.

Remove the oxtail from the sauce with a slotted spoon and place in a heatproof tureen. Place the watercress over the oxtail, cover, and keep warm.

Bring the sauce to a boil and reduce it until it is thick, about 10 minutes. Or combine the arrowroot with a little cold water and stir it in. Cook, stirring, until the sauce has thickened. Add the lime juice and pour the sauce over the oxtail.

Serve with polenta and Malagueta Pepper Sauce.

NOTE: To prepare the polenta, follow the recipe on page 176, eliminating the corn kernels and cheese. Turn the hot polenta out into an oiled shallow pan and spread with an oiled spatula about ½ inch thick. Allow to cool. Using a knife dipped in hot water, slice the polenta into rectangles about 2 x 4 inches. Generously brush a nonstick skillet with olive oil and brown the polenta over medium-high heat, about 3 minutes on each side. Serve with the oxtail and watercress.

SERVES 4

BELOW:
*Rabada, an
oxtail stew, is
one of my
favorite suppers
prepared by
Anita.*

by a fresh egg yolk, the liquid shoots through our veins, straight to our head. We feel better already.

A Goliath rack of beef ribs crusted in golden fat is wheeled to the table and carved, one large rib for each of us. The fat melts in your mouth, preceded by the sting of rough salt and fragrant pepper. We dip the tender morsels of moist, dark rib meat into grated horseradish, and it is the best rib I've ever tasted in my life. Tomatoes, onions, tender greens, parsley, and shaved carrots are deftly chopped to confetti in front of our eyes. Salt, pepper, mustard, vinegar, and olive oil are whisked with a fork to dress the salad. The cook then serves a rice dish that is a crazy concoction of chopped scallions, bacon, and fried matchstick potatoes, called *arroz de Rodeio* (page 33). Then three *picanha* are presented, ovals of dark, satiny, ruby meat encased in a thin ribbon of yellow fat—the hump of the cow, prized as the tenderest and most savory part. The captain slices them thin and grills the slices briefly, for a minute or two on each side, over the glowing embers in the grate of the brazier strategically situated near us. The picanha requires nothing more than a fork for cutting, and with it we sip our Brazilian Petit Syrah—as good as any California varietal. Laughing through the events of last evening, we finish with a cafezinho. Newly restored, we are ready for the rest of the day.

The Saturday before Christmas I prepare *moqueca* (page 24), the renowned fish stew from Bahia, for lunch. Sig, a friend, has brought Francisco, whom he describes as his guru. Francisco is an enormous, rich-coffee-colored black man with a majestic head framed by plaited dread-

Cuscuz Paulista, a dish loved by the locals.

locks and a smile that could light the sky. Turbaned, bedecked with strings of wooden beads and a sizable wooden cross and sparkling silver bracelets, he spends most of the time in the kitchen making caipirinhas and seriously watching me make his native dish.

"More chopped cilantro," he says. "Don't add the malagueta pepper oil. We never season dishes with this hot *pimenta* oil while cooking; we do it ourselves at the table. Brazilian food isn't hot. You make it hot!" Then "More dendê oil!" he cries, referring to the common name Brazilians use for palm oil. I refuse and he says, "Aaah, yes, Americano—they are afraid for the fat." Time enough, but I am learning the authentic Brazilian cooking style, nonetheless.

DATELINE: TIETÊ, IN THE NORTHWEST OF SÃO PAULO STATE, DECEMBER 24

The day before Christmas, we pack up and head to Peri Peri, the family fazenda (similar to our early plantation houses in the South), some two hundred kilometers northwest of the city. Dating back to the eighteenth century, these colonial seats made the fortunes for the coffee and cotton barons who made São Paulo the city it is today, and most are still working farms.

On the curvy, wavy highway to the little town of Tietê, the heat is intense, and every quarter mile or so on the side of the highway are square sheets of bright yellow canvas anchored to bamboo poles, protecting vendors and their wares from the sun. Some of these makeshift tents shade farmers' children selling boxes of loose eggs stacked in walls that reach the brim of the canvas. The light coming through the canvas roofs is so bright the yolks are actually visible through their translucent shells. Banks of mangoes and masses of oranges still tinged green look more golden in the transfused light. They beckon as we speed to our destination, and we stop for a refreshing drink at one selling *agua de cana.* Under the tent a woman is forcing poles of freshly cut sugarcane into the mouth of a funnel. This jerry-rigged machine looks more like the guts of a fuel-powered lawn mower sputtering and choking while clear juices flow into the pail beneath. Served with a generous squeeze of lime in ice-filled cups, the juice is nectar.

We arrive in the little town of Tietê—a collection of confectionery-colored small houses, tiny cafés, and a sizable white stucco church, with cobalt-blue doors and trim, that surround the town green. The mood is festive yet calm. Under flowering trees stands decorated with strings of fresh fruit sell *batidas,* fruit juices served with or without shots of cachaça, empadas, grilled sausages, and sweets. We find a table on the sidewalk of a small bar and join a bunch of older men sipping their icy beer, looking oddly like our western cowboys in their boots, jeans, plaid cotton shirts buttoned at the wrists, string ties, and straw cowboy hats. Like most farmers they pretend to be barely aware of us city folk.

We reach the fazenda by a winding dirt road covered in crimson petals falling from the flamboyant trees shading the way, catching glimpses here and there of fields of sugarcane and ponds and forests punctuated with exalted palms. The soft-orange-tiled roof seems to float over the circumscribed veranda of this sprawling white stucco house. On the soft-gray-painted main door a red-ribboned wreath joyously announces the season. We pass from soft-hued room to soft-hued room fringed with stencils suggesting ornamental pineapples and flowers in light blues and pinks; bowls of fragrant roses scent the rooms, and cousins, aunts, uncles, grandmother, and friends are greeted, kissed, and hugged. Lunch is on the veranda, overlooking the stretch of green rolling farmland. The mandatory Christmas fish dish, *mariscada de bacalhau* (page 29), is succulent with chunks of moist cod swimming in fresh tomatoes, sweet peppers, and herbs, served with fluffy white rice and robust red wine. The *pudim de leite* (page 28; a flan) is a triumph. The velvety custard is scented with flecks of orange zest and vanilla. And there's a macédoine of fresh tropical fruits to lighten us up. After cups of thick rich coffee we disband in groups for tours of the vegetable garden, filled with salad greens, herbs, and tomatoes and an alley of mango trees and stumpy papaya trees laden with clusters of ripening fruits, which leads to the hidden rose garden. Then a swim and a nap.

Back at the fazenda, after a trip into town for midnight mass, the Christmas tree is lit, champagne bottles pop, fresh mint tea and cookies are served, presents are opened, and I'm off to bed to be lulled to sleep by the hollow din of a small forest of huge bamboo lightly clattering in the breeze, sounding like flutes.

On Christmas Day, the kitchen is abuzz with activity.

When I remark on the rich mahogany color of the turkey, Maria, the cook, explains that during the last couple of hours of cooking she adds a cup of rich dark coffee with cream and sugar and bastes and bastes the bird. This little trick produces a delicious gravy. The Swedes do the same when roasting lamb.

The turkey, she tells me, has been marinating in white wine and herbs for more than a day. Brazilian cooks marinate their turkeys in cachaça, wine, or beer. Sometimes they inject the flesh, by inserting a hypodermic needle; on occasion the more modern kitchen will employ a bulb baster with a pointed needlelike attachment. Whatever the method, the result is a very moist and tender bird.

Lunch begins with a chilled heart of palm soup, followed by the turkey with a traditional stuffing of farofa meal, pork sausage, onions, celery, and seasonings. The bird is accompanied by mashed white sweet potatoes, fried bananas (page 37), and green beans. Desserts consist of an array of fruit *doces* (sweetened fruits, preserved through slow cooking, that are somewhere between a conserve and the crystallized sweet fruits from Provence), carambola (star fruit), strips of mango swimming in syrup, and guava paste served with a choice of rich clotted cream or soft Minas cheese, which is similar to our farmer cheese.

The doces began appearing on the tables of the great houses in the northern state of Minas Gerais in the seventeenth century, and that style of cooking filtered into the northern regions of São Paulo. My host explains during dinner that when fazendas were the center of country social and business life they served as both guest house and restaurant to visiting friends, family, ranch foremen, cattle sellers, and the brokers, bankers, lawyers, and accountants from the city. Visitors would arrive at all times of day, and the sideboard in the dining room groaned with foods and was constantly replenished. Everything appeared on the table—meat, fish when they had it, vegetables, beans, rice, potatoes, boiled manioc, fried bananas, cheeses, and desserts. "That is why," Joachim says, "all those starches appear at a Brazilian buffet party—it is because of years of having all these dishes presented to them at once. It isn't so odd for us to eat rice and beans with potatoes. And with the popularity of pasta today—you get some of that, too."

Part of the reason for marinating meats and sugaring fruits was to preserve and sustain the food because of rapid spoiling. There was no source of ice or refrigeration in the country, and what ice was available in the cities was affordable only by the wealthy. Dona Lucila, their sprightly septuagenarian mother, explains why meals are always served hot: simply because the heat of the food creates the illusion that the outside temperature is cooler. She said one reason the pressure cooker became so popular after its introduction in the forties was, in addition to a shorter cooking time requiring less fuel, the risk of beans, the household staple's, fermenting and souring while soaking was reduced. Meats were served soon after slaughter, the fresh or "green" meat, as they call it, immediately used or bartered for other staples from neighbors nearby, and the lesser cuts hung to dry in the sun or made into salami and sausages. One reason the vegetables and fruits sold at market are so good is due to farmers' picking only what is ripe and ready for eating that very same day. The excess abundance of fruits grown on these farms is made into delectable doces, marmalades, and jams.

I spend the next morning on the veranda with Dona Lucila, who regales me with talk of life at the fazenda in the old days. She speaks of the families who have worked for her family over the years on the farm and in the city, and although, or perhaps because, most of Brazil's population has always had economic difficulties, responsibilities of employers go beyond just giving their workers food and a roof. They help educate their children and care for them when they are old or sick. "There are too many for us to help them all," Dona Lucila laments. But I think Dona Lucila is an exception and exceptional.

She remains enchanted with the old ways and has no time for newfangled kitchen gadgets. No kitchen that prides itself on being truly Brazilian lacks a wicker sieve for sifting flour and pressing roots, an earthenware water jug, gourd cups, brooms of palm fronds, and a mortar and pestle, unbeatable for pounding corn, cod, and dried meats and for pulverizing nuts. These are the elements of the old colonial kitchens, and you can sense them in the food. Dona Lucila actually has a mortar, made of the best hardwood, that has been passed through her family from generation to generation for more than two hundred years. It stands thigh-high and requires kneeling before it, pestle gripped with two hands, and she uses it to make one of her favorite dishes: *paçoca,* a dish of mulled meat, sausage, and spices known only at the farms in Minas and northern São Paulo. She says, "I know a Mineira cook [a person from the state of Minas Gerais], and you will come to my house when you return to the city, and she will cook it for you. But I think it a good idea if you go to the kitchen and watch Maria make the *tutu*; this version is more Paulista—we don't mash the beans. Probably too much work today, or perhaps it is the style—to keep our individuality separate from the Mineiras."

The meat and sausage vendor at the street market sells all the basic meat ingredients for a feijoada.

Tutu is a creamy puree of beans, made famous in the hills of Minas Gerais (page 53). I'd heard it is among the Mineiras' treasured dishes and expected to taste it there. What I hadn't realized was that it is their variation of feijoada, nor did I know that in São Paulo it is served as a sort of leftover dish following Saturday's feijoada, called *virado de feijão*. Maria makes her version as they do in Minas—from scratch! But hers is not pureed. The beans, boiled in water with neither salt nor seasonings, are seasoned after cooking. In good olive oil she sautés onions, garlic, chopped tomato, a handful of parsley, a goodly amount of bean liquor, a generous taste of salt, and a steady stream of manioc flour. When thickened, this mixture is added to the beans. The flavors are preserved rather than diluted during cooking. Like the Brazilians, I now crave servings of these protein-filled legumes, and so will you.

While Maria finishes off the beans she is also busy preparing a farofa dish (page 37) to accompany a roasted chicken she will serve with tender mustard greens (page 36). She starts off sautéing some aromatics, then adding raisins. The farofa is toasted carefully, then the two mixtures are combined. She quickly sautés tiny sweet bananas, a traditional accompaniment, to round off the meal (page 37).

Cozido

BOILED MEATS AND VEGETABLES

This lusty meal is often served as a Sunday lunch. The origins of the dish are Portuguese, but the preparation and sauce are very similar to the *bollito misto* of Northern Italy and the *pot au feu* of northern France.

MEATS

1 pound salted pork ribs
½ pound smoked bacon, with rind, blanched
½ pound lingüiça sausage (spicy Portuguese sausage)
1½ pounds beef brisket or chuck
6 small marrow bones
2 celery ribs, trimmed
10 whole peppercorns
1 bay leaf
6 sprigs parsley

VEGETABLES

1 small green cabbage, trimmed, cored, and cut into 8 wedges
4 small carrots, peeled, cut diagonally in 1-inch lengths
1 pound pumpkin, rind removed and cut into 1-inch cubes
3 ripe plantains, peeled and cut into 3-inch rounds
Salt and freshly ground pepper to taste
4 ears corn, shucked and cut into 3-inch rounds

1 pound white sweet potatoes, peeled and cut into ½-inch rounds
½ pound green beans, trimmed and tied together with twine
½ pound okra, tops trimmed
2 medium xuxu (chayotes), trimmed, cored, and cut into 2-inch sticks

SAUCE

3 garlic cloves, finely chopped
1 cup chopped fresh parsley
1 small red onion, finely chopped
1 small hot chili pepper, seeded, deveined, and finely chopped
Juice of 3 limes
⅓ cup extra-virgin olive oil
Salt and freshly ground pepper to taste

ACCOMPANIMENTS

1 cup manioc flour (farinha de mandioca) for the pirão
Preserved malagueta peppers

To prepare the meats, rinse the pork ribs in cold water. Place them in a medium saucepan, cover with cold water, and bring to a boil. Reduce the heat and simmer for 20 minutes. Drain the ribs and repeat the process 3 more times, or until all the salt is removed. Drain the ribs and reserve.

Add the bacon and the sausage to 2 separate saucepans of cold water, bring to a boil, and simmer for 15 minutes. Cool each meat separately under cold running water and reserve.

In a large stockpot, add the beef and marrow bones, cover with cold water, then add the celery, peppercorns, bay leaf, and parsley. Bring to a boil, skimming off any impurities periodically, reduce the heat to low, and simmer until the meat is fork tender. Remove the veal knuckles after about 1 hour of cooking and reserve.

When the beef is cooked, after about 2 hours, remove it and reserve. Skim off the fat and strain the liquid into a clean kettle.

For the vegetables, add the cabbage, carrots, pumpkin, and plantains into the kettle with the strained liquid and simmer for 10 minutes. Season with salt and pepper and add the corn, potatoes, green beans, okra, xuxu, bacon, sausage, and beef and cook for 10 minutes, or until the vegetables are tender.

To make the sauce, in a nonreactive bowl, combine the garlic, parsley, onion, chili pepper, lime juice, olive oil, and salt and pepper and set aside.

Remove the meats from the pot with a slotted spoon, slice them, and arrange on a warm serving platter with the vegetables.

Place a marrow bone in individual heated soup plates. Strain the soup into a heated tureen and serve with accompaniments.

SERVES 6

NOTE: When setting the table place a small bowl with 2 tablespoons of manioc flour at each soup plate. The diner mixes the soup and manioc flour with a fork, creating a pirão, taking as much soup as he or she wishes to achieve the desired consistency. The meats and vegetables are eaten along with the pirão, the sauce, and the preserved malagueta peppers.

OVERLEAF:
Cozido, the classic boiled meat and vegetable dinner, awaits the guest.

Pudim de Bacalhau
CODFISH PUDDING

This is wonderful served with Stewed Tomato and Okra (see page 17) and a xuxu salad (see page 52).

- 1 **pound salted codfish**
- 1 **tablespoon white cider vinegar**
- ¾ **pound potatoes (about 2 medium), peeled and quartered**
- 2 **tablespoons olive oil**
- 1 **medium onion, chopped**
  Salt and freshly ground pepper to taste
- 1 **cup fresh or canned tomato juice**
- 2 **tablespoons (¼ stick) unsalted butter**
- ¼ **cup chopped fresh parsley**
- 6 **large egg yolks**
- 7 **large egg whites**
- 5 **tablespoons freshly grated Parmesan cheese**

Place the cod in a large bowl and cover with cold water. Refrigerate for 48 hours, changing the water 4 or 5 times. Drain.

In a large kettle, add the cod, vinegar, and enough cold water to cover. Bring to a boil and cook for 15 minutes. Drain and cool. Remove the skin and bones and shred the cod into fine needlelike pieces with a fork.

In a large kettle, add the potatoes and water to cover. Cover, bring to a boil, and cook 20 minutes, or until tender. Mash the potatoes well and set aside.

Preheat the oven to 350° F.

Heat the olive oil in a large skillet over medium heat. Add the onion and sauté for 3 minutes. Add the cod and sauté 1 more minute. Season with salt and pepper and remove from the heat.

Combine the cod mixture with the mashed potatoes. Cool slightly. Add the tomato juice, butter, and parsley and combine. Cool thoroughly.

Add the egg yolks one at a time and set aside.

In a mixing bowl, beat the egg whites with a pinch of salt until stiff and glossy and fold them into the cod mixture. Set aside.

Butter a 2-quart ovenproof soufflé pan and dust with 3 tablespoons of the Parmesan cheese. Tap out any extra cheese.

Add the pudding mixture and sprinkle with the remaining cheese. Bake for 45 minutes, or until golden and springy to the touch.

SERVES 8 TO 10

Pamonha

SWEET CORN PUREE STEAMED IN THE HUSKS

Like the tamales of Mexico, these sweet little puddings are sold by vendors in towns and cities. In late afternoon, trucks travel the residential areas of São Paulo as our Good Humor trucks once did, some ringing bells, others blaring pop tunes over a megaphone, and a voice shouts over the din *"Pamonha! Pamonha! Gostoso e fresca!"*—delicious and fresh. Wrapped individually in newspaper, they are still warm.

10 **ears sweet corn**
   About ⅓ cup milk
 2 **tablespoons sugar**
   Pinch of salt
 ¼ **teaspoon ground cinnamon**

 2 **tablespoons (¼ stick) unsalted butter, at room temperature**

   Malagueta Pepper Sauce (optional; see page 96), for serving

Remove the husks carefully, so they do not break, and reserve. Remove all the silk. Slice the kernels away from the cob and place them in a large bowl. Over the bowl, run a soup spoon down the cobs to scrape out any additional corn milk.

Place the corn kernels, about a cup at a time, in a food processor or blender and pulse on and off, adding a little milk until the corn is creamy but still lumpy. Turn each batch into a large bowl when it achieves the right consistency. Add the sugar, salt, cinnamon, and softened butter to the corn mixture and blend. Set aside.

Line a steamer basket with the tougher outer green corn husks and fill the bottom of the steamer with enough hot water to come ½ inch below the basket. Set aside.

Take one of the large pliable inner corn husks and spread it flat. Place about 2 tablespoons of the corn mixture in the lower, larger end of the husk. Roll up the husk loosely and fold the ends over the seam. Tie loosely with kitchen string, making a small package. Repeat until all the mixture is used. Stack the pamonha in the basket seam side up. Cover with a layer of husks, cover the steamer, and bring to a boil. Reduce the heat and simmer for 1 hour, or until the filling has a puddinglike consistency. Remove and cool for 20 minutes, or until the husk does not stick to the filling.

Serve the pamonha with Malagueta Pepper Sauce or with stews or grilled meats.

MAKES ABOUT 16 PAMONHA

Salada de Xuxu

ORANGE AND CHAYOTE SALAD

Xuxu, or chayote, is a crisp-textured, bland-tasting vegetable that mixes pleasingly with more dominant flavors. Its surface is oily and sticky, but a Brazilian cook taught me a little trick for easy handling. Cut the xuxu in half lengthwise and rub the halves back and forth under cold running water. The oil will rise to the surface and rinse off.

 4 **xuxu (chayotes), peeled, cored, and grated on the large side of the grater**
 4 **oranges, skin and pith removed and sectioned from the membranes**
 1 **large red onion, thinly sliced**

 ½ **cup fresh mint leaves, chopped**
 4 **tablespoons extra-virgin olive oil**
   Juice of 1 lime
   Salt and freshly ground pepper to taste

In a large nonreactive bowl, combine all of the ingredients. Toss to mix well and divide among 4 chilled plates.

SERVES 4

Tutu Peri Peri

An indigenous bean dish from Minas Gerais, usually made from scratch and served with fried pork chops, pork roasts, and sausages. In São Paulo it is a leftover dish made from Saturday's feijoada called *virado de feijão* (virado means "to turn," as in turned or stirred beans, meaning reheated). Serve with roast chicken, grilled pork chops, or sausages and accompany with Hot Pepper Salsa (see page 180).

1 **pound dried beans (Use** *carioca* **or** *mulatinho*—**"little mulatos"—in Brazil, cranberry or pinto in the United States. You can also use white or navy beans.)**
Salt to taste
¼ **cup vegetable oil**

1 **large onion, chopped**
3 **cloves garlic, chopped**
1 **large, firm tomato, chopped**
1 **cup flat-leaf parsley leaves, chopped**
½ **teaspoon fresh thyme leaves, chopped**
1 **cup manioc flour (farinha de mandioca)**

Soak the beans overnight in the refrigerator with water to cover.

Drain the beans. Put them in a large soup kettle with enough water to cover by five inches. Cover and bring to a boil over high heat, then reduce the heat and simmer for 1 hour, or until the beans are tender. Add more water if necessary. (You will need a lot of liquid to finish the beans—there should be at least 3 cups of liquid left in the stockpot when beans are tender.)

When the beans are tender, season with one tablespoon salt, or more to taste.

In a large saucepan, heat the oil over medium heat and sauté the onion and garlic for 5 minutes, or until translucent. Add the tomato and parsley and cook another minute or two. Add 3 cups of bean liquor to the mixture.

Reduce the heat and gradually pour in the farinha de mandioca in a thin stream, stirring constantly. Stir for 10 minutes, or until the mixture thickens. Add two-thirds of the beans and stir. If the mixture is thin, add more beans. Reserve any remaining beans for another use. The beans should be wet, but not soupy.

SERVES 8

rio de janeiro

Flying into Rio is a traveler's treat. We circle around cone-shaped hills, lush palm trees spiking out at every angle, as we brush clouds, coming too close to the hills. We can see the faces of the hang gliders fluttering off the peaks of São Conrado like butterflies as we curl around the shimmering loops of long sinuous beaches. The sea sparkles beneath us as

One of the hundreds of stands along the beach offering cool coconut water and refreshment for the thirsty

we approach Rio, heading toward the Santos Dumont airstrip in the middle of the city.

I'm headed down the beach to Ipanema to stay with Italian friends. A quick change into a bathing suit, and I'm in the sapphire sea in minutes. For me Brazil is the sea—all three thousand miles of its coastline. Waves crash and splash the nearest lazy bodies.

For refreshment, we join a bunch of beach-clad Cariocas at one of the palm-thatched *barzinho de praia* (open-air bar stands that line the beaches) selling iced green coconuts. One of the beach boys deftly hacks off the top of the fruit with his cutlass, and we sip the cooling sweet water through colored paper straws. Looking happy and festive, the barman offers us a shot of cachaça to spike up the juice, but we resist. When we finish, he cuts the coconut in half with one swift blow so we can eat the translucent white flesh—unlike any coconut meat I have ever eaten. An open farm truck pulls up, overflowing with clusters of coconuts still attached to their spikes, looking like bunches of bionic grapes. Fresh coconut might seem a bit exotic to us, but it's revered and regarded as the most important food for one-third of the population of this planet, and it plays a considerable role in the Brazilian kitchen.

We walk over amazing patterned curls, swirls, and swells of black-and-white marble streets to meet our friends for lunch. Luigi, my Italian friend, reminds me that these stones came from Portugal to weight down the ships in place of cargo until they returned with the gold, jewels, parrots, monkeys, Indians, and eventually cotton, coffee, and cocoa they came for. We weave our way through the crowded outdoor cafés and head to the backstreets, passing shops selling a variety of wares.

And people—waves of shades of tan, coffee, cocoa, copper, mahogany, and black; tall, thin, with dazzling white teeth, legs that go on for days; lightly dressed, if not in minute bathing suits; all lolling, walking, talking, smoking, playing, embracing, eating, and drinking.

The sights and aromas of street food envelop us.

Frying manioc, grilling meats, black coffee, bitter chocolate, garlic, and rich ripples of cooking oil filter through the breeze. Small cafés, stand-up bars, and street carts offer a dazzling array of snacks: fried codfish balls (page 64), freshly made shrimp and crab cakes, spicy hamburgers, hot dogs, sausages, steaming corn, fresh fruit ices, popcorn, and *cocadas*—irresistible chewy coconut sweets. We almost stumble over a little urchin who has set up his tin brazier on the curb, filled with burning embers; he is preparing chunks of cheese on wooden skewers to grill. He's as determined as any American kid setting up his first lemonade stand.

By late afternoon we are sitting in the Colombo, one of Rio's oldest cafés and gathering places—a nineteenth-century marvel of polished wood, brass, marble, etched mirrors, and sparkling globes with peachy glass shades diffusing the light. The aged marble-topped tables, the gilded cane chairs, the tubs of palms, and the overhead dome of frosty pastel stained glass have all the aura of a tropical Viennese coffeehouse. Spiffy waiters in black jackets glide through the room balancing trays of *suco misto*—tall iced glasses of fresh, lightly sweetened fruit juices made from any of a dozen fruits harvested as far away as the Amazon, guava, passion fruit, mango, melon, papaya, pineapple. The bright drinks look like rainbows whooshing through the room. We order a half dozen by color, including the pale green one—*limonada Suissa* (page 64)—a popular limeade brimming with specks of dark green lime rind. (*Limão* is the Portuguese word for "lime." Yellow lemons are not available in Brazil, or in South America for that matter, except on occasion at a staggering price. The Brazilian lime is a little sweeter than our lime and a little less acidic, but our lime is still the best proxy for this crowd-pleasing drink.) Tall glasses of shrimp cocktails (page 65) arrive looking like ice-cream sundaes—tiny pink baby bay shrimp laced among layers of velvety cool avocado cream and topped with a curl of sliced lime in place of a cherry.

It's late for lunch, and the available menu consists of a selection of sandwiches, and we settle on *bife com alho*—a serious white-bread sandwich filled with thinly sliced roast beef, melted cottage cheese, watercress, sliced gherkins, tomato, and shredded lettuce. Its elegant presentation belies its lustiness. The dessert tray arrives with pastries filled with rich dark chocolate, and vanilla and nut creams, and there are also fresh guava tarts and *quindim* (page 65)—a sugary puddinglike tart of rich custard and coconut.

Later that night we dine at one of those restaurants that is enjoying its fifteen minutes in the sun simply because its chef has just returned from a stint in France. But the evening is not a total disaster. I meet the divine Cesarina, a musician friend of Joachim's, and we are off for an evening of Brazilian folk music and jazz, finishing the evening at a samba school at the edge of one of the *favelas* (shantytowns). The favelas shelter tens of thousands of poor Cariocas in village clusters that literally hug the sides of the steep earthen hills that are among the unique natural wonders of Rio. We look up in awe at the corrugated rusting sheet metal and scrap lumber boxes that cling to the hill like houses of cards, twinkling with thousands of lightbulbs dangling from wire strings. In the stillness of the black night it looks beautiful. Luigi gasps and says, "It looks like Positano at night." Cesarina points out the reality by chiding him, "Not by day, *caro!*"

OVERLEAF:
Fruits and vegetables at the Leblon outdoor market. Clockwise from the left: manioc root, oranges, fresh malagueta peppers, guava, passion fruit, pineapples, and mangos.

Carnival is a month away, and students at the samba schools practice through the night from now until then at feverish frequency. The school is a cinder-block hall the length of a soccer field located at the base of the favela. Drums blare, thunder, roar, and boom the long *TRRAAHH-TRAAh-TRAah-tah-ta,* and your heart and head pound with the electrifying beat. Dancers assemble at one end of the hall and dance their parade, splashing the crowd outward against the walls as they move forward. The sensuousness and warmth belie the poverty, misery, and disease that afflict so many Brazilians and probably account for the tinge of sadness that pervades the music I've heard through the evening. Brazil's great storyteller Gilberto Freyre says, "The slave, even when well treated, felt vaguely nostalgic, which made his song one of sadness, though his dance was often of joy." This sadness invades me, giving rise to a feeling of wistfulness—what the Brazilians call *saudade.*

We have been invited to celebrate New Year's Eve with our Brazilian friend Nalita and her French husband, Gerard. Calls go back and forth all morning as our group expands. Nalita has no problem with issuing an enthusiastic ultimatum: "You must bring them all."

Late morning we spend at the Jardim Botânico, a veritable rain forest in the middle of Rio. Rio was a monoculture (first sugarcane and later coffee) in her early days, but under the aegis of Emperor Dom Pedro II, the destroyed surrounding hills and forests were revitalized. The long avenue of imperial palms in this garden are testament to his vision. Rocketing to the sky, they lead us to the playing fountain and on to an orchid house, ponds filled with lily pads large enough to float on, bamboo forests, Amazonian jungle plants and trees, and paths that lead to a waterfall barreling down from huge rocks. Barely visible in the canopy of trees above, parakeets, parrots, and monkeys screech and rustle in the leaves. In Brazil one is rarely far from the jungle—even in the large cities one feels it closing in, in a park, a private garden, and an abandoned lot and on the edges of the city. If I stand in one place too long, I feel the creeping vines, roots, and lianas that crawl and hang from the trees will entangle, even suffocate, me. It is quite oppressive sometimes.

Just before the celebration of the New Year approaches, the feeling in the streets is solemn. But by nightfall, all dressed in white to symbolize the birth of a new year, we move through the throng of graceful, unselfconscious, ogling white-clad Cariocas to join our friends on Copacabana for a prefatory glass of champagne, then on to our party.

High above Rio, glass doors open to the terrace, and we can almost touch the first of the string of conelike hills that meet Pão de Açúcar

(Sugar Loaf Mountain), named because it resembles the conical block of hard-packed refined or raw sugar that was common in kitchens throughout most of the civilized world until the end of the nineteenth century. Locals tell us the Tamoyo Indians poetically called the mountain Hill to Heaven. Spiraling down like a rope of pearls, natives slowly descend the nearest hill, stepping gingerly one behind the other, to the base that leaves them stranded on the opposite side of the beach, but with a perfect view of fireworks to come.

The sounds of samba bands echo from the beach below, and with one gigantic crack the bombardment of fireworks begins, illuminating us and the entire city for an hour, culminating with a seemingly endless waterfall of cascading white light. The surprise at being so close to the firing line of this pyrotechnic display of man, God, and nature leaves us dumbfounded, and at the stroke of midnight we roar, yelp, grin, and hug like children.

Our hostess, Nalita, entices us to the buffet table, and we help ourselves to a display of hams, turkey, roast pig, fish salads of lobster, squid, and shrimp of all sizes bathed in a subtle cilantro vinaigrette, salads of diced fresh vegetables glistening through mayonnaise, a casserole of shrimp and heart of palm (page 68), rice, beans, farofa, and potato salad. A sideboard of desserts, jammed with fresh fruit, crystallized fruits, spice cakes, and creams, sparkles in the candlelight.

When we bid our farewells, our hostess hands each of us a white rose and a reminder to toss it into the sea and make our wish to the sea goddess, Iemanjá. On the beach some celebrants surround campfires listening to the robed and bejeweled men or women dispensing voodoo blessings and magic while others pray over mounds of sand decorated with flowers and candles that cover the buried fruits and sweets offered to the hungry Iemanjá. Brazilians are above all people with a belief in the supernatural; every so often one feels the touch of strange influences, and I occasionally hear stories of apparitions, ghosts, and other enchantments.

Closer to the avenue bands are blaring, and we join the merrymakers, dancing our way from band to band. We pause at an all-night tropical-juice stand selling suco misto. Quickly surrounded by five smiling, dirty street kids, we buy drinks for them, too.

DATELINE: SÃO CONRADO, JANUARY 2

Cesarina lives in the dense, lush hills of São Conrado, pinned in by the erupting mountains and a view of sky and sea. She and her family have lived here since her Italian father took his Amazon-born wife to manage what was then one of Rio's last coffee plantations. The house is called the Villa Riso. "I love this house and this land too much *(continued on page 66)*

(continued on page 66)

OVERLEAF LEFT: *The mountain at São Conrado bordering Ipanema*

RIGHT, TOP: *An array of colorful sucos, drinks made from tropical fruits at the Colombo*

BOTTOM: *Bolinho de Bacalhau, fried codfish balls, are a very popular street food and cocktail tidbit.*

Bolinho de Bacalhau
FRIED CODFISH BALLS

2 medium baking potatoes, peeled
1 pound cooked and shredded salted
   codfish (see page 49)
1 tablespoon minced onion
2 tablespoons minced fresh parsley
1 garlic clove, minced
   Freshly ground pepper to taste
2 large eggs, separated

1 tablespoon all-purpose flour
   Pinch of salt
1 cup fine dry bread crumbs
   Vegetable or olive oil, for frying

Molho Campanha (see page 72) or
hot pepper sauce, for serving

Bring a large pot of water to a boil over high heat. Add the potatoes and cook until tender, about 20 minutes. Drain and cool. Pass the potatoes through a ricer or mash them well.

In a large mixing bowl, combine the potatoes, shredded cod, onion, parsley, garlic, pepper, and egg yolks. Sprinkle the flour over the mixture and combine.

In a large bowl, whisk the egg whites with the salt and beat into stiff peaks. Fold into the codfish mixture to combine. Do not overmix.

Form the mixture into balls about the size of a walnut. Roll the balls lightly in the bread crumbs, cover them with plastic wrap, and refrigerate for 1 hour or more, until ready to cook.

Remove the codfish balls from the refrigerator 15 minutes before frying.

In a deep, heavy saucepan, heat 1½ inches of oil over high heat until it shimmers and heat waves appear above the oil, about 350 to 360°F. Fry the balls a few at a time, turning them from time to time until golden, about 4 to 5 minutes. Remove with a slotted spoon and drain on paper towels.

Serve with Molho Campanha (Country Sauce) or hot pepper sauce.

MAKES 20 TO 24 FRITTERS

VARIATION: A whole boneless, skinless large chicken breast (about 4 ounces), finely chopped, can be substituted for the cod.

Limonada Suissa
SWISS LIMEADE

There are simply no lemons in Brazil, so it is the lime that is the dominant citrus flavor in the food.

1 lime
2 tablespoons superfine sugar,
   or to taste

Cracked ice cubes

Slice the lime in half starting at the stem end. With a sharp paring knife, remove the inner pith core of each half. Slice each half into 3 or 4 pieces. Place the pieces in a blender or food processor with the sugar and 4 to 5 cracked ice cubes. Pulse on and off until the lime is reduced to small green specks.

Add 4 more cracked ice cubes and blend or process for 3 seconds.

Add ice to a tall glass and pour or strain the juice into the glass, as preferred.

MAKES 1 DRINK

Coquetel de Camarão com Abacate

SHRIMP AND AVOCADO COCKTAIL

½ lime, sliced
1 pound tiny fresh bay shrimp or "t-ts,"
   frozen and defrosted

AVOCADO DRESSING
2 medium avocados
2 tablespoons fresh lime juice
1 tablespoon grated onion
1 garlic clove, chopped

1 teaspoon chopped fresh cilantro, or
   more to taste
1 malagueta pepper, chopped, or
   ¼ teaspoon chopped hot chili
   pepper, or more to taste
¼ cup extra-virgin olive oil
Salt to taste
½ oup mayonnaise
½ cup crème fraîche or sour cream

Bring a kettle of lightly salted water to a boil and add the lime slices and shrimp. Swirl the shrimp around and cook 1 minute or less, depending on their size, until pink. Drain and cool under cold running water. Drain again, cover, and refrigerate.

To make the dressing, pit and peel the avocados and place them in a food processor or blender. Add the lime juice, onion, garlic, cilantro, and hot pepper and puree. Gradually add the oil and season with a little salt to taste. Place the mixture in a bowl and whisk in the mayonnaise and crème fraîche and refrigerate.

Arrange layers of shrimp and dressing neatly in 4 chilled tall cocktail glasses so they look like parfaits, and refrigerate until chilled completely, then serve. This cocktail should be served icy cold.

SERVES 4

Quindão

COCONUT TORTE

The Brazilian affection for sugar and coconut is best expressed in this dessert. *Quindão*, the large "pie," or *quindim*, an individual tart the size of a silver dollar, is taken with afternoon tea or coffee and sold at pastry shops throughout the country.

10 large egg yolks
 2 large eggs
2½ cups sugar
 2 cups grated fresh or packaged unsweet-
    ened coconut (1 large coconut)

Pinch of ground cloves
½ tablespoon unsalted butter, softened

Preheat the oven to 325°F.

In a food processor, blender, or electric mixer, beat the egg yolks, whole eggs, and sugar until thick and lemon colored, about 5 minutes.

Add the coconut, cloves, and butter and beat another minute.

Butter a 9-inch pie pan and pour the mixture into the pan. Place the pan in a larger baking pan and add enough hot water to come two-thirds up the sides. Place in the center of the oven and bake for 40 minutes, until the top is dry and resilient to the touch. To test, insert a toothpick in the center; if not dry, bake another minute or two.

Cool for 15 minutes. Run the blade of a sharp paring knife around the quindim and place a serving platter over the pie dish. Invert and unmold. Serve at room temperature or refrigerate until ready to serve.

SERVES 10

Sopa de Castanha do Pará, a cream soup flavored with Brazil nuts, is flecked with pomegranate seeds.

and when my father died I knew I must keep it. The only way I could think was to hold big parties, and so I cater weddings and dinners and conferences, and every Sunday I have open house and people can come for feijoada. Always we have music: jazz quartets, folk dancing with whoever I can get when they are in town. It is not a museum, but it is a bit of Rio history."

Pools reflect walls with clinging foliage, punctuated with niches holding glazed ornamental pineapples and acorns. Courtyards with dancing fountains, hedged with paths of roses and filled with the scent of jasmine, lead to the porte cochere, and on the left, ancient carved wooden doors lead to a white-walled chapel. Another set of wooden doors open to the villa on the right: polished mahogany floors and a wide flight of steps take you to white-plastered rooms filled with colonial paintings of saints and myths; and dark carved-wood eighteenth-century consoles and dark leather chairs are sheltered under coffered ceilings. Cesarina guides us out to the terraces of polished, patterned white marble. Glazed terra-cotta pots overflowing with flowering hibiscus, plumbago, and agapanthus buffer the view of six imperial palms and hills of green crashing down to the Atlantic. The nearby sounds of leopards, monkeys, and an aviary of exotic birds can be heard from the menagerie belonging to a neighbor who has dedicated his life to the study of Amazonian wildlife.

Cesarina sends a tray of icy caipirinhas around while we marvel at the

surroundings and listen eagerly to her stories. The Portuguese introduced one-crop agriculture—sugarcane or coffee. Like the states of Bahia, which raised cocoa and coconuts, and Pernambuco, which grew sugarcane, Rio too was a monoculture and accumulated its wealth from coffee and sugar. The one-crop harvest led to the exhaustion of the land, and our hostess explains that "all the green that surrounds us was once stark, depleted, and dusty hills, like the moon. We killed the soil. During the middle of the nineteenth century we brought it back; the government and all the Cariocas who had land helped nourish it. So we are the first ecologists. Unfortunately, the burning of the land taking place in the Mato Grosso and the Amazon can be blamed on us, but big industry from your country is doing its share of the damage, too. We are working to improve this loss.

"Now we must take a swim and have lunch at my house," she says as she points up the hill. There a waterfall crashes into a black icy pool, and soon under the shade of umbrellas we serve ourselves pale cocoa-colored soup made from ground Brazil nuts and laced with cream and stock, speckled with ruby pomegranate seeds (page 69). A platter piled high with steamed crabs, langoustines, and various-sized shrimp flushed in colors from white to pink to scarlet is accompanied by bowls of green herb-flecked mayonnaise and *molho campanha* (page 72), a delicate sauce of chopped tomato, peppers, herbs, *(continued on page 71)*

A shrimp and heart of palm casserole, Camarões com Palmito

6 7

Camarões com Palmito

CASSEROLE OF SHRIMP AND HEART OF PALM

STOCK

Heads and shells from 3 pounds
medium shrimp
1 onion, peeled and quartered
2 garlic cloves, chopped
1 carrot, peeled and sliced
1 small bunch parsley stems
1 bay leaf
6 whole peppercorns

¼ cup extra-virgin olive oil
3 medium onions, finely chopped
1 green bell pepper, cored, deveined,
seeded, and finely chopped
18 large ripe plum tomatoes, peeled and
roughly chopped (juices reserved), or
1½ pounds canned plum tomatoes,
drained (juice reserved)

½ cup chopped fresh parsley
¼ cup chopped fresh cilantro
6 scallions, including most of the
green, trimmed and chopped
½ cup all-purpose flour
3 pounds medium shrimp, peeled and
deveined
Salt and freshly ground white pepper
to taste
2 14-ounce cans heart of palm, drained
and cut into thirds

Simple Boiled White Rice (see page
12), for serving

To make the shrimp stock, in a medium saucepan, combine the reserved shells and
heads, onion, garlic, carrot, parsley stems, bay leaf, peppercorns, and enough cold
water to cover by 1 inch.

Bring the stock to a boil, skim off the impurities, reduce the heat, and simmer for
40 minutes, skimming occasionally. Strain and reserve the stock, discarding the
solids. (You will need about 2 cups.)

In a large nonreactive casserole, heat the oil over medium heat. Add the onions
and sauté until wilted, about 5 minutes. Add the bell pepper and cook until almost
tender, about 4 minutes more. Add the tomatoes and their juices, cover, and simmer
for 10 minutes, or until the tomatoes give off most of their juice.

Add the 2 cups of shrimp stock and bring the mixture to a simmer again. Add ¼
cup of the chopped parsley, ⅛ cup of the the cilantro, and half the scallions and
cook for 2 minutes.

Place a medium saucepan over high heat. When the pan is hot, add the flour and
cook for 5 minutes, stirring constantly until the flour turns a deep beige color. Do not
allow the flour to burn. Remove the flour from the pan and set it aside.

Add the shrimp to the casserole mixture, season with salt and pepper, and simmer
for 2 to 3 minutes.

While the shrimp are cooking, add about 2 cups of the casserole liquid to the
saucepan used to cook the flour, place over medium heat, and gradually add 3 to 4
tablespoons of the toasted flour, one at a time, to the liquid, stirring constantly and
smoothing out any lumps with the back of a wooden spoon. When the sauce has
thickened to the desired consistency, return it to the casserole and combine thoroughly. Add the heart of palm and cook another 4 minutes, or until the heart of palm
is heated through.

Stir in the remaining ¼ cup parsley, ⅛ cup cilantro, and scallions and cook for 1
more minute.

Serve with boiled white rice.

SERVES 8

Sopa de Castanha do Pará
BRAZIL NUT SOUP

1½ cups Brazil nuts
6 cups rich homemade or canned low-sodium chicken stock
2 tablespoons (¼ stick) unsalted butter
2 tablespoon all-purpose flour

Salt and freshly ground white pepper to taste
¼ teaspoon ground mace
1 cup heavy cream
2 pomegranates

Preheat the oven to 400°F.

Place the nuts on a baking pan and bake for 10 minutes, stirring occasionally to toast evenly. Cool.

When the nuts are cool, rub off the skins. In a food processor, grind the nuts, pulsing on and off until they are finely ground. Reserve in the food processor.

In a large stockpot, heat the stock over medium heat. Add a ladle of the stock to the food processor, pulse until smooth, and set aside.

In a medium saucepan, melt the butter. When it begins to foam, remove the pan from the heat and whisk in the flour. Return the roux to the heat and whisk constantly, just until it begins to pull from the sides of the pan. Ladle 3 cups of the stock into the roux a little at a time, whisking constantly.

Whisk the flour and stock mixture and nut mixture into the stock. Season with salt, pepper, mace, and cream. Simmer gently for 20 minutes. If the soup is too thick, add a little more cream.

Cut 1 pomegranate in half, juice in a juicer, and strain into the soup.

Cut the remaining pomegranate in half and carefully scoop out the seeds, leaving them intact.

Serve the soup in warm soup plates and sprinkle the top with the pomegranate seeds.

SERVES 8

vinegar, and oil, the perfect accent for the delicate shellfish. We pass around platters of rice studded with raisins, almonds, and parsley, a grated xuxu salad, and the ubiquitous farofa, which is mixed with onion, parsley, cilantro, and strands of scrambled egg.

The table is cleared and glass bowls of chalk-white coconut mousse (page 76), golden passion fruit mousse (page 73), and pink guava mousse arrive with sauces to match, along with *pudim de Clara* (page 77), a carmelized baked meringue, and *papo de anjo* (page 81), little babas. The flavors are as round and as intense as the actual fruits. *Baba de moça* (page 77), a sauce of coconut milk, egg yolks, and sugar that accompanies the coconut mousse, is a sweet elixir but not cloying, and the passion fruit sauce (page 73) flecked with seeds is, Cesarina tells us, "sugar and juice melted over a low flame, then pureed in the blender while you count *um, dois, três*—so the seeds don't break up and blacken the sauce. The guava is the same idea—but you strain out the seeds and add the juice from maraschino cherries we preserve here at the house. It gives the sauce that beautiful ruby color."

The sun disappears and the sky turns ominous gray as we sip our cafezinho. When I pick up the little cup and peer at the residue of sugar inside, Cesarina tells us, "This habit of sweetening the coffee before serving comes from generations of drinking sugar water, as well as chewing on the cane as they do in the north."

We move indoors as the clouds darken, and we run for the house to drumrolls of thunder, crashes and flashes of lightning, lashing winds, bending palm trees, tumbling fern pots. Shutters bang and steel-gray sheets of drenching rain flood down.

DATELINE: RIO, JANUARY 6

Lionel, a Brazilian publisher friend, promises me a walking tour of old Rio and lunch where the true Cariocas eat. As luck has it, he and Cesarina are old friends, and the three of us meet at the creamy rococo customs house in the wilting sun on what everyone is calling the hottest day in Rio.

We linger at the ornate Victorian library and then take a brief look at the cloistered gardens of the Santo Antônio, with ancient Portuguese tiled walls, rinsed sky blue from years of washing, depicting flora, fauna, fountains, and the lives of saints. Then we're off to the Bar do Teatro, located in the opera house. The interior is a Byzantine *(continued on page 74)*

(continued on page 74)

Frutos do Mar
COLD SHELLFISH

6 small hard-shell crabs
6 prawns (large shrimp), in their shells
12 small shrimp (white river shrimp, if available), in their shells
6 langoustines (available at specialty fish markets), lobster culls, or large crayfish
8 cups (1 quart) beer
1 medium onion, thinly sliced

1 bay leaf
1 sprig thyme
1 tablespoon mustard seeds
6 whole peppercorns
1 allspice berry

Green Mayonnaise and Molho Campanha (recipes follow), for serving

Scrub the crabs and set aside. Wash the remaining shellfish and set aside.

In a large steamer, combine the remaining ingredients. Cover and bring to a boil.

Steam the shellfish, adding them in order of cooking times, beginning with the lobsters culls for 8 to 10 minutes; crabs about 5 minutes; large prawns for 4 minutes; small shrimp or river shrimp for 2 to 3 minutes. Langoustines cook in about 3 minutes and crayfish about 4 to 6, depending on their size. Let cool, then refrigerate, covered, until chilled. Serve with Green Mayonnaise and Molho Campanha.

SERVES 6

Maionese Verde
GREEN MAYONNAISE

1½ cups homemade or good-quality store-bought mayonnaise
3 scallions, including some of the green, chopped
2 tablespoons chopped fresh parsley
1 tablespoon chopped fresh cilantro
1 tablespoon snipped chives

1 tablespoon drained and rinsed capers, chopped
1 small sour pickle, chopped
1 large hard-boiled egg, chopped (optional)
Preserved malagueta pepper oil or hot pepper sauce to taste

Combine all the ingredients and mix thoroughly. Cover and refrigerate until ready to use, up to 3 days.

MAKES ABOUT 2 CUPS

Molho Campanha
COUNTRY SAUCE

1 red onion, finely chopped
1 small green bell pepper, cored, seeded, ribs removed, and finely diced
1 medium firm tomato, cored, seeded, and diced

Salt and freshly ground pepper to taste
¾ cup extra-virgin olive oil
½ cup light red or white wine vinegar

Combine the ingredients and mix thoroughly. Cover and refrigerate until ready to use.

MAKES ABOUT 2½ CUPS

Mousse de Maracujá
PASSION FRUIT MOUSSE

Despite their exotic name, these small aubergine globes are ripe only when they resemble withered old prunes. When you see them on a market shelf in this condition, then you know they will produce the most delicious juice.

Frozen passion fruit puree is available in 14-ounce packages at Latin American and Asian markets and some supermarkets. If using the frozen puree, use the remaining ¾ cup for Passion Fruit Sauce, decreasing the sugar to ¾ cup and the water to ⅓ cup.

1 cup strained fresh passion fruit juice, seeds reserved (about 18 passion fruit), or frozen passion fruit puree	1 cup superfine sugar
1 envelope unflavored gelatin	8 egg whites
1 can (1¼ cups) unsweetened condensed milk	Pinch of salt
	Passion Fruit Sauce (recipe follows), for serving

If using fresh passion fruit juice, place the passion fruit seeds in a blender or food processor and liquefy at a fast count of 1-2-3, so the broken seeds don't blacken the remaining juice. Strain the liquid into the juice and discard the seeds.

In a small nonreactive saucepan, heat ¼ cup of juice with the gelatin and dissolve over low heat. Add to the remaining juice and stir in the condensed milk and ½ cup of sugar. Reserve, stirring from time to time.

Beat the egg whites and the salt with an electric beater. When the mixture begins to whiten and stiffen, gradually add the remaining ½ cup sugar until stiff and glossy.

Add a large spoonful of meringue to the passion fruit mixture and combine thoroughly. Fold in the remaining meringue with a spatula, making sure not to overmix. Some streaks of white should show. Pour the mixture into a large glass serving bowl and place in the freezer for 2 hours, or until ready to serve.

Fresh passion fruit can sometimes separate and settle in the bottom of the bowl. Fold again once or twice after the first half hour of freezing if it should separate. Serve the mousse with Passion Fruit Sauce.

SERVES 10

Molho de Maracujá
PASSION FRUIT SAUCE

About 18 fresh passion fruit, or 1 cup frozen passion fruit puree	½ cup water
	1 cup sugar

If using fresh passion fruit, cut them in half and scoop out the pulp and juice. Strain the mixture and reserve the juice and seeds separately.

In a nonreactive saucepan, heat the water and sugar over medium heat. When the sugar dissolves, cook another 3 minutes, then add the passion fruit juice or puree and stir until the sauce begins to thicken, about 8 minutes. Remove from the heat. Cool and add the seeds if using fresh passion fruit. Chill, covered.

Serve with Passion Fruit Mousse or Coconut Mousse.

MAKES ABOUT 2½ CUPS

spectacle decorated with earth-color ribbed tiles. Winged griffins leafed in gold decorate wooden beams that connect with columns capped with life-sized bulls' heads, and marine-green tiles surround gilded mirrors. Ballroom chairs are set around tables covered in white cloths, and waiters mill among the few patrons, serving drinks. We pause for a soda water, and Lionel explains, "The opera is closed. It's been closed for six months and this is the opera season. It's a good opera—the best singers come here, but the unions are killing it." Lionel was Rio's last secretary of culture and has strong opinions regarding Rio's internal governmental problems.

As we walk to lunch we walk past shops selling random merchandise that clashes with the splendor of their cast-iron facades and we arrive at the restaurant Penafiel. The buzz of the trattoria's overhead fans and the whiteness of the walls cool us mentally, and we faint into our chairs. The burly waiter delivers plates of olives plump as prunes, a bowl of whole tomatoes, a plate of shredded tender lettuce, olive oil, vinegar, and a few halved limes. We order beer and water while Lionel apologizes for the heat as though it were his fault and orders marinated baby octopus (page 84), which we nibble. Then plates of thinly sliced tender beef tongue in a tomato and sweet pepper sauce (page 84) arrive, alongside white rice and beans. This is typical Carioca fare—"What we call our *prato feito*—and what you might call your blue plate special—a balanced meal." Not complicated or overwhelming, but good.

Mousse de Côco

COCONUT MOUSSE

Though packaged coconut can be substituted for fresh in many recipes in this book, the moist texture of fresh coconut is necessary to produce this excellent dessert. I've tried the packaged and it isn't worth the effort.

2 cups grated fresh coconut (about 1 large coconut)
1 envelope unflavored gelatin
¼ cup cachaça or white rum
8 large egg whites
  Pinch of salt
1 cup sugar
1¾ cups fresh or canned unsweetened coconut milk

1 teaspoon or more sweet almond, canola, or neutral vegetable oil

Baba de Moça (see opposite) or Passion Fruit Sauce (see page 73), for serving

Place 1 cup of coconut meat in the bowl of a food processor with the metal blade. Pulse on and off for a minute or two until the meat is uniformly chopped, then continue to pulse until finely grated. Reserve.

In a small saucepan, sprinkle the gelatin over the liquor and place over low heat until the gelatin dissolves. Set aside.

In the bowl of an electric mixer, beat the egg whites with the salt until they begin to form stiff peaks. Gradually add the sugar until the whites form stiff and glossy peaks.

In a large mixing bowl, combine the coconut milk with the dissolved gelatin. Add the finely ground coconut and a large spoonful of beaten egg whites and combine thoroughly. Gently fold the mixture into the remaining beaten egg whites, making sure not to overmix.

Moisten a sheet of paper towel with the oil and lightly oil a 3-quart mold or round stainless-steel bowl. Gently spoon in the mixture and freeze for 2 hours or more.

When ready to serve the mousse, dip the mold in a warm water bath for about 1 minute. Run the blade of a paring knife around the inside of the mousse. Place a serving plate over the bowl, invert, and unmold. Cover the top and sides with the reserved coconut and serve with Baba de Moça or Passion Fruit Sauce.

SERVES 10

Baba de Moça ("Baby's Dribble")
C O C O N U T   S A U C E

6 large egg yolks
2 cups sugar
½ cup water

1 tablespoon unsalted butter
1 cup fresh or canned unsweetened coconut milk

Pass the yolks through a fine-mesh sieve into a small bowl and set aside.

In a medium saucepan, combine the sugar and water and set over medium heat. When the sugar has dissolved, stir in the butter. Add the coconut milk and simmer for 1 minute.

Gradually whisk in the yolks. Swirl some of the coconut milk mixture into the bowl that held the yolks to remove all yolk residue, then return it to the saucepan.

Continue to cook over medium heat at a low bubble, mixing with a wooden spoon until the mixture thickens and the coconut essence becomes intense, about 8 to 10 minutes.

Cool and chill, covered, at least 2 hours or up to 2 days. Serve with Coconut Mousse (see opposite).

MAKES ABOUT 3 CUPS

Pudim de Clara
M E R I N G U E   S O U F F L É

CARAMEL
½ cup sugar

1 cup sugar
1 teaspoon grated lime zest

MERINGUE
5 large egg whites

Fresh berries or tropical fruit, for serving

Preheat the oven to 500°F.

For the caramel, in a medium saucepan, melt the sugar over medium-high heat, stirring and making sure the sugar doesn't burn. Reduce the heat and cook until the syrup turns a dark amber caramel, swirling the pan.

Lightly oil a 2½-quart tube mold. Add a drop or two of water and lightly rub it around the interior of the mold. Pour the caramel into the mold and rotate, covering as much of the surface as possible, working quickly so the caramel doesn't harden. Set aside.

For the meringue, in the bowl of an electric mixer, gradually whisk the egg whites until foamy. Increase the speed and gradually add the sugar. When the meringue forms stiff peaks, fold in the grated lime zest.

Using a rubber spatula, gently spoon the meringue into the mold. Place the soufflé in the oven and bake for 5 minutes, or until the surface is golden brown. Cool for 10 minutes and refrigerate, covered, for at least 2 hours or overnight.

To serve, run a sharp thin knife around the inside of the mold and inside tube. Place a serving plate over the mold, invert, and tap the surface. Remove the pan and serve with fresh berries or tropical fruit.

SERVES 8

OVERLEAF:
The Brazilian affection for sweets includes (clockwise from top left) Pudim de Clara (meringue soufflé), Papo de Anjo (angels' chins in syrup), Molho de Marinha (guava sauce), and Mousse de Maracujá (passion fruit mousse).

Molho de Limão
LIME SAUCE

10 limes
2½ cups sugar

3 cups cold water

Trim the ends off the limes and cut away the zest. Squeeze the pulp and reserve the juice for another use. Cut the zest into ¼-inch dice. You should have 1¾ cups diced zest.

In a nonreactive medium saucepan, combine the diced lime zest and 4 cups cold water. Bring to a boil over high heat and boil for 10 minutes. Drain the zest and cool under cold water. Repeat this process 2 more times with fresh cold water and drain.

In a clean saucepan, add the sugar, lime zest, and 3 cups cold water and bring to a boil over high heat. Reduce the heat to a simmer and cook for 45 minutes, or until the limes are almost opaque and the liquid is syrupy. Remove the sauce from the heat and cool it completely. Pour it into sterilized jars, cover, and refrigerate.

Lime Sauce will keep 6 months or more refrigerated. Serve with other fruit doces or Coconut Mousse (see page 76).

MAKES ABOUT 5 CUPS

Mousse de Goiaba
GUAVA MOUSSE

2 pounds fresh guava, peeled and chopped, or 1½ cups frozen guava puree
10 maraschino cherries (look for the dark variety cooked in heavy syrup)
1 tablespoon maraschino syrup

8 large egg whites
Pinch of salt
¾ cup superfine sugar, or a little more depending on the sweetness of the fruit
1 tablespoon unflavored gelatin

In a food processor, puree the guava with the cherries in 2 batches, pulsing on and off until smooth. Strain the mixture through a fine sieve, pushing down with a rubber spatula to remove the seeds.

In a small saucepan, stir the maraschino syrup with the gelatin mixed with 1 tablespoon of warm water over low heat. When dissolved, fold into the guava puree, cover and cool, but do not allow to set.

In the bowl of an electric mixer beat the egg whites with the salt. When the mixture begins to stiffen, gradually add the sugar and continue to beat until it forms glossy, stiff (but not dry) peaks. Add a large spoonful of the meringue to the guava mixture and combine thoroughly. Fold in the remaining meringue with a spatula, making sure not to overmix. Some white streaks should remain.

Moisten a sheet of paper towel with oil and lightly oil a 3-quart mold. Using a rubber spatula, fill the mold with the guava mixture, cover with plastic wrap, and freeze for 3 hours or longer.

When ready to serve, run a sharp paring knife around the interior of the mold and place in a warm water bath for a minute or two. Remove and dry the exterior of the mold. Place a serving platter over the top and invert. If the mousse does not come out easily, place a damp warm towel over the inverted mold for a minute and give the mold a few taps with the handle of a knife. Remove the mold and serve with the guava sauce.

SERVES 10 OR MORE

Molho de Marinha
GUAVA SAUCE

¾ pound fresh guava, or 1 cup frozen
   guava puree
1 tablespoon maraschino syrup

¼ cup sugar, or more depending on the
   sweetness of the fruit

If using fresh guavas, cut the fruit in half and scoop the pulp from the shells.

Place the guava pulp, maraschino syrup, and sugar in a saucepan over medium heat and bring to a boil. Reduce the heat and simmer for 10 minutes or until the sugar is dissolved. Strain and chill (see Note). Serve with the mousse.

MAKES ABOUT 1¼ CUPS

NOTE: Guava sauce will keep up to 3 days when refrigerated.

Papo de Anjo
ANGEL'S CHIN

These little babas are named after the second chin of a chubby angel. Dipped in sugar syrup, they are served as often as we serve cookies. The texture of the soaked papo is like that of moist sponge cake. You will need 24 1¼-inch metal tartlet shells to make these.

SYRUP
4 cups cold water
12 whole cloves
1 cinnamon stick
   Zest of 1 small orange

1 cup plus 1 tablespoon sugar

5 large egg yolks
1 tablespoon clarified butter
   (see page 32)

For the syrup, in a medium saucepan, combine the water, cloves, cinnamon stick, and orange zest and bring to a boil over high heat. Add the sugar and mix with a wooden spoon until the sugar dissolves. Reduce the heat and simmer for 15 to 20 minutes, or until the mixture is slightly thick and syrupy. Strain the mixture into a heatproof bowl and cool completely.

Preheat the oven to 500°F.

In the bowl of an electric mixer, beat the yolks, gradually increasing the speed, for 8 to 12 minutes, or until lemon colored and thick enough to make a peak on the end of your finger.

Butter 24 1¼-inch tartlet shells and place on a baking sheet. Fill the shells half full of the mixture.

Place the sheet in the oven and bake for 3 to 4 minutes, or until the tops are lightly glazed and tinged a pale brown.

Using a rounded paring knife, run the tip of the blade around the inside of the tart shells and carefully drop the papo into the syrup and coat thoroughly. Cool completely in the liquid, cover, and refrigerate. Serve with the syrup.

These keep for 3 days.

MAKES ABOUT 24 PAPOS

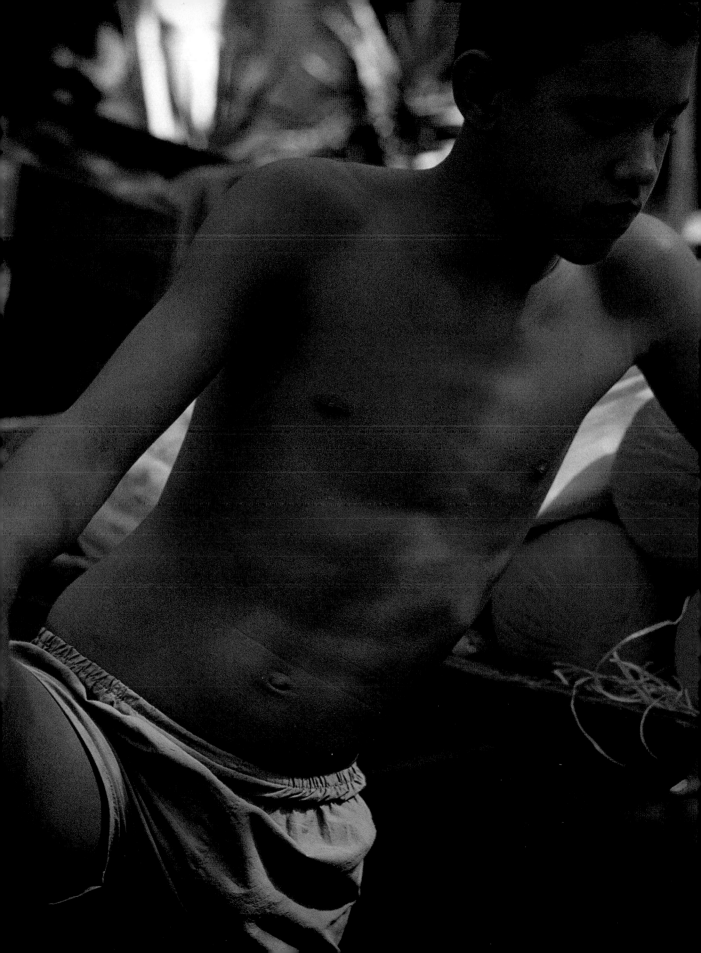

Salada de Polvo
BABY OCTOPUS VINAIGRETTE

The octopus used in this salad are the size of shooter marbles, sweet and succulent—there is nothing quite like them. Try to buy the smallest you can find.

2 pounds baby octopus
1 large red onion, finely chopped
½ cup chopped fresh flat-leaf parsley
¼ cup chopped cilantro, or more to taste
¼ cup finely chopped green bell pepper
¼ cup finely chopped red bell pepper
3 limes, halved

¾ cup extra-virgin olive oil
Salt and freshly ground pepper to taste
1 head Boston or butterleaf type lettuce, washed, dried, and thinly sliced

Malagueta Pepper Sauce (see page 96), for serving

Clean the octopus by turning it inside out and removing the eyes and the small bone at the bottom of the head. Wash thoroughly in cold water.

Bring a large pot of salted water to boil, over medium-high heat. Cook the octopus for 30 to 40 minutes, depending on their size, or until they can be easliy pierced with a fork. Drain and cool under cold running water. (It is necessary to peel larger octopus.)

In a large bowl combine the onion, parsley, cilantro, green and red pepper, the juice of ½ lime, and olive oil. Season with salt and pepper. Set aside.

Cut the octopus in quarter-inch slices. Add to the onion mixture and marinate for ½ hour.

Transfer to a large platter and squeeze the remaining limes over the octopus. Cover and set aside to marinate for another half-hour.

Serve with mounds of the julienned lettuce and Malagueta Pepper Sauce.

SERVES 6

Língua de Vaca Assada
BRAISED TONGUE

2 medium onions
2 whole cloves
1 beef tongue (about 2½ pounds), or 4 small fresh veal tongues
1 celery rib, chopped
1 carrot, peeled and sliced
1 bay leaf
3 garlic cloves
2 tablespoons extra-virgin olive oil
3 large ripe tomatoes, peeled, cored, seeded, and chopped

1 teaspoon chopped fresh oregano, or ¼ teaspoon dried oregano
2 green bell peppers, cored, seeded, ribs removed, and diced
Salt and freshly ground pepper to taste
2 tablespoons chopped fresh parsley

Simple Boiled White Rice (see page 12) and White Beans (see opposite), for serving

Stud one of the onions with the cloves.

In a medium saucepan, add the tongue, the clove-studded onion, celery, carrot, bay leaf, 1 whole garlic clove, and enough water to barely cover. Cover and bring to a boil over high heat. Skim off any impurities and reduce the heat. Simmer for 2 hours, or until the tongue is almost tender (if using veal tongues simmer for 1 hour, as they are much smaller).

Remove the tongue and cool. Strain and reserve the cooking liquid. When the tongue is cool enough to handle, peel away the outer skin casing.

Preheat the oven to 350°F.

Chop the remaining onion and 2 garlic cloves and set aside.

In a medium casserole or Dutch oven, heat the oil over medium heat, add the chopped onion and garlic, and cook for 8 minutes, or until the onions are lightly browned. Add the tomatoes and oregano and bring to a simmer. Skim any fat from the reserved stock and add 1½ cups of the stock to the tomato mixture. Add the green pepper and season with salt and pepper. Add the tongue, cover, and bake for 1 hour, or until the tongue is tender and can easily be pierced with a fork or paring knife.

Remove the tongue and cut it into thin slices. Arrange the serving plate, sprinkle with parsley, and serve with the cooking sauce, boiled white rice, and beans.

SERVES 6

OVERLEAF:
*Carioca cooks
gossiping from the
balcony.*

Feijão Branco
WHITE BEANS

½ pound white or navy beans, washed
   and picked clean
1 tablespoon extra-virgin olive oil
1 small onion, chopped
1 garlic clove, chopped
1 sprig fresh thyme
1 medium tomato, peeled, seeded, and
   chopped

2 tablespoons chopped fresh parsley
2 tablespoons chopped scallions,
   green part only
   Salt and freshly ground pepper
   Malagueta pepper oil or Tabasco
   sauce, to taste

Soak the beans overnight with water to cover by several inches.

Drain the beans and place them in a large soup kettle with fresh water to cover by 2 inches. Bring to a boil over medium-high heat and skim off any foam or impurities. Reduce the heat to a simmer and cook for 45 minutes, stirring from time to time so the beans do not stick to the kettle.

In a sauté pan, add the olive oil and place over medium heat. Add the onion and garlic and sauté for about 5 minutes, or until the onion is translucent. Add the tomato and cook another 4 minutes.

Add the tomato mixture to the beans. When the beans are soft and tender, add the parsley and scallions, and season them with salt, pepper, and malagueta pepper oil to taste.

Remove the beans with a slotted spoon and serve with the tongue.

Sopa Fria de Feijão Preto

COLD BLACK BEAN SOUP

Beans of any kind are always served hot in Brazil. This version of a traditional soup was served chilled on a very hot night and everyone admitted it was a refreshing change.

3 cups cooked black or cranberry beans, drained (see Note)

2 to 3 cups homemade or canned low-sodium chicken or beef stock

1 cup (about 14) small peeled shrimp

1 tablespoon extra-virgin olive oil
Salt and freshly ground pepper to taste

¼ cup fresh or canned unsweetened coconut milk
Malagueta pepper oil or hot pepper sauce to taste

¼ cup heavy cream

1 tablespoon fresh lime juice

6 to 8 thin lime slices

Puree the cooked beans in a food processor or blender with a little of the stock. Place the mixture in a large bowl and whisk in 2 cups stock. If too thick, add a little more stock. Cover and chill.

Reserve 6 to 8 shrimp to decorate the soup and finely chop the remaining shrimp.

Coat a medium skillet with the olive oil and sauté the whole shrimp for 1 minute. Add the chopped shrimp and cook for 2 more minutes, or until the shrimp become pink and glazed. Season with salt and pepper and mix in 2 tablespoons coconut milk. Set the whole shrimp aside and stir the chopped shrimp into the stock mixture, along with a few drops of malagueta pepper oil or hot pepper sauce. Whisk in the heavy cream, remaining coconut milk, and lime juice. Cover and chill the soup and whole shrimp separately.

To serve, ladle the soup into chilled soup plates and float a lime slice and 1 shrimp in the center of each plate.

SERVES 6 TO 8

NOTE: Prepare the beans according to the Tutu à Mineira recipe (see page 177) or use the Tutu Peri Peri recipe (see page 53), eliminating the manioc flour. The beans and stock can be prepared and pureed a day ahead.

Robalo com Coentro da Jupira

JUPIRA'S BAKED SNAPPER WITH CILANTRO SAUCE

- 1 6-pound whole red snapper, bass, or grouper
- Salt and freshly ground white pepper to taste
- Juice of 1 lime
- 1 large tomato, peeled, seeded, and chopped
- 3 sprigs parsley
- 4 sprigs cilantro

- 1 medium onion, sliced
- ¼ cup olive oil
- ½ cup chopped fresh cilantro

- Malagueta Pepper Sauce (see page 96), Simple Boiled White Rice (see page 12), and Simple Farofa (see page 109), for serving

Wash and dry the fish. Place the fish in a baking pan on lightly oiled foil. Season the cavity and skin of the fish with salt, pepper, and lime juice, cover, and refrigerate for 1 hour or more.

Preheat the oven to 400° F.

Cover the fish with the tomato, herb sprigs, and onion and drizzle the oil over the fish.

Enclose the fish tightly in foil and bake for 20 minutes, or until the flesh is opaque and springy to the touch. Remove the fish from the pan to a warm serving platter. Place the juices and vegetables in a food processor or blender and puree.

In a small saucepan, add the pureed juices and chopped cilantro and warm over medium heat.

Pour the sauce over the fish and serve.

Serve with Malagueta Pepper Sauce, white rice, and farofa.

SERVES 6 TO 8

Pavé de Maracujá

PASSON FRUIT PAVÉ

- About 18 champagne finger biscuits (available at specialty stores and some supermarkets)
- Scant 2½ cups sweetened condensed milk

- 6 large egg yolks
- 1¼ cups fresh or bottled unsweetened passion fruit juice
- 4 tablespoons mascarpone cheese
- 1 cup milk

Measure the biscuits to fit the bottom and sides of a 2-quart serving bowl.

In a food processor or blender, blend the condensed milk, egg yolks, and fruit juice for 1 minute. Add the mascarpone cheese and pulse another second, or until blended. Cover the bottom of the serving bowl with 1 cup of the mixture.

Pour the milk into a bowl. Reserve 1 biscuit and briefly dip the remaining biscuits in the milk one by one. Cover the bottom and sides of the bowl with the biscuits, fitting them snugly, side by side.

Add half the remaining passion fruit mixture and cover with another layer of biscuits. Top with the remaining mixture. Crumble the reserved dry biscuit and sprinkle over the top.

Chill, covered, for 3 hours or longer before serving.

SERVES 8 TO 10

bahia

I drive along the recently completed road that is a direct route from Rio to Bahia. North of Victoria I speed up and down the highway, making hairpin turns through the lush jungle hills, weaving around brown cone-shaped rock mountains. A sign warns drivers of possible panthers shooting across the road. Two hours later, at the crest of a hill, a boy sits on the edge of a rickety wooden cart surrounded by a heap

A batida, a refreshing drink of cachaça and passion fruit, at a remote beach bar

of pineapples that sparkle like gold against the emerald hills. I stop to stretch and taste this juicy refreshment that he prepares for me—he holds the peeled fruit by the bristly spiked leaves and hands it to me as if it were a big lollipop. This fruit, native to Brazil and still called by its Indian name, *abacaxi,* is smaller than the varieties we are accustomed to eating, sweeter and juicier, too.

Hours later I emerge from the luxurious forest and descend onto the parched plains—burned to grow acres of eucalyptus. The saplings look dwarfed and pathetic sticking through the nettle of dried curled roots. After the trees mature and are cut down, the earth will remain barren for ages.

The serpentine road curls down to the sea through plantations of coconut palms, and I reach the small fishing village where Pedro Alvares Cabral landed with his thirteen caravels in 1500 and called it Puerto Seguro—"Safe Harbor."

I drive through the town lined with two-story colonial row houses, dusty streets, bars packed with lightly clad vacationers, and fishermen sitting on walls mending nets. I grab my knapsack, lock the car in a lot, and join a small group waiting for the ferry at the dusty wharf. The heavy smell of palm oil floats over us, and with a turn of my head I zero in on its source. A woman, imperious, a mahogany black with an aquiline nose, high rouged cheekbones, a long graceful neck, and languid hands, sits at a makeshift table covered with a white fringed cloth. She wears a white lace tunic, billowy cotton skirts, and a lacy turban. A jangle of beads, crosses, and chains dangling from a clenched ebony-black fist to protect her from the evil eye are strung about her neck, and her arms are heavy with silver and wooden bracelets. She's overseeing shiny tin pans gleaming like silver and filled with batter, shrimp, and spices. A cauldron of ruby dendê oil bubbles at her side. With a long wooden spoon she shapes the batter to the size of a big egg. This mixture is made of dried beans called *fradinho,* similar to black-eyed peas, that have been soaked, peeled, mashed, and mixed with ground dried shrimp. She lowers the spoon into the hot oil, and the *acarajé* (page 96) floats and dances on the surface as she turns the bobbing fritter until it puffs up and the crust turns deep crimson-orange. She drains it on a tray covered with cloth to absorb the grease; pries open the center and adds a saucy paste of blended peppers, both sweet and hot, ground dried shrimp, onions, ginger, and dendê oil; then seals it and randomly presses three small fresh-cooked shrimp on top. Starving after the eight-hour drive, I eat my first acarajé. It is cholesterol nectar, foreign and familiar all at once.

Acarajé is a variation on the *accra* served in the Creole communities of the Caribbean and the beanie cakes in our U.S. South, both derivative of the black-eyed-pea fritters of West African origin.

The African slaves brought the dendê palm (*Elaeis guineensis*) with them from West Africa along with their style of cooking, making Bahian food unlike that of the rest of Brazil. The crimson-colored oil is disappointingly tasteless until heated. Primarily used for frying, the oil is often added to a dish near the end of cooking to give color and flavor. And though cooks and food writers often suggest combining vegetable oil with paprika or annatto oil as a substitute, dendê has a flavor that can thrill the palate. Dendê is very high in saturated fat—a staggering 51 percent—and this does not sit well with Americans who worry about cardiovascular disease. It does not, however, seem to affect the health or figures of the Baianos.

I rejoin the ferry passengers, board the wooden canopied skiff, and putter across the river. We shift to a ramshackle wooden bus and climb a rutted, dusty hill. Finally, at dusk, on top of a bluff, I reach the remote coastal town called Trancoso. The ultimate escape.

Drums beat furiously and a circle of folks surround four barefoot young men gripping two yard-tall vaulting sticks of bamboo, playing out a sequence of martial-art movements in graceful dance form. They are enacting the *capoeira*—what was once the slaves' only means of self-defense.

Beyond the crowd a great lawn spreads to the sea. Lined on one side are colonial cottages washed in baby-clothes-colored pastels, topped with clay-tiled roofs. On the other side, similar cottages house bars and restaurants offering up a competing cacophony of sounds and smells. A fifteenth-century whitewashed church stands like a cardboard silhouette at the far end, protected by the Southern Cross, the three Marias, and a canopy of stars that dip into the ocean. And I head toward the cottage of some Brazilian friends in the heart of this little hamlet.

Dusty and tired, I'm anxious for a cool shower, a drink, a snack, and a bed enveloped in mosquito netting. My sleep is fitful, and in the light of a glaring moon my ears and eyes become accustomed to the new sounds and sights. Palm leaves scratch the stucco wall outside, and moonlight shines through the shutter slats, throwing light on the lizard on the wall hunting the spider the size of a silver dollar. These insects bite, and by morning I will wear their imprint on my chest like a red tattoo. I hear the buzz of mosquitoes and flies and the lightning bug that has lost its way into the eaves. The first cock crows at 2:00 A.M.; cats pat across the roof anticipating a skirmish. A chorus of roosters go at it noisily. At sunrise, a tropical downpour overcomes the din, and I hear a twittering of birds, the neighborhood dogs barking, and the laughter and cries of little children. We breakfast on a small terrace overlooking the great lawn. Platters of cool papaya, mangoes, and pineapples appear with bowls of warm tapioca

swimming in sweet milk and cinnamon, plus coffee, rolls, and jam.

In Bahia the pleasure of simple, unadorned food can be found nearly everywhere. On the hillside down to the beach, there are little shacks nestled in a grove of palm trees, offering refreshment and protection from the sun. At lunchtime, Bahian children run out of the green sierra bearing basins filled with empadas and pastel, pastries of meat or fish or chopped heart of palm mixed with green olives and cheese. Lunch under a palm umbrella on the beach consists of fried squid, with a squeeze of lime, fried whitefish from the river, or a grilled grouper with fried potatoes. A platter of shrimp sautéed in their shells with crusty flakes of garlic is served with a bowl of cut limes and malagueta pepper. Bars and lean-to stands offer little plates of sun-dried salted shrimp (page 97) for a cocktail tidbit, and for meat eaters, there is *carne de sol,* a tough jerky made from flanks of fresh beef that has been salted and sun dried, served warm and dotted with pimente. This classic meat is also known as carne seca and *charque,* pronounced "sharkey." The meat keeps well in hot climates and rehydrates well.

When languishing on the beach becomes routine, we bargain with a local fisherman to sail us five miles out to sea to a sandbar protecting a coral reef island. With snorkel gear and sneakers to protect our feet, we cross the coral and a minefield of sea urchins before reaching head-deep pools filled with multicolored fish. Our "captain" snares the urchins and deftly opens them with his machete. We eat these raw delicate treats with a drop of lime juice and cold white wine from our cache.

Evenings in Bahia are relaxed. We grill shrimp and tiny clawless lobsters and roast dull breadfruit that comes alive with *(continued on page 98)*

OPPOSITE:
A local fisherman gutting his catch

BELOW:
A bowl of fried whitebait is served for a mid-morning snack.

Acarajé
BEAN FRITTERS

If you want to taste the authentic acarajé, use dendê oil.

1 pound dried black-eyed peas
1 medium onion, peeled and quartered
1 preserved malagueta pepper, mashed, or ¼ teaspoon hot pepper sauce
Salt and freshly ground white pepper to taste
1½ cups Vatapá with shrimp (optional) or Malagueta Pepper Sauce

3 cups vegetable oil
1 cup good-quality dendê oil
20 small Dried Shrimp (see opposite)

Vatapá (see page 120; see Note) or Malagueta Pepper Sauce (see below), for serving

Soak the peas in water to cover for 24 hours, changing the water once.

Drain the peas and add fresh water to cover. Rub the peas between the palms of your hands to remove the outer skin. Allow the peas to settle and the skins will float to the top. Skim off the skins and drain the peas.

In a food processor or blender, puree the peas with the quartered onion in 2 batches.

In a mixing bowl, combine the puree with the malagueta pepper, salt, and pepper.

In a double boiler, heat the Vatapá, if using. Meanwhile, in a deep fryer, heat the vegetable and dendê oils to 350° F. Using 2 oval soup spoons, form some of the bean mixture into an egg-shaped oval. Tuck 1 dried shrimp in the flatter part of the oval and cover the edges slightly with the puree to keep its shape. Do not cover the shrimp completely. Repeat until all the puree is used.

Working in small batches, fry the Acarajé in the oil for 5 minutes, or until golden, turning them from time to time with a slotted spoon. Drain on paper towels and keep them warm in a low oven.

Split the Acarajé slightly in half lengthwise and fill with a teaspoon of warm Vatapá or Malagueta Pepper Sauce. Serve hot.

MAKES 18 TO 20 SMALL ACARAJÉ

NOTE: If serving with Vatapá, cut the Vatapá recipe in half.

Molho de Pimenta Malagueta
MALAGUETA PEPPER SAUCE

This sauce can accompany any dish requiring hot malagueta peppers. The green malagueta is milder than the red. Other hot chilies may be substituted but the taste will not be quite the same.

1 tablespoon (about 6 to 8) fresh green malagueta peppers (see Note) or bottled malagueta in cachaça or vinegar
2 tablespoons red wine vinegar

¼ cup good-quality dendê oil
1 small yellow onion, chopped
1 teaspoon grated fresh ginger
1 tablespoon salt, or more to taste

If using fresh malagueta peppers, remove the stems and steep the peppers in vinegar for 24 hours.

In a small skillet, heat the oil over low heat, add the onion, and sauté until it is translucent, about 5 minutes.

Drain the peppers and add them to the pan, stirring from time to time until they become limp and mushy, about 15 minutes. Add the ginger and cook for another minute.

Add the salt and stir, pressing down on the mixture with a wooden spoon. Place the mixture in a sterilized jar, cool, and cover.

The sauce will keep for 1 month or more refrigerated

MAKES ABOUT ½ CUP

NOTE: Scotch bonnet peppers or other hot varieties may be substituted. Unlike the malagueta, they must be seeded and deveined before steeping in vinegar.

Camarão Seco
DRIED SHRIMP

Dried shrimp are one of the more important ingredients used in Bahian cooking. In fishing towns along the Bahia coast one sees fishermen mixing their catch of little shrimp with dendê to give them that delicious taste and brilliant crimson color. In the scorching sun, hills of shrimp are tossed and raked over and over again, then at night covered with a tarp. The process is repeated over the next couple of days until the shells are crisp and crunchy and the flesh tender but a little chewy.

Though store-bought dried shrimp are tougher, they can be substituted for homemade in the recipes in this book, although your homemade ones will be better. If you can't get dendê oil, use store-bought dried shrimp.

1 pound small shrimp, preferably with heads intact if possible	**½ cup good-quality dendê oil** **Salt to taste**

Preheat the oven to 500° F.

Place the shrimp on a foil-lined pan and toss with the dendê. Place the pan in the oven and bake for 18 to 20 minutes, turning the shrimp 2 or 3 times so they cook evenly. When the shells are lightly crunchy, preheat the broiler, place the pan 4 inches away from the heat of the broiler, and crisp up for 1 or 2 minutes. Do not allow the shrimp to blacken or overcook. The shrimp should be an even crimson-gold color. Remove them from the pan and season with a generous amount of salt.

Cool the shrimp completely and store in tightly closed plastic bags. Refrigerate if not using immediately. These will keep for 1 week.

MAKES ¾ POUND

a simple sauce of chopped peppers, tomatoes, and lime juice. A salad of
ripe tomatoes, onions, and mint is refreshing in the evening heat.
Sometimes we make a fire of dried coconut shells, and when the embers
are just glowing we grill shrimp and pineapple skewered on sticks of
spliced sugarcane (page 101). This luscious dish was the genius of my
host. Soaked in a marinade made with tamarind, the shrimp tastes like
crusty marshmallows on a stick. One memorable meal is served up by my
friends Mariza and Frey—a pineapple shell filled with lobster scented
with sweet onion, cream, and pineapple juice is dusted with a little
Parmesan (lugged up from São Paulo) and braised till golden and bubbly
(page 104). We walk to the edge of the village for the best sorbets of passion fruit, mango (page 104), lime, and burnt coconut, bought from the
boy who walks up and down the beach hawking his fruit-filled ices.

The evening before my departure to Salvador, Mariza makes two Bahian
specialties, *vatapá* (page 120) and *xinxim* (page 108), a quick sauté of
skinless, cubed boneless chicken cooked in dendê and peanut oil with
onions, garlic, tomato, green peppers, spiked with fresh cilantro. A little
lime juice is usually added last, but when she realizes there are no limes
she goes to the garden in the back of the house and picks an almost
translucent, pale green fruit covered with soft spiny nubs and called *biri-
biri,* cuts it in slices, and adds it to the pot. She offers me a slice, and I like

its tart lemony flavor and its slightly resistant texture, like crunchy cucumbers. Now I know why everything we've been cooking and eating has been so remarkable. Like the natives around us and the original tribes before them, we have been supplying our table with the bounty nature has provided, taking only what is immediately available from the sea, the fruits that ripen on a nearby tree, and the few necessities bought from little patch farms up in the hills behind us.

A local Baiano anticipates his lunch.

DATELINE: SALVADOR, FEBRUARY 17

I've made arrangements with Francisco, my priest friend, to find rooms for me in Salvador. I'm surprised to see him dressed in shorts, a flowery shirt, and with only a couple of layers of beads and the cross hanging about his neck to hint of his holy profession. He's found me a hotel in the oldest section of the city. Going up the steps he points to a plaque commemorating Jorge Amado, Brazil's leading novelist, who once lived in one of the hotel apartments. Amado's books celebrate the life and food of Bahia; *Gabriela, Cravo e Canela* ("Cloves and Cinnamon") portrays life in a harbor town and describes with zest the heavenly dishes prepared by a beautiful cook for a local barkeeper. Her ardor turns to pathos when he falls out of love with her and her cooking goes to hell. This to date is all I know of Bahian life. *(continued on page 103)*

Peixe Frito
FRIED WHITE FISH

Sundays along the beaches are reserved for idling in the sun and water, and the main event of the day is lunch. The meal begins with icy caipirinhas, and my favorite part is the battered fried fish, piles of it, that might include all varieties of small fish, and whitebait and other bigger fish cut up in chunks. It is served with the ubiquitous accompaniment of rice and beans and the bowls of Molho Campanha to mix with the beans.

2 pounds whitefish fillets, such as black bass, grouper, snapper, cut into 2-inch cubes (see Note)

½ cup fresh lime juice
Salt and freshly ground pepper to taste

6 large eggs, separated

1½ cups all-purpose flour, sifted
Vegetable oil, for frying

4 or more limes, halved, Molho Campanha (see page 72), and Malagueta Pepper Sauce (see page 96), for serving

In a large bowl, toss the fish cubes with the lime juice and season with salt and pepper. Marinate for 30 minutes.

In the bowl of an electric mixer, add the egg whites and ⅛ teaspoon salt and beat until they form stiff peaks. With a wire whisk, lightly beat in the yolks, one at a time. Sprinkle the surface with a tablespoon of the flour and slowly fold it into the egg-white mixture.

Pour 2 inches of oil into a deep, large skillet, or use a fryer with a basket and heat over medium-high heat until it begins to lightly smoke or reaches 350° F.

Pour the remaining flour into a shallow dish. Drain the fish cubes and pat dry, then dredge them in the flour, shaking off any excess. Dip the cubes in the batter and fry them in batches until golden, about 2 minutes on each side. Drain on paper towels and serve hot with lime sections, the Molho Campanha, and pepper sauce.

SERVES 6

NOTE: Small fish like whiting, smelt, whitebait, etc., can be left whole and prepared in the same manner.

Lula Frita
FRIED SQUID

2 pounds small squid, cleaned

1 cup all-purpose flour

¼ teaspoon cayenne pepper
Salt and white pepper to taste

About ⅓ cup extra-virgin olive oil or vegetable oil, for frying

Lime sections, for serving

Cut the squid into ¾-inch rounds, keeping the tentacles intact. Dry thoroughly.

Sift the flour with the cayenne, salt, and pepper into a shallow dish or pie pan. Set aside.

In a large heavy skillet, heat the oil until it is hot and begins to smoke. Dredge the squid in the flour mixture and shake in a sieve to remove any excess flour. Add in batches to the hot oil and sauté for a minute or two until golden. If the squid slices are thin, they will cook in a minute. Remove with a slotted spoon to a paper towel to drain.

Serve hot with lots of fresh lime sections.

SERVES 4

Cana de Açúcar com Camarão

GRILLED SHRIMP ON SUGARCANE SPEARS

24 prawns (large shrimp), in their shells
3 garlic cloves, chopped
1 tablespoon chopped fresh cilantro
1 tablespoon fresh or canned tamarind
  paste
  Kosher or freshly ground sea salt
  to taste
1 tablespoon fresh black peppercorns,
  crushed

Juice of 1 lime
½ cup extra-virgin olive oil
6 18-inch lengths of spliced sugarcane,
  about ¼ inch wide (see Note), or
  wooden or metal skewers

Grilled mango and pineapple
spears or Vatapá (see page 120),
for serving

Wash and dry the prawns and place them in a shallow pan.

In a medium bowl, combine the garlic, cilantro, tamarind paste, salt, and crushed peppercorns and mix thoroughly. Whisk in the lime juice and olive oil.

Toss the mixture with the shrimp, cover, and refrigerate for an hour or longer.

Meanwhile, prepare a fire of dried coconut shells or charcoal or a combination of the two.

Skewer 4 shrimp on each sugarcane spear or skewer, passing the sugarcane or skewer through both the tail and top end. (If using wooden skewers, soak them in water for 20 minutes so they will not burn. The sugarcane skewers are moist enough and do not require soaking.)

When the coconuts or coals have a dusty glow, place the shrimp on the grill for 3 to 4 minutes on each side, basting with the remaining marinade. If using a broiler, cook the shrimp 4 inches from the heat source for the same amount of time. Serve with grilled mango and pineapple spears or Vatapá.

SERVES 6

NOTE: Sugarcane is available at many Brazilian and Latin American markets.

The white light reflecting off the bay illuminates the hotel's wide marble corridor, and cool breezes blow through the lobby from the distant terrace. Francisco checks me in and promises to pick me up in the early evening to have dinner at home with his family.

In my room from the balcony window I can look out to the brightly painted colonial villas—soft pinks, blues, mint greens, and creamy yellows, accented with apricot, cobalt, lime-green, and bright yellow trim. It looks like a mountain of tropical sherbets punctuated by baroque and rococo spires and domes of churches and chapels. Hundreds of these religious houses were established throughout the city during the tenure of the Portuguese viceroy, and one can supposedly go to mass every day of the year and never enter the same church twice. Windows open to another balcony that faces the shimmering Bay of All Saints. Three years after the explorer Cabral quit Brazil in search of his Eden, Amerigo Vespucci entered this bay. For the next two hundred years, Salvador would be both the capital and the most important port city in Brazil, until the government shifted to Rio in 1763.

Aimlessly I meander through the city soaking up the tatty beauty and the smells of food. The streets are overrun with tourists and visitors who have come for a week of Carnival. Everyone seems bent on having a party now, even though the real party doesn't officially start for three more days. Shopkeepers stand in doorways, mostly *(continued on page 107)*

OPPOSITE:
Lunch at a barraquinha, a beach bar, features fried squid and beer.

ABOVE:
Baked pineapple stuffed with a creamy lobster filling

103

Abacaxi com Lagosta Capim Santo
BAKED PINEAPPLE WITH LOBSTER

2 live lobsters (about 1¼ pounds each)
1 cup heavy cream
1 small ripe pineapple
2 tablespoons (¼ stick) unsalted butter
2 shallots, minced

Salt and freshly ground white pepper to taste
4 tablespoons freshly grated Parmesan cheese

Preheat the oven to 500° F.

Bring a very large pot of salted water to a boil. Plunge the lobsters headfirst into the boiling water and cook for 10 minutes. Drain and cool under cold running water.

When the lobsters are cool enough to handle, remove the lobster meat, cut into 1-inch chunks, and reserve.

In a small saucepan, heat the cream over medium heat and reduce by half, about 10 minutes.

Meanwhile, cut the pineapple in half lengthwise, starting at the base, including the leaves. Cut the flesh away from the skin, leaving a ½-inch "wall" of flesh in the shell. Place the pineapple halves upside down on a baking sheet to drain and set aside.

Squeeze the pineapple flesh through a sieve, pressing down on the pulp; discard the pulp and reserve the juice.

In a medium nonreactive saucepan, melt the butter over medium heat and sauté the shallots until they are translucent, about 5 minutes. Add the lobster meat, ½ cup of the reserved pineapple juice (see Note), and season with salt and pepper.

Stir quickly and add the reduced cream and bring to a boil. Divide the lobster mixture between the pineapple halves, dust with the cheese, and bake for 10 minutes, or until the surface has a rich golden glaze. Serve immediately.

SERVES 2

NOTE: Pineapple juice acts as a tenderizer and will soften the lobster to the point of making it spongy if the lobster is cooked too long.

Sorvete de Manga
MANGO SORBET

¾ cup sugar
½ cup water
3 pounds very ripe mangoes

Juice of 2 limes
1 tablespoon white rum or vodka (optional)

In a small saucepan, bring the sugar and ½ cup of water to a boil for 5 minutes. Remove from the heat and cool.

Peel away the skins of the mangoes and slice the fruit off their pits, holding them over a bowl to catch their juices. Place half the fruit and juices in the bowl in a food processor with half of the lime juice and puree. Repeat with the remaining mango slices and lime juice and add to the first batch. (Makes about 3½ cups.) Add the cool syrup and the alcohol, if using, then cover and chill. (The alcohol makes the sorbet smooth.)

Freeze in an ice-cream maker according to the manufacturer's directions.

MAKES ABOUT 1 QUART

Sorvete de Abacaxi
PINEAPPLE SORBET

1 large or 2 small very ripe pineapples
½ cup superfine sugar

1 tablespoon white rum or vodka
(optional)

Cut the stem end and bottom off the pineapple, slice off the skin, and remove the eyes with a small, sharp paring knife. Slice the fruit in quarters lengthwise and cut away the core. Slice the pineapple in chunks and puree them in a food processor or blender. Strain the mixture through a sieve, pressing down with a rubber spatula to extract all the juice from the pulp. You should have about 4 cups juice.

In a small nonreactive saucepan, bring the sugar and 1 cup of juice to a simmer over low heat. Add to the remaining juice, then add the alcohol, if using, cover, and chill.

Freeze in an ice-cream maker according to the manufacturer's directions.

MAKES ABOUT 1 QUART

Sorvete de Carambola
STAR FRUIT SORBET

1 cup sugar
¾ cup water
2½ pounds carambola (star fruit)

1 tablespoon cachaça or white rum,
or vodka (optional)

In a nonreactive saucepan, combine the sugar with ⅔ cup water and boil for 5 minutes. Cool.

Trim away the brown points of the carambola and roughly chop them. Puree in a blender or food processor, pulsing on and off until smooth. Strain the mixture through a sieve, pressing down with a rubber spatula to extract all the juices.

Add the cool syrup and the alcohol, if using, and chill. Freeze in an ice-cream maker according to the manfacturer's directions.

MAKES ABOUT 1 QUART

Pudim de Goiaba
GUAVA PUDDING

6 ripe guavas, peeled
½ cup superfine sugar, or more depending on the sweetness of the fruit

⅔ cup heavy cream

In a food processor or blender combine the guavas and sugar and pulse on and off until pureed. Taste for sweetness. Strain the puree through a sieve to remove the seeds. Chill thoroughly.

One hour before serving, whip the cream in a chilled bowl to form soft peaks. Gently fold it into the fruit puree. Do not overmix; the pudding should be streaked with white cream. Cover and refrigerate until ready to serve. Serve with sugar cookies, plain cake, or as a sauce for fresh or poached fruit.

SERVES 4 TO 6

Baiana women who smile shyly as you pass, hoping to lure you in to buy a little primitive painting, a silver trinket, or maybe some fine embroidered linen. They're wrapped in layers of starched white cottony skirts and billowy blouses, and their silver bracelets and necklaces catch the light. I move up and down cobblestone streets peeking into flowering palm-filled gardens, window-shopping with everyone else. My attention is arrested as I pass a storefront beauty parlor. In the dark of this room I gaze at three women in form-fitting white dresses buttoned from neck to knee, appearing more like nurses or attendants at a spa. Three men as elegant as blackamoors sit bare-chested in ballooning sapphire silk pants, their white leather slippers curling up in Oriental fashion. At the base of each chair baskets of white cotton ribbon unfurl to the hands of the attendants, who engulf the crowns of each man's head in an elaborate turban of snow, then buckle a stage-sapphire pin to the cloth above each forehead. They are members of an old African guild who will march in Carnival. Farther up the street a band of some dozen men in ruby silk trousers and bright white shirts play drums and gongs and blow on ornamental pipes attached to pig bladders—the rhythms and sounds intensely African.

OPPOSITE: *Pastel, little pastries filled with shrimp and heart of palm*

ABOVE: *Rei do Milho, the King of Corn, with his steam wagon*

I wander into Terreiro de Jesus (Jesus' Yard), a moderate-sized square surrounded by six churches and a couple of convents. The yard is a bazaar of stands and tents, and I hustle through, trying to avoid the vendors hawking hammocks, tin lanterns, table linens, and endless racks of T-shirts and jeans. Like any sweaty, fatigued tourist, I retreat to a church for a rest. Adjusting to the somber light, I gaze at the wood-planked vaulted ceiling perspectively painted with a host of saints bursting through Tiepoloesque sky and clouds; plaster walls and altars drip with gold leaf. Refreshed, I reenter the bright city. On the steps a doce vendor has set up her tray of tapioca sticks—a dense creamy bar of tapioca. She takes my few cruzeiros and dips the bar in a pot of white sweet condensed cream. It's as sweet and as cool as the air blowing off the bay. *(continued on page 111)*

Xinxim
CHICKEN AND SHRIMP STEW

2 3½-pound chickens, backbones and wing tips removed, cut into 8 pieces
Salt and freshly ground pepper to taste
2 limes, halved
1 pound medium fresh shrimp, peeled, tails intact, and deveined
½ cup vegetable oil
2 to 3 tablespoons extra-virgin olive oil
2 medium onions, chopped
2 garlic cloves, minced
1 green bell pepper, cored, seeded, ribs removed, and diced
3 large tomatoes, peeled, seeded, and chopped
2 cups homemade or canned low-sodium chicken stock

4 malagueta peppers, or 1 small hot chili pepper, chopped
¼ cup ground roasted cashews
¼ cup ground roasted peanuts
½ cup ground dried shrimp (see page 97)
½ teaspoon grated fresh ginger
2 tablespoons dendê oil
½ cup chopped fresh cilantro
½ cup fresh or canned unsweetened coconut milk

Simple Boiled White Rice (see page 12), Simple Farofa (see opposite), Vatapá (see page 120), and Malagueta Pepper Sauce (see page 96), for serving

Wash and pat dry the chicken pieces and season with salt and pepper. In a large bowl, toss the chicken pieces with the juice of 1 lime and set aside for 30 minutes.

Meanwhile, in a medium bowl, season the shrimp with salt and pepper, toss with the juice of half a lime, and set aside for 15 minutes.

Heat 2 tablespoons of vegetable oil in a large skillet over high heat. Add the shrimp and sauté briefly, until they are pink, about 2 minutes. Remove and reserve.

Add half the remaining vegetable oil to the pan. When the oil is hot, add the chicken in batches, skin side down, and brown until golden, adding more oil as needed. Repeat until all the chicken is well browned and reserve.

Drain the oil, add 2 tablespoons of olive oil to the pan, and sauté the onions and garlic until soft and translucent, about 5 minutes. Add the green pepper and cook another 5 minutes. Add the tomatoes and the stock, bring to a boil, reduce the heat, and add the chicken. Cover and cook for 35 minutes, or until the chicken is tender and cooked through, stirring from time to time so the chicken does not stick to the bottom of the pan.

Mix the ground cashews and peanuts with the ground dried shrimp.

Remove the chicken from the pan and whisk in the ground dried shrimp and nut mixture, ginger, and salt and pepper. Bring to a simmer, add 1 tablespoon dendê oil, then return the chicken to the pan and add the shrimp. Add the cilantro, bring to a simmer, and cook about 5 minutes, or until hot. Squeeze the juice of the remaining lime half over the Xinxim, add the remaining dendê oil and the coconut milk, and cook until heated through, about 3 minutes.

Place the Xinxim in a heated serving bowl and serve with the boiled white rice, farofa, Vatapá, and pepper sauce.

SERVES 6 TO 8

Simple Farofa

When farinha de mandioca (manioc flour) is toasted, it is called farofa. Farofa accompanies all Brazilian dishes, and the taste and texture are similar to that of very fine bread crumbs. In the south of Brazil the manioc flour is warmed in a pan with butter or olive oil or sometimes just heated plain. In the north, particularly in Bahia, it is always toasted with dendê oil, and in Minas Gerais and the northeast (the states bordering the Amazon) it is usually toasted without any oils or fat.

1 cup manioc flour (farinha de mandioca)	**1 tablespoon unsalted butter, olive oil, or dendê oil (optional)**

Heat a medium skillet over medium-high heat. Add the oil or butter and warm for about 1 minute, until the butter foam subsides or the oil gets hot.

Add the manioc flour and stir slowly for 3 minutes or until the oil or butter is incorporated and the flour has a lightly toasted color and is warm throughout.

Place in a small bowl and serve as an accompaniment to recommended dishes.

MAKES ENOUGH FOR 6 SERVINGS

NOTE: For a fancier variation of this Brazilian staple, try the Farofa Peri Peri (see page 37).

Côco Queimado
BURNT COCONUT SWEETS

2 packed cups grated fresh or packaged unsweetened coconut	**⅛ teaspoon ground cloves**
½ teaspoon ground cinnamon	**2 packed cups dark brown sugar**
	2 large egg whites

In a large bowl, toss the coconut with the cinnamon and cloves and set aside.

Lightly oil 2 baking pans with vegetable oil.

In a heavy-bottomed saucepan, melt the sugar over medium-low heat, stirring until it melts. Stir in the coconut mixture, reduce the heat, and stir for 5 minutes, or until the mixture thickens. Remove from the heat and immerse the pan in cold water, without allowing any water to enter the pan, to stop the cooking.

Whisk the egg whites until white and frothy but not stiff. Fold this into the coconut mixture and with a large soup spoon, scoop the mixture onto the baking pans, separating each spoonful by 3 inches. The Côco Queimado will spread as it cools. Set the baking pans in a dry place and cool for 2 hours, or until set.

Store in a covered container.

MAKES 16 SMALL CÔCO QUEIMADO

I walk down to the Largo do Pelourinho, where I smell the cauldrons of boiling dendê that a couple of old black women have set up for frying their acarajé. The Pelourinho, the Place of the Pillory, once housed the whipping post where African slaves were publicly punished. These imposing stunted columns, white and decorated in gold paint, are in every old colonial town, a perpetual monument and reminder. In the great Praça da Sé, reviewing stands are rigged, flags unfurl from lampposts and buildings, and a small band rehearses Brazilian songs to a rock beat on an elevated stage. Some women are busily setting up their portable kitchens to make acarajé, while others arrange trays of paçoca, a soft candy brittle chock full of cashew nuts (here in Bahia it's candy, not a meat dish), coconut candies, and little freezer boxes filled with fruit ices.

The Brazilian fondness for sweets at almost any time of day goes back to precolonial Salvador when kitchens were run by the black slaves. To support themselves when they were freed, the women took their craft to the streets or helped the nuns who made convent sweets and cakes. Now at every hour, at every train station, bus depot, ferry launch, and post office, women claim their concessional turf. When they become too old, that space is handed over to their daughters or a close relative. (Only pushcarts serving up popcorn, steamed corn, hot dogs, and soda pop are "manned" by the male population.) The cakes made in convents were perceived as aphrodisiacs, and the sweets' names had a suggestive (if not obscene) boldness to them. Some can still be found in sweet shops or on the trays of the older Baianas as the nuns named them: little kisses, weaned sucklings, rise-the-old-man, maiden's tongue, love's caresses, jealous sighs, breasts of Venus, nun's belly, angel's throat (miniature egg-yolk babas soaked in sugar syrup and supposedly the shape of the lower part of a double chin), and mother-in-law's eyes (a reconstituted dried prune filled with a vermicelli of sugared egg yolk). In more naive times, when Brazilian sons arrived at the age to "know" a woman, (continued on page 114)

OPPOSITE:
Bahian specialties include Xinxim, a flavorful stew of chicken and shrimp, and Vatapá, a creamy puree of shrimp, spices, and ground cashews and peanuts, all accompanied by farofa, the starch of Brazil.

BELOW:
Cachaça perfumed with a snake is an aphrodisiac.

Sopa de Caranguejo
CRAB SOUP

The Brazilian Atlantic crab is slightly smaller than the famed blue crabs found along our Eastern Shore of Maryland, which are equally delicious and sweet.

2 onions
1 cup cachaça (optional)
1 bay leaf
2 whole cloves
3 sprigs parsley
2 sprigs cilantro
3 garlic cloves
12 small live blue crabs, washed and scrubbed (see Note)
2 tablespoons extra-virgin olive oil
1 celery rib, chopped
2 large tomatoes, peeled, seeded, and chopped
1 small hot chili pepper, seeded, deveined, and chopped

1 tablespoon chopped fresh parsley
2 tablespoons chopped fresh cilantro
1 tablespoon chopped fresh basil
Salt and freshly ground pepper to taste
1 cup fresh or canned unsweetened coconut milk
1 teaspoon dendê oil (optional)

3 limes, halved, and Malagueta Pepper Sauce (see page 96) or hot pepper sauce, for serving

Slice one of the onions. In a steamer, add the cachaça, if using, the sliced onion, bay leaf, cloves, parsley and cilantro sprigs, and 1 garlic clove along with enough cold water to fill by 3 inches. Cover and bring to a boil.

Place the crabs in the steamer basket, lower them into the pot, cover, and steam for 5 minutes. Remove the crabs and set them aside to cool. Strain the liquid and reserve.

Remove the top shells from the crabs and cut the bodies in half lengthwise. Pick out the meat and reserve, along with any yellow or crimson egg sac. Crack the claws, remove the meat, and reserve.

Return the hard and soft shells and claw shells to the pot. Add the crab steaming liquid and enough water to cover. Bring to a simmer and cook for 20 minutes. Strain and set aside.

Chop the remaining onion and garlic cloves and set aside.

In a large nonreactive kettle, heat the oil over medium heat. Add the onion, garlic, and celery and sauté until translucent, about 5 minutes. Add the tomatoes and chili pepper and cook another 5 minutes. Add the chopped parsley, 1 tablespoon cilantro, basil, and crab broth and season with salt and pepper. Bring to a boil, reduce the heat, and simmer for 15 minutes.

Add the coconut milk and crabmeat and swirl in the reserved egg roe. Add the dendê oil and simmer for 5 minutes, or until hot.

Serve in heated bowls, sprinkled with a little remaining chopped cilantro, and serve with lime halves and pepper sauce.

SERVES 6 TO 8

NOTE: The soup can be made by substituting 2 pounds fresh crabmeat, picked clean, for the live crabs and substituting fish stock for the crab stock. It's good—but not the real McCoy.

Caruru com Coentro
OKRA WITH CILANTRO

1 pound small okra, ends removed
   and sliced in ¾-inch rounds
2 tablespoons good quality dendê oil
   or extra-virgin olive oil
2 medium onions, finely chopped

1 clove garlic, minced
   Salt and freshly ground pepper
   to taste
2 tablespoons chopped fresh cilantro

Heat a medium-heavy skillet over medium heat. When very hot, add the okra and cook for 10 minutes, stirring constantly with a wooden spoon. The gum of the okra will stick to the side of the pan.

In a separate pan, heat the oil over medium heat. Add the onion and garlic and sauté until soft and translucent, about 5 minutes. Add the okra and season with salt and pepper. Add the cilantro, toss, and serve with fish dishes.

SERVES 4

Doce de Banana
BANANA BUTTER

Bananas being such a prolific fruit in the tropics, I'm sure this recipe came about early in Brazilian cooking. It is sheer delight. The consistency is similar to that of apple butter, and it requires hours of cooking, as does apple butter. It can be done in a double boiler with an occasional stir and a watchful eye, making sure the lower pan stays filled with hot water.

12 ripe bananas
½ cup sugar

2 whole cloves
½ cup water

Peel the bananas and slice them in long thin slices. In the top of a double boiler, add the bananas with the sugar, cloves, and water. Place the pot directly over medium heat and stir until the sugar dissolves. Then place the pot on top of a double boiler over hot boiling water. Stir from time to time, making sure the water does not evaporate. Cook for 5 to 6 hours, or until the mixture becomes a deep rich brown color and the consistency of apple butter.

Cool and serve with whipped cream, crème fraîche, or ice cream.

Banana butter should be stored in a sealed container and refrigerated. It keeps for weeks.

MAKES ABOUT 1¼ PINTS

RIGHT: *Crab soup, a seaside favorite*

OPPOSITE: *Bobó e Acaçá, a mixture of prawns and fresh manioc, served with a coconut-scented steamed pudding made with rice flour that has been cut into diamond shapes*

their fathers were in the habit of giving them "money to buy a cake"—the meaning of which now is quite clear.

Dinner with Francisco is a party in the kitchen. Parents, relatives, siblings, and friends all gather in this happy room. Shiny white tiles go halfway up the wall to meet a border of green fruits stenciled on the white plaster walls above, and a wood-burning stove sputters sparks. At the end of the room, doors open onto a veranda, and on this a long dining table is set overlooking a garden of palms, limes, and mango trees. Cages haphazardly hang from the rafters with parrots, parakeets, and a small black bird with a brilliant orange beak who is quite pleased with its very melodic song.

In the center of the room a marble table is laden with piles of tiny orange dried shrimp, fresh pink shrimp, and huge white prawns, onions, garlic, tomatoes, peeled manioc roots soaking in a bowl of water, gingerroots, balls of nutmeg, cashews and peanuts, red bell peppers, limes, bouquets of parsley and cilantro, and pitchers of coconut milk, olive oil, and dendê. Francisco announces with a broad smile that tonight is my Bahian cooking lesson, and "we" will make two famous specialties—*bobó e acaçá* and *vatapá*. "And we will drink!" Francisco's mother, dressed all in white, pounds the dried shrimp with a static solid beat. A brother slices limes for the caipirinhas, and someone else cracks ice over the sink. I peel shrimp and am instructed to save the heads and shells for stock. When I reach for an onion and a little parsley to add to my stock, Francisco shakes his head. "*Não, não*!! We want to taste shrimp—not onions; they come later in the sauce."

Bowls and platters are brought to the table to *(continued on page 126)*

Bobó e Acaçá
RICE FLOUR PUDDING AND SHRIMP

Bobó is a classic Bahian dish of shrimp and spices ladled over acaçá—a stark-white silken pudding made of rice flour, similar to polenta.

2 pounds prawns (large shrimp), peeled and deveined (reserve heads and shells if making stock)

2 pounds manioc root (cassava)

2 cups shrimp stock or light fish stock
Juice of 1 lime
Salt and freshly ground white pepper to taste

1 large onion, quartered

2 whole cloves

1 bay leaf

3 tablespoons extra-virgin olive oil

2 medium onions, finely chopped

2 garlic cloves, chopped

6 large tomatoes, peeled, seeded, and chopped

1 tablespoon tomato paste

1 cup milk

1 cup fresh or canned unsweetened coconut milk

2 tablespoons dendê oil

3 tablespoons heavy cream

½ cup chopped fresh parsley

¼ cup chopped fresh cilantro, or more to taste

Acaçá (see opposite), for serving

Clean the shrimp and set aside.

With a sharp paring knife, peel away the manioc skin and cut the manioc root in half lengthwise. In a large bowl, cover the manioc in cold water and set aside for 1 hour or more.

Meanwhile, if using homemade shrimp stock, combine the shrimp heads, shells, and enough cold water to cover in a saucepan. Bring to a boil, skim, reduce the heat, and simmer for 15 minutes. Strain through a fine mesh strainer and reserve the broth, about 2 cups.

In a medium bowl, mix the lime juice with the salt and white pepper and mix until the salt dissolves. Stir in the shrimp and set aside.

Drain the manioc and place in a large kettle of lightly salted water. Stud 1 onion quarter with the cloves and add it and the remaining quarters and bay leaf to the manioc.

Bring to a boil and cook for 20 minutes, or until the manioc is fork tender. Drain and cool slightly. Remove the fibrous central cords from the manioc, remove the bay leaf and the cloves from the onion quarter, and discard. Set the manioc and onion aside.

In a large skillet, heat the olive oil over medium heat. Add the chopped onions and garlic and cook until the onions are lightly browned, about 8 minutes. Add the shrimp and cook for another 3 minutes, or until they turn a bright pink. Drain the shrimp and set aside. Add the tomatoes, tomato paste, and stock to the skillet. Season with salt and pepper, bring to a boil, reduce the heat, and simmer for 10 minutes, stirring from time to time.

Working in 2 or 3 batches, in a food processor, puree the boiled manioc and onions with the tomato mixture, adding the milk, coconut milk, and dendê as you pulse the mixture. Place the pureed mixture in a large nonstick saucepan and set over medium heat. Add the cream, season with salt and pepper, and cook for 5 minutes, stirring constantly. If the sauce is too thick, thin it out with a little milk or stock. Add the reserved shrimp, parsley, and cilantro and cook for another 2 minutes. Serve over sliced Acaçá.

SERVES 4 TO 6

Acaçá
STEAMED RICE FLOUR PUDDING

Acaçá is also served with hot fish soup in place of pirão, and as an accompaniment to sautéed and grilled shrimp. It is also wrapped in banana leaves and steamed and sold as a popular snack by street vendors.

OVERLEAF:
*Scenes along
the beaches from
sunrise till dusk*

2 tablespoons extra-virgin olive oil
1⅓ cups fresh or canned unsweetened
coconut milk
1 cup milk
Salt and freshly ground white pepper
to taste

1½ cups rice flour (available at Latin
American and specialty food stores)
⅓ cup heavy cream

In a large saucepan, mix together the olive oil, coconut milk, milk, and salt and pepper and bring to a simmer over high heat. Reduce the heat to medium and whisk in the rice flour a little at a time, stirring constantly until the mixture is smooth and thick, about 8 minutes.

Gradually add the cream, mix, and pour into a lightly oiled 8 × 8-inch shallow ovenproof pan. Cool, covered, until ready to serve.

When the pudding is ready to serve, allow it to come to room temperature if chilled for a long time. Cut it into small squares or diamond shapes and serve with the bobó.

MAKES ABOUT 12 SQUARES

Vatapá
S E A F O O D   C R E A M

This puree of fish or shrimp has no equivalent in English and the only vague parallel it might have is a spicy quenelle. Though the classic accompaniment is Xinxim (see page 108), it is also served with Açaçá (see page 117), grilled prawns, and as a filling for Acarajé (see page 96).

FISH
- 1 **pound fresh nonoily, white fish fillets, such as snapper, bass, or grouper (heads and tails reserved for homemade stock; optional)**
- 1 **pound heads and tails for stock or substitute 4 cups fish stock**
- 1 **small onion, sliced**
- 2 **sprigs cilantro**
- 1 **garlic clove, crushed**
  Salt to taste

VATAPÁ
- ½ **loaf stale French bread**
- 2 **cups milk**
- ¾ **cup ground dried shrimp**
- ½ **cup ground roasted unsalted peanuts**
- ½ **cup ground roasted unsalted cashews**

- 1 **medium onion, quartered**
- 1 **garlic clove**
- 2 **sprigs cilantro**
- ½ **teaspoon grated fresh ginger**
  Generous pinch of nutmeg
  Salt and freshly ground pepper to taste
  Juice of 1 lime
- 1 **tablespoon dendê oil (optional)**
- 1 **teaspoon malagueta pepper oil or hot sauce**
- ½ **cup fresh or unsweetened canned coconut milk**

Simple Boiled White Rice (see page 12) and Simple Farofa (see page 109), for serving

For homemade stock, in a large nonreactive saucepan, combine the fish heads, bones, tails, onions, cilantro, garlic, salt, and enough water to cover, about 4 cups. Bring to a boil over high heat, reduce the heat, and simmer for 15 minutes. Strain the stock and reserve the fish bones. Pour the homemade broth or the fish stock into a large, clean saucepan and return to the heat. Add the fish and poach for 10 minutes, or until the flesh is firm and slightly resilient to the touch. Remove the fish from the broth with a slotted spoon, then strain the broth and reserve.

To make the Vatapá, soak the bread in the milk and set aside.

When the fish bones are cool enough to handle, remove the skin and flake away the fish from the bones, including the cheeks, and reserve.

Wring the bread dry to extract all the milk (about 2 cups when wrung dry) and puree the bread and flaked fish in a food processor or blender until smooth.

In a nonreactive pan, combine the ground dried shrimp, peanuts, cashews, and pureed bread and fish, then whisk in the reserved stock a little at a time. The consistency should be light and slightly fluffy. You may not use all of the stock.

Add the ginger and nutmeg and season with salt and pepper. Bring just to a low boil over medium-high heat reduce the heat, and simmer, stirring constantly, for about 10 minutes. Stir in the lime juice and the dendê and cook another 2 minutes.

Add the hot pepper oil and coconut milk and cook another few minutes until thoroughly hot.

Serve with boiled rice and farofa.

SERVES 8 TO 10

VARIATION: Vatapá is also made with fresh shrimp puree. Substitute 1 pound (about 12) large shrimp, peeled and deveined, for the fish. Puree the raw shrimp in a processor, finish the recipe as given, and add 10 minutes to the cooking time of the Vatapá.

Casquinha de Siri
STUFFED BAKED CRABS

The word *siri* in the Tupi language means "to run, glide, or walk backward," which is what crabs do.

- Meat from 12 small cooked blue crabs, picked clean, or 1 pound fresh lump crabmeat, picked clean
- 2 slices stale French bread
- ¼ cup milk
- 1 tablespoon extra-virgin olive oil
- 1 shallot, minced
- 1 small garlic clove, minced
- 1 large medium-ripe tomato, peeled, seeded, and chopped
- ⅓ cup white wine
- Salt and freshly ground pepper to taste
- 3 tablespoons unsalted butter
- ½ teaspoon chopped fresh basil
- ½ teaspoon chopped fresh cilantro
- ½ teaspoon chopped fresh parsley
- A few gratings of nutmeg
- ½ teaspoon dendê oil, or extra-virgin olive oil
- 1 tablespoon heavy cream
- ⅓ cup freshly grated Parmesan cheese or manioc flour (farinha de mandioca)

- Lime sections and Malagueta Pepper Sauce (see page 96) or hot pepper sauce, for serving

Preheat the oven to 400° F.

Lightly grease 8 crab shells or 8 shallow ovenproof porcelain ramekins.

Finely shred the crabmeat and set aside.

Soak the bread in the milk and set aside.

Heat the olive oil in a small saucepan over medium heat. Add the shallot and cook for 2 minutes, or until it begins to sweat. Add the garlic and cook another minute. Add the tomato and white wine, bring to a boil, reduce the heat, and simmer 5 minutes. Season with salt and pepper. Remove the tomato sauce from the heat and reserve.

Squeeze the bread dry and shread finely with a fork. Fold it into the tomato sauce.

In a clean skillet, melt the butter over medium heat and sauté the crabmeat for a minute or two. Add the tomato sauce, basil, cilantro, parsley, nutmeg, and dendê oil. Add the cream, stirring for 1 minute.

Stuff the mixture into the crab shells or ramekins, dust with the Parmesan or manioc flour, and bake for 10 minutes, or until piping hot and the surface is golden.

Accompany with lime sections and Malagueta Pepper Sauce or hot sauce.

SERVES 4

OVERLEAF, LEFT: *The Big House breakfast includes sweet breads made with manioc flour (Bôlo de Aipim) and corn (Broa de Fubá), tapioca crepes, and French toast filled with mild cheese (Pão Doce com Queijo).*

RIGHT: *Casquinha de Siri, stuffed baked crabs, are filled with a rich mixture of crab-meat, bread, herbs, and spices.*

Pão Doce com Queijo
FRENCH TOAST AND CHEESE

3 cups milk
1 3-inch cinnamon stick
½ cup raw or crystallized sugar

SYRUP
2 cups raw or granulated sugar
2 cups water
1 2-inch cinnamon stick
1 strip lime zest

6 thin slices mild cheese, such as Muenster or Monterey Jack, sliced to fit the bread (mild Brazilian cheese is similar to our packaged cheeses, and Bel Paese is a good substitute)

12 ¾-inch-thick slices good-quality day-old white bread
4 large eggs, lightly beaten
12 tablespoons (1½ sticks) unsalted butter
2 tablespoons vegetable oil

Raw or crystallized sugar and ground cinnamon

In a saucepan, combine the milk, cinnamon stick, and sugar and bring to a simmer over medium heat, stirring until the sugar dissolves. Allow the mixture to simmer for 5 minutes, then remove from the heat and cool. (The milk mixture may be prepared the night before and refrigerated, covered.)

To make the syrup, in a medium saucepan, mix the sugar, water, the cinnamon stick, and lime zest and bring to a boil, stirring with a wooden spoon until the sugar dissolves. Continue to simmer until the syrup thickens and begins to turn a medium-amber color. Set aside and keep warm. (The syrup may be prepared the night before and reheated in a double boiler.)

Place a slice of cheese between each 2 slices of bread and trim away the crusts.

Stir the cooled milk mixture into the beaten eggs and place in a shallow baking pan. Soak the "sandwiches" in the egg mixture, thoroughly drenching the bread. Place the soaked sandwiches on a wire rack over a baking sheet and set aside.

In a large heavy skillet, heat half the butter and vegetable oil over medium heat. Fry the "sandwiches" in batches for 2 to 3 minutes on each side until golden, adding the rest of the butter as needed. Place on warm plates and dust with sugar and cinnamon. Accompany with the syrup.

SERVES 4 TO 6

Bôlo de Aipim
MANIOC BREAKFAST CAKE

As you travel from state to state, words change as fast as the scenery and as diversely as the regional dishes. In the north the word for "manioc root" is *aipim*. This delicious breakfast cake needs neither jam nor butter.

2 pounds manioc root (cassava)
14 tablespoons (1¾ sticks) unsalted butter, at room temperature
2 cups sugar
4 large eggs
Scant 2 cups (less 2 tablespoons) all-purpose flour

1 teaspoon baking powder
2 cups milk
2 cups fresh or canned unsweetened coconut milk

Preheat the oven to 300° F. Generously butter a 2-inch-deep 9 × 13-inch baking pan. Flour the pan and tap out any excess.

Peel the manioc root and grate as finely as possible, removing all threads. Set aside.

In the bowl of an electric mixer, blend the butter and sugar. Beat in the eggs one at a time, then add the flour and baking powder and beat until smooth.

Fold in the grated manioc root and gradually add the milk and coconut milk.

Pour the batter into the pan and bake for 30 minutes. Cool on a rack and cut into squares or diamond shapes when ready to serve.

Keeps for 2 days covered and refrigerated.

SERVES 8 TO 10

Broa de Fubá
BREAKFAST CORN CAKE

14 tablespoons (1¾ sticks) unsalted butter, at room temperature
2 cups sugar
4 large eggs
1 cup all-purpose flour
1 teaspoon baking powder

2 cups milk
1 cup very fine yellow cornmeal
¼ cup plus 1 tablespoon brewed anise-flavored tea
1 cup vegetable oil

Preheat the oven to 300° F. Butter and flour a 2-inch-deep 9 × 13-inch baking pan and tap out any excess flour.

In the bowl of an electric mixer, beat the butter with the sugar. Add the eggs one at a time. Gradually add the flour, baking powder, and milk. Add the cornmeal and gradually add the tea and oil.

Pour the batter into the pan and bake for 30 minutes.

Cool slightly in the pan on a rack and cut into squares or diamond shapes when ready to serve. Serve warm or at room temperature.

MAKES ABOUT 12 SQUARES

A *diver with his lobster catch ready for the hungry lunch crowd*

begin the evening meal. Francisco's mood is suddenly reverential—extending his hands he delivers a heartfelt prayer in his euphonious voice, then looks up and grins at us all, and we eat with gusto. First, there is a delicious, rich crab soup (page 112). Then we have the *bobó* (page 116), a stew of shrimp cooked in a velvety sauce of tomato, garlic, onions, and stock, accented with cilantro and lime juice and smoothed with a little coconut milk and dendê. It is served over cubes of *acaça* (page 117), a dense cake of rice flour whipped with coconut milk and cream and cooked like polenta or grits. He also serves a side dish of *caruru* (page 113). The *vatapá* (page 120) is a creamy paste of pureed dried and fresh shrimp, ground peanuts and cashews, flavored with ginger and nutmeg, which is blended with coconut milk and spiked with malagueta pepper oil, cilantro, and lime juice. Francisco tosses some leftover shrimp on the top of the stove to sputter and char—we dip them, shells and all, into the vatapá. The meal is a triumph of tastes.

Dinner ends with a platter of pineapple, fresh *caju* (the fruit of the cashew nut), mangoes, papayas, and then a bowl of banana doce (page 113), which is similar to apple butter. The ripe bananas stew at a slow heat until they resemble this condiment, but softer, creamier, with hints of chocolate and coffee. Sweetened cream is poured on top.

The Mercado Modelo, Salvador's main produce market, is a great maze of wooden shacks and stalls strung out along the *(continued on page 130)*

Lula Manacau

GRILLED SQUID MANACAU

This dish was made famous by Edinho at his restaurant Manaca in the village of Camburi on the São Paulo coast.

MARINADE

Juice of 3 limes (2 rinds reserved)

1 tablespoon extra-virgin olive oil, plus extra for cooking

1 teaspoon salt, or more to taste

¼ teaspoon freshly ground white pepper

1½ pounds medium squid, cleaned

¼ cup extra-virgin olive oil

8 garlic cloves, minced

¼ cup dry white wine

2 tablespoons minced fresh parsley

Lime sections and preserved malagueta pepper oil or hot pepper sauce, for serving

To make the marinade, in a nonreactive bowl, mix the lime juice, oil, salt, and pepper and allow to stand 5 minutes, or until the salt dissolves.

Slice off the heads of the squid, place the heads and bodies in a large bowl, and add enough marinade to moisten the squid. You may not need all of it.

For the fried garlic, heat the oil over medium heat in a small heavy-bottomed saucepan. Add the garlic and cook just until lightly golden. Immediately remove the pan from the heat and remove the garlic with a slotted spoon. Set aside.

Heat a large cast-iron skillet or griddle. When it is very hot, rub it with the lime rinds, add a tablespoon or more of vegetable oil, then carefully wipe dry with a kitchen cloth or paper towel. (This method is often used throughout Brazilian houses and small restaurants for seasoning pans before cooking, and for cleaning afterwards.)

Add the remaining tablespoon of olive oil or enough to coat the skillet or griddle. Add the squid and sauté on each side until it is a streaked rich mahogany color, about 4 minutes on each side. Sprinkle the fried garlic over the squid. Splash the white wine over the squid, add the parsley, toss for 1 minute, and place on a warm serving platter. Serve immediately with additional lime sections and malagueta pepper oil or hot pepper sauce on the side.

SERVES 4

Moqueca do Cândido

FISH STEW CANDIDO

In the fishing village of Guarujá, just outside Rio, you can sample this Bahian dish that elegantly hints of coconut milk, dendê oil, and fresh herbs. This famous dish can be made with either fish or shrimp, or a combination of both.

1 pound firm whitefish steaks, such as swordfish, monkfish, or tilefish

½ pound prawns (large shrimp), peeled and deveined

Salt and freshly ground pepper to taste

2 tablespoons extra-virgin olive oil

1 medium onion, sliced in rounds

2 tablespoons tomato sauce

1 medium tomato, peeled, seeded, and chopped

½ red bell pepper, seeded, deveined, and chopped

1 cup fresh or canned unsweetened coconut milk

1 tablespoon good-quality dendê oil

6 to 8 sprigs cilantro

¼ cup chopped cashew nuts

Simple Boiled White Rice (see page 12), Simple Farofa (see page 109), and Malagueta Pepper Sauce (page 96), for serving

Preheat the oven to 400° F.

Season the fish and prawns with salt and pepper and set aside.

In a deep skillet, heat the olive oil over medium heat. Add the onion and sauté until wilted, about 5 minutes. Add the tomato sauce and cook another minute. Add the tomato and red pepper and cook another 8 minutes, or until the mixture thickens.

Stir in the coconut milk, dendê oil, and 2 tablespoons of water.

Place the fish in a lightly oiled Dutch oven and pour the sauce over the fish. Cover and bake in the oven for 5 minutes. Add the shrimp and toss gently to cover with some of the sauce.

Add 4 sprigs of cilantro, cover, and bake another 5 minutes, or until the fish is opaque, the shrimp tender, and the sauce is bubbling slightly.

Sprinkle the cashews over the fish, bruise the remaining cilantro sprigs, and scatter them over the top.

Serve with boiled white rice, farofa, and pepper sauce.

SERVES 2 HANDSOMELY

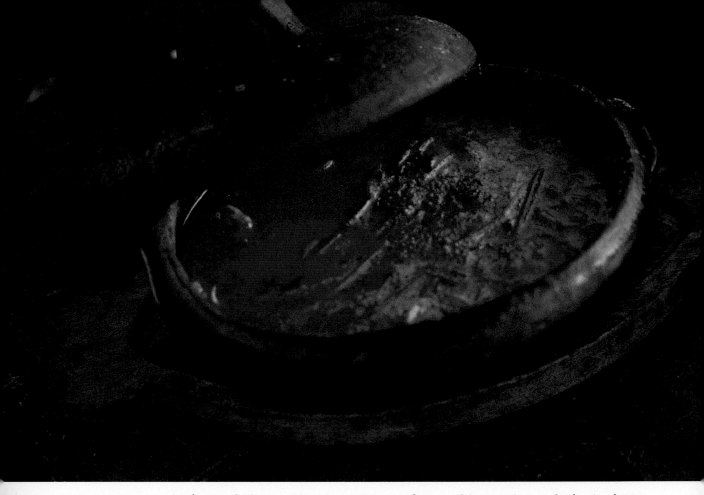

harbor and close to the piers where tankers and luxury liners dock. At 6:00 A.M. the sun is already hot as I follow the crowds through an obstacle course of hills of pineapples and melons set up on the curb, dart out of the way of barrels, filled with limes, charging through. Boys run with stalks of bananas balanced on their heads, others with bundles of sugarcane that could impale you as they speed by. I'm pushed through a narrow opening and press myself against a wall goggling at a table loaded with rosy-gold caju.

Down one tight alley I pass stall after stall of green, rose, gold, and purple mangoes, and I'm offered a taste of the purple one, called the royal mango. Its flesh is silky, warm, juicy, and the flavor and scent more like an exotic perfume than the mango flavor I know. The sweet fragrances float above the stench of rotting fruit skins that cover my path. The briny odor of fresh silvery fish also mingles with the stink of rotting guts, and I slip and slide on a muddy path covered with fish scales.

Under the shade of a wooden awning a woman hugs an hourglass-shaped mortar with her knees and thumps a pestle as thin and tall as she into the bowl. Pounding to a slow count of four, she pulverizes purple-brown seeds into gritty cocoa powder. A burlap bag of seeds rests against her thigh, and stacked behind her are elongated cacao pods with elevated ribs of purple and gold. The dusty aroma of chocolate fills the air.

A platter of fresh raw mussels starts lunch.

An old vendor reading his morning paper is almost hidden behind his bank of fresh red, green, and yellow lilliputian malagueta peppers; another hut offers yard-long wooden spoons used to mix the batter for acarajé. At one stall bottles of crimson dendê heavy with solidified white sediment are tied to poles with cord, and small tables are laid out with burlap-lined baskets brimming with dried oregano, wide barks of cinnamon, heaps of cloves, bay leaves, and urucum of all shades of red—the tasteless powder made from the leaves of the plant of the same name used to brighten stews. Across the way a man sits on his haunches in front of a low flat basket filled with a mound of strung brown beads the size of large peas. I pick one up, I take a bite, and beneath the shiny brown skin is white coconut meat. They will make fun little edible presents. I wander out toward the dock, and farm trucks are spilling over with mountains of papayas, oranges, onions, and peppers—none of them boxed. Shirtless workers sparkle with sweat, moving like mercury. Stalls in one long line sell the sinister trappings and props for macumba and candomblé—the voodoo rites so ingrained in the Bahian culture. Anxious goats rustle in a stall of hay—the sacrificial animal, cooked and presented at the altar of one's patron saint. One stall sells bundles of herbs and grasses reserved only for the preparation of foods to be offered to *(continued on page 136)*

Carne de Sol do Arco-Iris

BEEF JERKY FROM THE RAINBOW INN

1 pound carne de sol, shredded (salted dried meat, such as tender jerked or corned beef, makes a good substitute)

3 large Idaho potatoes, peeled

8 tablespoons (1 stick) unsalted butter

1 tablespoon extra-virgin olive oil

1 medium onion, chopped

1 green bell pepper, cored, seeded, ribs removed, and cut in thin strips

1 red bell pepper, cored, seeded, ribs removed, and cut in thin strips

1 yellow bell pepper, cored, seeded, ribs removed, and cut in thin strips

1 tablespoon vegetable oil

3 slices smoked bacon, cut ¼ inch thick and diced

2 large carrots, peeled and grated

1½ cups manioc flour (farinha de mandioca)

2 large eggs, lightly beaten

1 tablespoon chopped fresh parsley

2 firm sweet bananas, peeled and sliced ½ inch thick on the diagonal

In a medium saucepan, add the meat and enough water to cover. Bring to a rolling boil over medium-high heat for 5 minutes and remove the meat. Depending on the saltiness of the meat, repeat the process up to 3 more times with fresh water to remove the salt. If the meat is still too salty, repeat the process one more time with fresh water. During the last water change, reduce the heat and simmer for 15 to 20 minutes, or until the meat is fork tender. Cool, then shred the meat with a fork and reserve.

While the meat is cooking, cut the potatoes into ½-inch cubes, rinse in cold water, and bring to a boil in a pot of lightly salted water. Cook for 5 minutes, drain, and set aside.

In a large skillet, melt 2 tablespoons of the butter with the olive oil over medium heat. Add the onion and sauté for 5 minutes, or until it is translucent. Add the green, red, and yellow peppers and sauté another 5 minutes, or until the peppers are limp. Fold in the meat, mix, and set aside.

In a separate skillet, melt 4 tablespoons of the butter with the vegetable oil over medium heat and sauté the potatoes until crisp and golden, about 10 minutes. Remove with a slotted spoon and add to the meat mixture.

Drain off any fat from the skillet, add the bacon, and cook over medium heat until golden and crisp, about 5 minutes. Remove with a slotted spoon and add to the meat mixture.

Add the remaining 2 tablespoons of butter to the bacon fat and quickly sauté the carrots for 1 or 2 minutes over medium heat. With a wooden spoon, add the manioc flour to the carrots and toast for 1 minute. Mix in the eggs and cook for 2 to 3 minutes, or until the eggs become lightly scrambled.

Arrange the manioc flour mixture around the sides of a warm serving platter, making a well. Spoon the meat and vegetable mixture into the center, sprinkle with the parsley, and scatter the bananas randomly over the top.

SERVES 4 TO 6

Mariscos do Baiana
MUSSELS BAHIA-STYLE

OVERLEAF:
*A remote beach
along the coast*

Be sure to clean and debeard the mussels just before cooking, as they will spoil if debearded too early.

2 quarts mussels, scrubbed and beards removed
1 cup dry white wine
1 bay leaf
3 tablespoons extra-virgin olive oil
1 large onion, chopped
2 garlic cloves, minced
1½ cups uncooked long-grain white rice
1½ cups peeled, seeded, and chopped fresh ripe tomatoes or chopped and drained canned plum tomatoes
1 3-inch strip orange zest

1 cup warm light fish stock or hot water
1 tablespoon chopped fresh parsley
1 tablespoon chopped fresh basil
1 teaspoon chopped fresh cilantro
Salt and freshly ground pepper to taste
½ cup fresh or canned unsweetened coconut milk
1 tablespoon dendê oil (optional)

Malagueta Pepper Sauce (see page 96) or hot sauce, for serving

Place the clean mussels in a steamer basket or colander and set in the freezer for 10 minutes before cooking. (This enables the mussels to open faster when they hit the steam.)

In a large, heavy soup kettle or steamer, add the wine and bay leaf, cover, and bring to a boil.

Uncover and lower the steamer basket or colander into the kettle. Cover and steam over high heat for 5 to 6 minutes. Remove the lid, lift out the mussels as they open, and place them in a bowl. Discard any mussels that do not open. Cool slightly, then pour off most of the mussel liquor, strain if sandy, and reserve.

In a large, deep heavy-bottomed sauté pan, heat the oil over medium heat, add the onion and garlic, and sauté for 5 minutes, or until the onion is translucent. Add the rice and sauté until the grains absorb the oil, stirring constantly. Add the tomatoes and cook another 2 minutes. Add the orange zest, mussel liquor, and stock or water, then cover and bring to a boil. Lower the heat, cover, and simmer for 10 minutes, stirring from time to time. Add the parsley, basil, cilantro, and salt and pepper and continue cooking until the rice is almost tender, about 5 more minutes.

Stir in the coconut milk and cook another minute. Add the dendê oil and fold in the mussels and any excess juices. Cover and continue cooking until the rice is tender, a few minutes more.

Serve in warm soup plates and accompany with Malagueta Pepper Sauce or hot sauce.

SERVES 4

one's protector, which must be better than anything you cook for yourself. Cotton-stuffed voodoo dolls in colorful costumes are hung by threads, and I buy one dressed all in white and wearing a chef's toque.

At the edge of the bay, wooden fishing boats are being washed down. An extension of long narrow planks extends from the bow of one moored skiff to the seawall, and three men bounce back and forth over the boards and down the narrow wall, unloading bundles of sugarcane. A half-dozen sows are taking a scrub at the water's edge. On my way out of the maze, I pass a vendor standing next to a monstrously long ovoid called *jaca,* referenced as "jackfruit" in English. The prickly bumps of Kool-Aid-green skin are similar to the skin covering a pineapple, and the knobby stem is as hard as wood. This one must weigh twenty-five pounds. He cuts it lengthwise to reveal banana-yellow stringy pulp. The aroma is strongly perfumy and the taste cloyingly sweet. The texture surrounding the slippery plum-sized seeds is mucilaginous and not appealing to me. It is the sweetest-tasting fruit in the world.

I meet up with Francisco, who has suggested a drive through the city and then lunch at Casa da Gamboa, one of Salvador's most wonderful restaurants. Tucked down a quiet little street, this old, elegant white colonial house hangs on a steep cliff. We are the only guests. During Carnival, eating hours are topsy-turvy; Baianos and visitors alike are too busy arranging for the nights of partying, and days of recovering. The rooms are quiet, and the only sounds come from the clatter of spoons and whisks in the kitchen. A couple of waitresses outfitted in regulation white dresses and bandanas quietly shuffle in with menus and drinks. We dine on *casquinha de siri* (page 121)—small blue crab shells gutted and restuffed with shredded crabmeat, spices, cream, and a gratin of cheese. The main course is another xinxim and a chicken stew called *frango molio pardo*—cooked in vinegar and its own blood. It's a close cousin to coq au vin. We finish with a coconut blancmange with a lime sauce.

Hour by hour the crowds swell into the streets, and I'm not sure if dawn is the start or finish of partying and dancing. A truck the size of a tour bus, outfitted with speakers that blare out the music played by a live band set up on the vehicle's roof, moves through the crowd, surrounded by spinning dancers. From my window I can see the endless stream of bands and dancers whirling and reeling up the cobblestone streets and avenues.

During Carnival, balls are held every night in hotels and homes throughout the city. I attend one held in an old villa, in an enormous room with windows opening out to balconies overlooking the bay. The ceiling is covered with balloons and streamers and sparkling lights; the floor rustles with the sound of silk rubbing satin rubbing velvet. Women and transvestites are wrapped in sequined caps supporting sprays of ostrich plumes, egret and peacock feathers, and whirligigs that sway, sparkle, and fan the air, like the heads of exotic birds attached to human bodies. Some wear almost nothing, but their plumage is so elaborate you barely notice. The crowded room is pulsating with music and the hoots from revelers determined to dance in the same place till they drop. All I can do is grip the balustrade and enjoy the pandemonium and color of this spectacle.

But a week of constant partying is not why I came to Salvador. It is my fortune that Carnival fits into my travel schedule. But I'm here for the food. At night the restaurants are packed, and dining from stands in the street cheek by jowl has limited charms; I need sleep.

DATELINE: ITAPARICA, FEBRUARY 20

I've heard of a *pousada* (country inn) across the bay on the island of Itaparica. In twenty minutes a blue-and-white-painted skiff ferries us across the bay, pulling to shore to be greeted by thrill-seeking youths who have swum out to meet us. I'm just off the dock, and I already like this place. I can see a few bathers along the stretch of white-sand beach, and the town square surrounded by a church, a small café, a little boutique featuring swimsuits and suntan lotions. Off to the side a *sorvete* stand sells homemade tropical ices. I try a scoop of pineapple (page 105), then the passion fruit that has become my addiction. The vendor gives me directions to Arco-Iris—the Rainbow Inn.

I walk up a shaded dusty road, past neat little houses surrounded by flowering shrubs. At the end of the street, iron gates open up to an alley of freshly raked sand, lined with palms leading up to the veranda steps. I introduce myself to one of the owners, hoping I might find a room for a few days. The patron goes by his nickname, Godje—a derivative of "God." All the rooms are booked, but he has a little one-room cottage out back. It's quieter, he tells me, and I say I'll take it. He insists I must see it first. He leads me through a small garden, past an aviary of parrots—a loose one hops on his shoulder and playfully pecks at his ear. Godje picks a banana, and the parrot peels it and begins to nibble away. We walk under the shade of magnificent old mango trees, the gray sand beneath littered with the orange-rouged fruit. He signals me to look up—they might drop on my head. A Dutch door leads to a small entryway, and in a glance I catch a chameleon frozen to a white wall speckled with sunlight that filters through the clay-tiled ceiling. The bed is covered in netting, and a fan overhead turns without generating a breeze. The amenities are

OVERLEAF, CLOCKWISE: *An unpriced menu board at a barraquinha, Junior's lunch wagon, a beach restaurant sign announcing fresh oysters and shrimp*

BEBIDAS

	NCZ$
CAIPIRA LIMÃO	
" MARACUJA	
" ABACAXI	
" CÔCÔ	
REFRIGERANTE	
CERVEJA	
PASTEL DE QUEIJO	
" CAMARÃO	
" FRANGO	
FILE DE CAÇÃO	
ANCHOVA	
LULA	
AIMPIM FRITO	
ATATA FRITA	

basic, and the room is mine for twenty U.S. dollars a night, including breakfast. I'm happy.

When I return from my day trip to Salvador, Godje invites me for a nightcap. The outdoor dining room and bar are a series of open-walled rooms shielded by lush vegetation. They are comfortable, easy, dimly lit. A fountain gurgles in the background, embers glow from a stone grill set out by the kitchen, and the music, unobtrusively low, is hip American.

The bar is filled with familiar brands of liquors and bowls piled with limes and fruits. He asks what I want to drink, and I tell him to give me something with fruit and cachaça. He takes two golden carambolas and slices them into stars, puts them in a glass with a little sugar, cachaça, and some ice and gives it a stir. Delicious: finally, I like this fruit. I'm introduced to a couple from Belém in the Amazon Delta—old friends of Godje. They invite me to bike with them to a beach in the morning, which I happily accept.

I crawl into bed beneath the gauze. The quiet whirl of the fan and the slow-burning repellent keeps the bugs at bay, an occasional thud on the roof is nothing more than a falling ripe mango, and I'm lulled to sleep by the cool breeze perfumed with the scent of this luscious mushed fruit.

Breakfast starts with a platter of fruit, then the waiter brings a tray of glass pitchers of freshly made juices—mango, pineapple, orange, and passion fruit. Then a basket of hot sweet breads, including a breakfast corn cake (page 125), a manioc cake (page 125), and something that looks like a rolled crisp white crepe made with tapioca gum, and pots of coffee and hot milk to wake me up. Then comes a plate of warm and fragrantly spiced bread—their version of French toast (page 124)—golden-crisp egg-soaked bread sandwiching a melting layer of slightly sharp cheese with cinnamon and crystal sugar dust melting on top. A truly delicious sensation. These big, hearty early morning breakfasts were very common at the big plantation houses throughout Bahia and Pernambuco. The great mahogany tables are still laid with china, linens, crystal, and lots of flowers, and the range and amount of food offered are always staggering.

Caito, the man from Belém, arrives with big smiles and joins my table. He takes the crepe with his coffee, and I ask him how it's made. "It's white tapioca we call *goma de tapioca*. You put it in a hot pan, and it comes out like a crepe." What binds it? I ask. The reply: "Nothing, it just does that."

Caito is very proprietary of this place—and everything he does is in the interest of friendship and fun. He can't stay still. He takes a swig of coffee. He looks for his wife. He gets the bikes, including one for me, and we are off to the beach.

My lunches over the next few days consist of sampling all manner of moquecas and eating quantities of squid and crab, fried fish, and ample amounts of fruit. A foray or two to Salvador to view the parades, but then back in time for dinner to talk about the Amazon with Caito and his wife, Angela, whose family owns the newspaper and Globo TV franchise network in Belém. I also discuss food with Godje and his partner, Renaldo, who has returned from a business trip.

Dona Figuinha, Godje's head cook, has been at the pousada some dozen years. She worked at one of the old plantations in the days when cocoa was big business in Bahia and has brought her traditions with her. Her small kitchen is dominated by four large mortars—one to pound dried shrimp, one for nuts, another for her fish pirão, and the last to pound jerky. She buys her chickens live and oversees one of her assistants in the killing, plucking, and gutting in the kitchen yard, and she buys her fish from one fisherman who delivers his daily catch at her kitchen door. Her herb garden is supplied with all she needs to season her dishes. Godje is happy to have her: "The only consistent worker in the place," he says. "Mostly the waiters and maids come for a few weeks, make some money, fall in love, and leave." So Godje plays all roles and performs all tasks, including cooking when the kitchen is understaffed.

Godje or Dona Figuinha usually decides what I will have for dinner. Godje feels I need a good substantial meal the night before I leave because I will be traveling most of the next day. We nibble on peanuts and drink *caipiroska*—the Russian version of a caipirinha, made with vodka. The platter arrives—a riot of colors or maybe a tribute to the national colors of Dona Figuinha's African heritage: strips of red and green peppers are splashed over bits of cubed bacon and onion, which have been mixed with threads of rust-brown shredded jerky (page 132). This mixture surrounds a mound of crisp sautéed potatoes and golden farofa (manioc flour) blended with shredded carrots, scrambled eggs, and bananas. Jerky is elevated to wonderful heights in this presentation.

The next morning I sit on the dock waiting for the launch to take me back to the city. The sun is pushing itself up above the rim of the ocean, bathing the bay in light. The distant high-rises and towers of new Salvador sparkle like sugar cubes. My drive to the airport is quiet and fast. The spiritual capital of Bahia is asleep.

the
amazon

DATELINE: BELÉM, ENTRANCE TO THE AMAZON, MARCH 3

I'm not prepared for the Amazon. Few of my Brazilian friends have ever visited the jungle, and well-intentioned friends in New York who are investing heavily to save the trees of a forest they've never seen aren't much help, either. And no one I know has specifically gone there for the reason I am going—for the food.

Palm trees and a canopy of vegetation slip by as we travel upriver.

My flight to the Amazon is in one of those puddle jumpers and takes the good part of the day. One of the stops is at Recife, an old Pernambuco town along the coast that attracts lots of European vacationers—especially male travelers because the female population outnumbers the male five to one, and hotels and restaurants are cheap. Arcing around the top of Brazil to Fortaleza and São Luis, over the thousands of miles of flat green terrain on one side and the Atlantic blue on the other, we approach the Amazon Delta, and land in Belém, the capital city of Pará, a port on the equator and the Amazon's major city.

Caito has kept his promise to guide me, arranging a room for me at the Equatorial Palace. He spends his working hours going up and down the Amazon in search of locations and accommodations for film crews. His credits include *The Emerald Forest, The Mission,* and more recently *At Play in the Fields of the Lord.* There is a bit of Hollywood savvy mixed in with his Brazilian sweetness.

Caito tells me to have an early dinner and suggests a restaurant close to the hotel. He will pick me up at 5:00 A.M. for breakfast and a tour of the Ver-o-Peso market, which literally translates to "see the weight (on the scale)." "And watch the mangoes," he says. "They're ripe and falling from the trees—they dent our cars!" This seems to be a running hazard.

The restaurant is a casual stroll through a tunnel of old mango trees covered in moss, their damp trunks as large as those of American elms. Behind fences and walls, through iron gates and beyond the dark vegetation and the camouflage of flowering vines, I can hear water plop from leaf to leaf, and, through the shadows, residential houses reveal themselves. What light filters out through closed shutters illuminates elaborate stone Beaux Arts and baroque façades encrusted with enameled Portuguese and French tiles, and Victorian gabled spires and roofs are outlined with fanciful iron filigree. The streets are quiet and heavy with moist air. I have no sense of place but somehow find my way to La em Casa. An unassuming alley leads to a garden of trees and bush palms protecting diners from the misty dark sky. Tables covered in red cloths are symmetrically set around the trees, and I am ushered to my place. The menu is beyond my comprehension, and the waiter is of no help. Nor is my kitchen Portuguese of much help, either. I can identify spaghetti and one dish I've heard of called *pato no tucupi* (page 149). I order the pato, and the waiter gives me a strained smile. The dish is indigenous to the Amazon—pato, a wild duck similar to our Muscovy, is roasted, then simmered in tucupi, the extracted juices from the leaves of a plant of the same name. Tucupi is slightly poisonous until fermented. It is considered the king of sauces among the Indians, who serve it with game meats and fish. From a clay tureen the waiter ladles out the dank sea-colored soup with chunks of duck and long strands of dark green leaves they call *jambu*. It looks like spinach. From a small bowl he fills a spoon with white pellets and sprinkles it over the top of my soup plate. He tells me it's manioc. The pellets begin to swell up like Rice Krispies. I taste one from the bowl—it's hard as buckshot, and chomping down I chip a tooth. I take a few minutes to examine the sharp edges with my tongue. Digging into the soup, I find the tucupi hints of spinach and chicory, and the duck flavor is intense, the meat strong and stringy. The taste is followed by a stinging and a numbing sensation around my lips. The jambu has the faint taste of samphire (saline marsh grass) and seaweed. It's a relative of the coca plant (the source of cocaine), and it's weird but good. The waiter seems to think I'm not satisfied with my meal and arrives bearing a bowl of *caldeirada de peixe* (page 148), a fish stew, which is indeed more familiar tasting. I order coffee and am offered my choice of sherbet—pineapple, chocolate, and *açaí*. I go for broke and order the açaí. Dark royal purple, the açaí is silken, nutty, a little chalky, but smooth and refreshing in the clammy heat. The fruit is the size of wild cherries and is gathered from the tops of the fecund açaí palm, where it grows in long cascading sprays. They look like beads strung on braided string. The crushed juice may or may not be sweetened and it is the Coca-Cola of the local youth, leaving their lips and tongue black-purple for hours.

I take a quick stroll around to the Praça da República, a grand square planted with elegant palms and luxurious mango trees, and past an equally grand opera house. I walk up the steps to the lobby of the Hilton, just because it looks so familiar: doormen in uniform, pretty Brazilian girls at the front desk, pert and businesslike in their blue suits, white blouses, and flimsy cravats. I could be anywhere.

At 4:45 A.M. Caito is in the lobby wide-awake, bouncing happily, ready to take me off to the Ver-o-Peso market in time for the sunrise. We park near the river's edge, where a couple hundred boats have come downriver during the night to bring produce from forest and farms as far as two hundred miles away. The hulls and double-canopied decks are whitewashed, blunted smokestacks painted in candy-colored stripes. These solid-wood vessels are halfway between a stunted galleon and a yacht. A V-shaped board, like a riverine bumper, extends out from the hull at water level to push away floating debris and trees on the river.

Across the gangplanks baskets of fruits and bundles of greens are rapidly shuffled from boats to dock: hundreds of tightly woven bushel-sized baskets filled with the dark açaí are gently lined up on the cobblestone

wharf. Tubes and sacks of intricately woven grasses and palm leaves hold all manner and shapes of exotic fruits. Caito is pointing and rattling off words like *babaçu, bacaba, pupunha, bacuri, tucumã, taperebá, cupuaçu*. I barely notice the sacks of crabs bound with familiar fan-shaped palm fronds, slender leaves knotted to hold the wriggling shellfish. Some fruits Caito peels and stuffs into my hand; others he cleans on his shirt and tells me to eat it all. I tell him to stop, go slower, wait. Dawn is just breaking, and I want a sharper look at these fruits. A farmer takes his machete and cracks the top off a rough brown ball the size of a soccer ball. He places it on top of others, and I look into the opening—a symmetrical circle of packed, perfectly formed triangular nuts. *"Castanha do Pará,"* Caito says. "Brazil nuts to you!" He tells me they have as much nutrition as milk, that two nuts are equal to one egg for breakfast, and that the oil from the nut is used for cooking and as a base for perfume; the pulp is used to make a kind of primitive bread and also for animal fodder.

Once it gets light I ask Caito to take me around again and explain the different fruits that I've seen and eaten in the dark. He goes back to the remaining baskets of açaí, the fruit used for the sorbet I had tasted the night before. It is indigenous to the jungle around us and has been a source of food for millennia. It grows wild in cluster patches in the forest, but is threatened by industry and the cattle rancher who burns the land. When the berry goes to seed on a tree, it falls and *(continued on page 152)*

OPPOSITE: *Fresh pimenta-de-cheiro, the cherry pepper, is used in the Amazon to season dishes as the rest of Brazil uses the malagueta pepper.*

ABOVE: *Pato no Tucupi, duck first roasted then cooked in tucupi juice with jambu leaves and coarse manioc flour, is as representative of Amazonian Indian cuisine as one can get.*

Caldeirada de Peixe
AMAZONIAN FISH AND VEGETABLE STEW

FISH

½ cup chopped fresh parsley
⅓ cup chopped fresh cilantro
4 garlic cloves, chopped
Salt and freshly ground white pepper to taste
Juice of 2 limes
4 pounds firm white fish fillets (filhote), such as monkfish or tilefish, skin removed

VEGETABLES

2 pounds potatoes, peeled and quartered
Salt to taste
3 large carrots, peeled and sliced diagonally
⅓ cup olive oil
1 medium onion, sliced
2 garlic cloves, finely chopped
1 red bell pepper, cored, seeded, ribs removed, and sliced
2 firm ripe tomatoes, cored and sliced

Freshly ground pepper to taste
½ small head white cabbage, cored and cut in very thin strips
4 large hard-boiled eggs

PIRÃO

¼ cup extra-virgin olive oil
1 onion, finely diced
1 garlic clove, minced
2 green bell peppers, cored, seeded, ribs removed, and finely diced
2 tomatoes, peeled, seeded, and diced
2 tablespoons white wine vinegar
Salt and freshly ground pepper to taste
1 cup manioc flour (coarse if possible)

1 small bunch jambu leaves or watercress, stems removed (optional)

Pimenta-de-cheiro (see page 160) or hot pepper sauce, for serving

To prepare the fish, in a large nonreactive bowl, combine the parsley, cilantro, garlic, salt and pepper, and lime juice and set aside. Cut the fish into 2-inch cubes and combine with the marinade. Set aside for 1 hour.

For the vegetables, place the potatoes in a medium saucepan with 6 cups of cold water to cover. Bring to a boil, add salt, and simmer until the potatoes are tender, about 20 minutes. Remove with a slotted spoon. Add the carrots to the boiling water and cook until tender, about 4 minutes. Drain, reserving the cooking liquid.

In a large nonreactive saucepan over medium heat, add the ⅓ cup olive oil. Sauté the sliced onion until wilted, about 5 minutes. Add the garlic, red bell pepper, and tomatoes and season with salt and pepper. When the vegetables are wilted, about 5 minutes, add the cabbage and 3 cups of the reserved cooking liquid, and simmer for 10 minutes. Add the whole hard-cooked eggs and remove from the heat.

To make the pirão, in a medium nonstick saucepan, heat the ¼ cup olive oil and sauté the diced onion and garlic for 5 minutes, until the onion is translucent. Add the peppers and cook another 5 minutes. Add the tomatoes, vinegar, and salt and pepper to taste. Add the manioc flour, pour in 1 cup reserved cooking liquid, and mix. Gradually add the remaining 2 cups of reserved cooking liquid or a little more from the pot so the pirão is the consistency of light Cream of Wheat. Set the pirão aside and keep it warm.

To finish the dish, add the potatoes and carrots to the cabbage mixture and bring to a simmer over medium heat. Add the cubed fish and simmer 8 to 10 minutes, or until the fish is opaque and slightly springy to the touch. Add the jambu or watercress, if using, and stir just until wilted.

Serve the soup in warm soup plates with the pirão and pimenta-de-cheiro or hot pepper sauce on the side.

SERVES 8

Pato no Tucupi
DUCK SOUP

Tucupi is the juice extracted from the manioc plant. The juice is boiled to release its toxins, then bottled, usually with pimenta-de-cheiro.

The tale of the tuber's origin has been passed down from the Tupi Indians. As the legend goes, a mother had no food and watched her starving infant die. The grieving woman could not part with her babe and so buried him under the floor of her hut. During the night, a wood spirit, or *mani,* visited the hut and transformed the child's body into the roots of a plant. She called the plant *mani oca*—wood spirit root—and it grew to feed all the Indians in the forest.

Juice of 1½ limes
2 garlic cloves, minced
Salt and freshly ground pepper to taste
1 bay leaf, crumbled
1 4-pound duck, preferably Muscovy
5 cups tucupi juice
2 cups (about 1½ bunches) jambu leaves or 2 cups sorrel

2 cups chopped chicory, washed and drained

Simple Boiled White Rice (see page 12), Simple Farofa (see page 109), and pimenta-de-cheiro sauce (see page 160), for serving

Preheat the oven to 300° F.

Combine the lime juice, garlic, salt and pepper, and bay leaf in a large bowl. Add the duck, turn to coat, cover, and marinate, refrigerated, for 2 hours, turning the duck once.

Place the duck on a rack in a roasting pan. Place the pan on the lower oven shelf and roast for 3 hours, or until the skin is crisp and the juices run clear when the thigh is pricked with a fork. Cool and cut into 8 pieces, removing the backbone and wing tips.

In a large nonreactive saucepan, combine the duck with the tucupi juice and bring to a simmer.

Bring a pot of water to a boil and plunge in the jambu leaves for 1 minute. Drain and add to the tucupi. If using sorrel, add directly to the tucupi.

Add the chicory and simmer for 7 minutes, or until the chicory is soft and tender.

Serve with white rice, farofa, and pimenta-de-cheiro.

SERVES 6

OVERLEAF:
Ver-o-Peso market (clockwise left to right): cupuaçu and piquia fruits; sacks of various manioc flours; pupunha, a berry from the pupunha palm tree; boys stripping the maniva leaf for maniçoba, the feijoada of the Amazon; tucupi juice; an assortment of market snack food, including breads and farofa-coated crab legs to be dipped in tucupi sauce; urucum, a flavorless cooking powder beloved by the Brazilian Indians and used to color their stews and paint their faces; and bowls of hot tapioca, corn, and banana porridges dusted with cinnamon

sprouts almost immediately. To make his point he guides me nearer to the dock. Beneath a ramp berries have fallen between the slats in transport, and little sprouts can be seen poking through. Little palm shoots grow taller and straighter on the sides of the path. When the shoots sprout they are called palm cabbage, boiled, and eaten. The fronds are used for thatching houses and the stems for lath. "We love the juice. Wherever you see a little red flag flying above a doorway, that is where you can buy the açaí. It has no nourishment, it just fills the stomach. It's been part of the Indian diet forever. We add a little to the pirão {farofa-based sauce} we serve with fish dishes just like the Indian does. And we drink it more from habit and addiction than for the taste."

He points to the babaçu—limpid stalks covered with hundreds of date-like nubs. They, too, are the fruit of a large palm. The sharply pointed, golden-green casing of tough skin encases an oily, floury pulp. The seeds are the edible part. The leaves are used for making baskets and thatching, the shells are ground for cattle fodder, and the sap, when fermented, becomes a popular local drink. The heart of the tree is supposedly as delicious as the *palmito* (heart of palm). And when a tree falls and rots, it attracts the gongo beetle, which makes good fish bait for the locals who live on the river's edge. Leftover beetles are fried and eaten as an appetizer before dinner, and Caito says they taste like burnt coconut.

The bacaba, the white açaí, is the berry from another palm. It has a yellowish creamy pulp that is oily and tastes surprisingly like chocolate. The berries are pressed and mixed with fermented manioc flour, and the resulting drink is considered a rare treat. The extracted oil can be used for cooking, and natives along the rivers use it in their oil lamps.

Bunches of pupunha piled on the side of the curb show off their splashy red, orange, green, and mahogany colors in the sunlight. Raw, their taste is flat and sweet, and the texture is a chalky paste. We buy a bunch, and later that day we will submerge the cluster in boiling water. As each one falls from the stem it is removed from the pot—cooked. The hot fruit is mashed with butter and salt, then pureed, resulting in a soup similar to a vichyssoise. We eat it chilled, mixed with mayonnaise and shrimp, and later still sample it in ice cream from a local store.

Some of the fruits attract me because of their exotic coloring and shapes. The buriti is perhaps the most beautiful, and this is the fruit of yet another species of palm. Dainty, lacquer-red, fan-shaped scales cover the plum-sized fruit. It looks like a precious handcrafted enamel object. Pried open, it reveals spongy, oily, orange-colored flesh. Caito says that deep in the Amazon one can dine on hearts of palm from the buriti tree braised in buriti oil, washed down with buriti wine, and end with a confection of sweet buriti pulp. After this woodland feast, one cools oneself with a fan made of buriti straw and then naps in a hammock made of buriti hemp. The palm is king.

Another exquisite fruit is the clusters of guarana—paperlike bright crimson pods, some popping open; inside, yellow linings protect a shiny white nut with a centered black eye. From this they make the apple juice and cream soda that is bottled and drunk either fizzy or flat all over the country. It tastes sort of like apple juice. A natural stimulant, it contains three times more caffeine than coffee. Guarana is also prepared in powdered and brick form and locals take it with their morning fruit juice.

The bacupari, a riverbank tree, is the size of a Ping-Pong ball, with a soft orangelike skin and thin juicy pith surrounding creamy sweet aromatic pulp, resembling fried eggs, sunny-side up. And the bacuri—a pedestrian-looking dull-yellow fruit speckled with green—has a thick but fragile rind that reveals, when cut, a snow-white, cottony orb of edible pulp surrounding four edible seeds. One of the seeds does not develop, and its dense pulp is considered the tastiest part.

They call the cupuaçu a berry, but this rust-colored fruit weighs up to two pounds. With its hard and pointed shell it looks more threatening than ugly. I learn later that the berry has more than sixty culinary uses, among them juices, mousses, puddings, and ice cream. The berries can be roasted and used in place of chocolate, but are more commonly crushed and served as a fruit drink. Cupuaçu is another relative of the coca (cocaine) plant, and this drink has a tranquilizing effect; when I sample it, the taste seems to register at the top of my head, not on my tongue.

None of these fruits remind me of anything else. I can't tell you that some have hints of mango, coconut, caramel, vanilla, cinnamon, lemon, or peach. Every taste is new.

Empty baskets are piled and carted back to the boats, and the containers and sacks made of palm leaves, grasses, and hemp are swept into piles and pushed to the edge of the river to disintegrate. Not a plastic bag in sight.

We walk around the edge of the harbor toward the wholesale fish hall, dodging hand trucks loaded with fresh river fish and bales of neatly packaged salted piranhas—flat and dead but still scary. The piranha is the Amazon's salted codfish. Fishermen sell the bigger fish from their boats. When a purchase is made, a porter arranges a knotted circular padded cloth on top of his head, the fish is placed on a large wooden plank, and then hoisted up and balanced on the pad. If a fish weighs more than four hundred pounds two men share the same duty, running off like Siamese twins in an operetta.

The fish hall is an elegant cast-iron structure   *(continued on page 158)*

OVERLEAF, TOP LEFT: *Land crabs stuffed with their own sweet meat and a heavy dusting of farofa served with tucupi, washed down with caiparinhas*

BOTTOM LEFT: *Maniçoba, a type of local feijoada prepared with maniva leaves. Maniva leaves are toxic; after being ground, the paste is boiled for six days to extract the poison. On the seventh day it rests, just as in a certain story we know. This is tradition and truth, not claptrap.*

RIGHT: *Caranguejo is the local crab boil. Just take your mallet, toc-toc, and dip the tender pieces in the accompanying sauce and farofa.*

Tacacá

SHRIMP AND JAMBU SOUP

Tacacá is the everyday soup of the Amazon—and what a soup it is. Served at the Ver-o-Peso market in Belém and in large settlements in the states of Parà and Amazonas, the ingredients are exclusively Indian. Though one can sample it at Arataca, Rio's only restaurant specializing in Amazonian food, this dish as well as most dishes from the Amazon region are not available in the rest of Brazil. The diner experiences a strong tingling sensation that numbs the lips and tongue after eating the jambu leaves, which are related to the coca leaf. Goma de tapioca (tapioca gum) thickens the soup like arrowroot and the aromatic pepper called pimenta-de-cheiro (the malagueta of the Amazon) provides the heat for the soup. I include the recipe just in case you visit the Amazon. You will have an idea of what the ingredients are.

4 cups tucupi juice
Pimenta-de-cheiro sauce (see page 160) to taste
1¾ cups tapioca gum

1 small bunch jambu leaves, blanched
½ pound dried shrimp (see page 97)
½ pound fresh shrimp, in their shells

In a large soup pot, combine the tucupi with the pimenta-de-cheiro and bring to a boil. Reduce the heat to a simmer and stir the tapioca gum, jambu leaves, and dried shrimp into the tucupi mixture. Simmer for 4 minutes and add the fresh shrimp in their shells. Simmer for another 4 minutes.

Serve the soup in warmed bowls, dividing the shrimp evenly in each of the bowls.

SERVES 6

Caranguejo Toc-Toc

CRAB BOIL

Similar to our own southern crab boil, the crabs are served on a plank and usually eaten out-of-doors or under a thatch-roofed hut. The crabs are piled high, and a wooden mallet is placed by each guest.

12 live large blue crabs (about 3 per person)

SAUCE
¾ cup white wine vinegar
1 firm ripe tomato, seeded and diced
1 medium red onion, diced

1 green bell pepper, cored, seeded, ribs removed, and diced

1 cup manioc flour
Pimenta-de-cheiro sauce (see page 160) or hot pepper sauce to taste

Bring a soup pot of lightly salted water to a boil and add the crabs. Cook for 5 minutes, then drain.

For the sauce, in a medium bowl, combine the vinegar, tomato, onion, and green pepper and set aside.

In a medium dry skillet, toast the manioc flour over medium heat for 1 or 2 minutes, stirring until it begins to turn a deep beige. Place in a separate serving bowl.

Serve the crabs on boards or an old wooden picnic table with wooden mallets to crack them.

Serve the manioc flour in little bowls with some of the tomato-pepper sauce poured over. Add a dash or two of pimenta-de-cheiro or hot pepper sauce and dip the shelled crab pieces into the manioc flour.

SERVES 4

Mikie Grilhado
GRILLED MIKIE

1½ pounds mikie fillets, or other firm white fish fillet such as monkfish, tilefish, cod, or halibut, cut into 1½-inch cubes

3 tablespoons extra-virgin olive oil

1 medium tomato, peeled, seeded, and chopped

1 small onion, peeled and quartered

¼ teaspoon chopped fresh chili pepper, or to taste

1 tablespoon chopped fresh cilantro, or more to taste

Salt to taste

Place 4 to 5 cubes of fish on long metal skewers or wooden skewers that have been soaked in water for 30 minutes. Set aside. In a food processor, add the oil, tomato, onion, and chili and pulse on and off until it is a smooth purée. Add the cilantro and salt to taste and pulse another second. Spoon the mixture over the skewers and set aside while you prepare a charcoal fire.

When the coals have a dusty red glow, place the skewers on the grill and cook for 6 to 8 minutes, turning every minute or so until the fish is lightly charred and the flesh opaque. Brush with the remaining marinade and serve with Bean Salad (see page 161).

SERVES 4

NOTE: The fish can be cooked under a hot broiler as well.

the size of a hockey rink. Dozens of varieties of river fish, shrimp, and crab are artfully arranged on granite slabs, gutted, hosed down, filleted, and cut into steaks and chunks. In just a couple of hours the hall is sold out of the delicate *tucunaré,* a troutlike fish with a speckled tail punctuated with a pair of black spots enclosed within yellow circles. I see the popular sweet *pescada,* which feeds on volumes of small river shrimp, and the *tambaqui,* encased in viridian scales tinged with vibrant pink, that lives off the fruits and nuts that fall from trees along the river. Their scales are large enough to be used as spoons. The *piraíba*—a blubbery miniature whale of a fish, cloaked in leathery skin—is the granddaddy of the delicate *filhote,* or "little son," as he is called. Weighing more than a hundred kilos, the piraíba is older, fatter, and not as choice. The filhote lives on the bottom of the river; its texture is similar to that of monkfish, and the taste is very sweet.

Out behind the market we walk by stalls selling bowls made of gourds, baskets, hammocks, colorful clay vessels, exotic birds, parrots, snakes, and

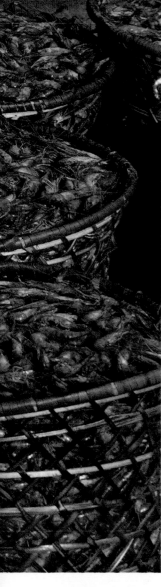

monkeys. Bottles hang from the poles of tents, displaying bugs, spiders, crabs, snakes, and the rather large gen-
italia of a male species of fish, preserved in moonshine.
Some of these pickled items are supposedly aphrodisiacs,
and others will just get you drunk. Caito stops to point
up at one of the bottles of fish genitals and tell me a tale.
The lower Amazon is the home of the bôto-tucuxi (the
pink dolphin), smaller than the Atlantic dolphin but
truly pink. The story goes that women would never
bathe in the river for fear that a male dolphin would
saddle up and impregnate them. On the night of the full
moon the dolphin would arrive in the city dressed in a
white linen suit and wearing a straw hat to cover the
blowhole on the crown of his head. The women were
enchanted and had eyes only for him. He points again
to the bottle and says ladies' boyfriends and husbands
would slip some of the liquid into the women's báths—
and win their love back forever.

   We move up to a stand surrounded by hungry
workers. A smiling woman with heaps of jet-black hair
stands behind large cauldrons bubbling with sweet-
smelling porridges of banana, corn, manioc, and tapioca. She ladles big portions into smooth, thin gourd
bowls coated with black palm pitch. I take a tapioca,
translucent pearls in creamy sweet milk dusted with
cinnamon, and feel like I'm tasting home.

   Walking back toward the river Caito suggests a bowl of *tacacá* (page 156)
before lunch. From late morning through lunchtime you can sample this
soup as innate to the city as hot dogs are to New York City. Close to the
pier two women are busily stirring and adding hand-measured amounts of
ingredients to two steaming cauldrons of murky brew. The base of the soup
is the juice of tucupi, to which the older woman adds ground dried shrimp
and a little tapioca gum (processed from the manioc) *(continued on page 164)*

LEFT: *Baskets
of fresh-water
shrimp*

BELOW LEFT:
*A woman sells
hot coffee and
sweet buns. Pre-
Columbian–style
cooking vessels
from the nearby
island of
Marajoara are
for sale just
beyond her.*

BELOW RIGHT:
*Tacacá, the mid-
morning pick-me-
up soup, is sold
all around the
market by
women called
tacacazeiras.*

Pata Grande de Caranguejo com Molho de Pimenta-de-Cheiro
CRAB CLAWS WITH HOT PEPPER SAUCE

24 large precooked fresh or canned crab
   claws, shelled

SAUCE
3 or 4 pimenta-de-cheiro or malagueta
   peppers, chopped, or 1 tablespoon
   mild hot chili pepper

1 small red onion, chopped
1 medium ripe tomato, chopped
¼ cup chopped fresh flat-leaf parsley
1 garlic clove, chopped
¼ cup fresh lime juice
½ cup extra-virgin olive oil
   Salt to taste

In a medium bowl, combine the sauce ingredients. Cover and set aside for 1 hour before serving. Use the sauce for dipping.

MAKES ABOUT 2 CUPS

Casquinha de Caranguejo
SWEET-WATER LAND CRABS

3 tablespoons extra-virgin olive oil
1 medium onion, finely chopped
1 large tomato, peeled, seeded, and
   chopped
1 tablespoon lime juice
2 tablespoons chopped fresh parsley
1 pimenta-de-cheiro or ¼ teaspoon
   seeded, deveined, and minced
   hot red chili pepper
   Salt to taste
3 cups cooked picked-over fresh hard-
   shell crabmeat (about 12 to 16 small
   live hard-shell blue crabs or land crabs
   if available) or picked-over canned
   lump crabmeat

1 tablespoon extra-virgin olive oil
1 cup farofa
2 or 3 pitted green or black olives,
   sliced

Lime sections and pimenta-de-cheiro
sauce (above), steeped in tucupi
juice, or hot sauce, for serving

Lightly grease the 6 crab shells or custard cups with olive oil.

In a skillet, heat 2 tablespoons olive oil over medium-low heat and sauté the onion until translucent, about 5 minutes. Add the tomato and cook another 5 minutes, or until the tomato has given up most of its juice. Add the lime juice, parsley, pimenta-de-cheiro or chili pepper, and season with salt. Toss in the crabmeat and stir gently for 1 minute to heat through.

Fill the shells or custard cups evenly with the mixture and set aside, loosely covered.

In a medium pan, add the dendê or olive oil and warm over medium heat. Add the farofa and cook for 1 minute, stirring with a wooden spoon.

Cover the crabmeat with a ⅛-inch layer of farofa and garnish with slices of green or black olives.

Serve warm with lime sections and pimenta-de-cheiro steeped in tucupi juice or hot sauce.

SERVES 6

Feijão em Salada

BEAN SALAD

½ pound great northern beans, soaked
  overnight
1 medium red onion, finely chopped
1 small green bell pepper, cored,
  deveined, and finely chopped
1 medium tomato, peeled, seeded, and
  chopped

3 tablespoons parsley, chopped
¼ cup cilantro, chopped
  Salt and freshly ground pepper
  to taste
¼ cup white wine vinegar
3 tablespoons olive oil, or more to taste

In a large saucepan add the beans and enough water to cover by 3 inches. Bring to a boil, skim, reduce the heat, and cook for 45 minutes, or until tender.

When cool, drain and place them in a large bowl. Add the remaining ingredients and combine. Serve warm with Grilled Mikie (page 157).

SERVES 8

Castanha do Pará com Chocolate

BRAZIL NUTS DIPPED IN CHOCOLATE

When faced with a bowl of mixed nuts, I tend to pick around the Brazil nuts. Eating them fresh from the shell, however, is quite another experience, and the creamy nut dipped in tempered chocolate is a particular delight. Serve them with strong espresso.

Brazil nuts are very oily and should be used soon after shelling. Keep tightly sealed and refrigerated for about 3 weeks; after that they go bad.

1 pound shelled fresh Brazil nuts
8 ounces semisweet chocolate

1 tablespoon hazelnut or almond oil

Preheat the oven to 400° F.

Place the shelled nuts on a baking sheet and put in the oven for 8 minutes, stirring once. Cool and rub off the skins with a clean kitchen cloth. Set aside.

In a heavy saucepan, melt the chocolate with ½ teaspoon of the oil over a double boiler. Remove from the heat and stir in the remaining oil. Cool to 80° F., a little warmer than room temperature.

Dip each nut halfway into the chocolate and place on a sheet of wax paper. Let cool completely to set.

MAKES 1 POUND

OVERLEAF, CLOCKWISE: *Riverboats and fishing boats in the Bay of Guarajará dock at the Ver-o-Peso market. A fish hauler rushes the catch to the nearby icehouse. Piles of filhote, or "little son," and tucunaré are some of the river's sweet, white-fleshed fish. The market offers a variety of salt-cured and dried Amazonian fish, including piranha—the local variant of salt cod.*

while the other gives it a vigorous stir. She adds a healthy splash of the hot pimenta-de-cheiro and a couple of handfuls of numbing jambu leaves and then ladles the hot broth into gourd bowls, adding a few fresh river shrimp to the aromatic broth. The flavor is peculiar if not downright weird to my Western palate, and it numbs my tongue and lips.

I will later try to reproduce these tastes at home with domestic ingredients, but it will be impossible. There are no substitutes for tucupi and jambu, so there's no point. I offer the authentic recipe anyway; someday you may have the opportunity to cook in Brazil, or if you taste the real thing, at least you'll know what you're eating.

The Belém harbor is buzzing with activity, and the tide is rising rapidly, the hulls of the boats climbing to reach the docks. We walk around the harbor, pushing our way through congested sidewalks and honking traffic, past disheveled sailors cleaning up their boats, and down a narrow cobbled street into the Praça Frei Caetano Brandão. The square opens onto a grand lawn surrounded by magnificent palms, setting the stage for the sugar-white backdrop of the great colonial Catedral-Sé. We pass a stately palace that was the bishop's residence until finances demanded that the government occupy it. Next to the palace two soldiers guard a courtyard entrance that leads to the old colonial fort and a restaurant.

On the veranda of the Restaurante do Círculo Militar, breezes blow wet and warm. We drink chilled glasses of exotic fruit juices. Caito just orders them all: *abricó-do-Pará,* which literally means "apricot from Pará," the state Belém is in, but we know it as the mammeapple. The bright orange nectar is pleasant and perfumy. The *pitanga,* originally a plant called the Surinam cherry once native to Barbados, is a delightful crimson, thick as wet lacquer, and hits the back of my tongue flat, then lightly tart. The heady cupuaçu is delicious, and the passion fruit the most familiar.

Lunch begins with a pair of land-crab shells stuffed with sweet juicy crabmeat, thickly dusted with fine manioc farofa, served with crab claws, both accompanied with a squeeze of fresh lime juice and a sprinkling of pimenta-de-cheiro (page 160). These little yellow and red peppers serve the same purpose as the malagueta pepper so popular in the rest of Brazil. A salad of white beans, chopped onion, green pepper, and cilantro is a welcome surprise (page 161). Small pots of hot olive oil accompany the dishes with a big green olive bobbing on the surface to intensify its flavor. *Mikie,* a firm-fleshed white fish, has been very simply grilled and tastes like candy to me (page 157); it rounds out a very satisfying and abundant lunch.

DATELINE: ON THE AMAZON, MARCH 7

Caito has arranged a visit to a manioc-flour mill, and in minutes Belém disappears behind us as we head up the river in his Chris-Craft. The route he chooses meanders through the small estuaries. The water becomes as silky as pearly black opals, and the earthy vapors from the river and the forest intoxicate. Dense palms and ancient gnarled trees thick with vines and lianas slide endlessly by. The only sounds are those of the occasional flock of glorious hyacinth macaws that fly overhead, shrieking as they streak the sky. Iridescent blue butterflies follow us upstream, and one lands for a moment on my hand, its nervous wings shimmering like blue foil. Occasionally we pass a lone man paddling his canoe, carved from the great trunk of a tree. Palms arc and meet, covering the sky, and some bend and weep into the narrows, creating a mirror reflection that gives me the dizzying sensation of moving through a green-black tube.

The tributary narrows, and I'm flat on my stomach, stretched over the bow watching for felled rotted trees to push from our path, guiding Caito around sunken stumps that I can see under the surface of the shallow waters. We ease our way through the serpentine waterway as the river bends and opens up to a clearing. A narrow ladder with rungs secured with knotted hemp reaches twenty feet up to a planked dock that leads to a palm-thatched hut. "I'm lost!" Caito announces. I keep the motor idling as he makes his wobbling ascent. Running back he shouts, "Just twenty minutes more." I inquire about the incredible height of the ladder, and I'm told that before the afternoon ends I will see the river swell and rise to meet the top of the docks.

Bugs and flies sting through my clothes. I'm beginning to feel very clammy, like I've been dragged through the river. The channel opens quickly and broadly, and we pass a few thatched huts, charming, graceful, and lonely. A young boy stands in the middle of his canoe and with one artful sweep tosses out a fishnet as big as a cloud. He smiles broadly and gives a nod of thanks for our slowing down and not throwing him off in our wake.

The settlement is built on stilts, and we tie the boat to the nearest ladder and climb up to the small dock. Thatch-roofed huts and houses with haphazardly nailed sun-bleached wood-board siding are joined by narrow boardwalks that connect one dwelling to the next. The largest hut is circular and sheltered by a coned dome covered in palm fronds. Inside, a rusting red Coca-Cola ice chest is planted near the entry to the kitchen, and a few old men are drinking beer at worn wooden tables. Caito announces that after lunch we will visit the place where they make the manioc flour. It's turtle season and the kitchen knows we are here to eat it.

OVERLEAF, LEFT: *Wherever you see this red flag or sign, açaí juice is sold.*

RIGHT: *The açaí palm grows wild in the forest. The fruit grows in clusters at the top of the tree; it is picked and packed in baskets and covered with aruma leaves. Brought by boat and dugout canoe, the berry is sold at the dockside markets.*

But first, we are served a pile of boiled crabs stacked on a wooden plank. We are handed a small club with which we crack the shells to extract the chunks of crabmeat. As soon as we finish, two small, smooth brown-and-yellow shells are placed before us belly up—chunks of meat sputtering in a dark brown sauce. The breeding season has just begun, and the endangered turtles crowd the sandbanks at night to dig pits and lay their eggs, which have been harvested and sold by the Indians for centuries. These are ingrained traditions, not easily changed. The taste is sweet, the meat plump and tender, the sauce brown and rich. "Cooked in their own blood," Caito announces. Then the next course arrives in a beaten old tin pot, a stew of dark juices, slippery boiled slices of manioc, and gray meat. The tough meat is filled with spindly sharp bones and to me tastes like squirrel. I must look a little disappointed. Caito grins and gives a little wink. "Take some more farofa and a lot more pepper sauce. Should have brought the ketchup—this is monkey!"

Behind the settlement, the boardwalk extends through vegetation and abruptly stops in the middle of a clearing. We hop down and walk about a quarter of a mile past a shack that serves as the local schoolhouse and into denser vegetation. Caito points out the large dark *maniva* leaves of the manioc plant they use for *maniçoba*—a dish of pork, beef, chicken, and spices that is considered the feijoada of the Amazon. This leaf, so popular in so many Amazonian dishes, grows wild. They are ground at the marketplace in a hand-cranked meat chopper. The "puree" is then cooked for seven days before incorporating it into the maniçoba. One rarely, if ever, experiences this dish in any other part of Brazil.

We walk down a narrow winding path and into another large clearing. Huge hardwood poles support an open-sided hut, the flour mill, and we step inside. At one end a primitive round brick stove warming up a five-foot-round shallow copper pan is being stoked with small bits of logs. Caito approaches the women busily preparing the manioc. He is especially friendly with one in particular, who seems to be in charge, and asks her to take me through the preparation from start to finish. Women come from the surrounding neighborhood and bring the manioc they have farmed and process it together. They take what they need, and some is sold at the settlement store—their cooperative. What's left over is sent to the Ver-o-Peso market in Belém. Troughs gutted from tree trunks are filled with water to soak the manioc tubers, which are then grated. Other troughs are filled with the wet white mush, and others still are filled with the finished dry grains.

The roots are first peeled, washed, and left to soak. After the soaking period, they are grated on a large beveled stone grater and poured into large clay bowls. After that the pulp is poured into a long cylindrical tube called a *tipiti,* made from plaited palm leaves and hemp. Both ends are pulled taut in a jerking movement, and the liquid is forced out, leaving the damp meal. The meal flour is sieved over a clean trough and then toasted in the hot copper pan. One of the women stands over the pan stirring it with a long wooden hoe. The utensils and process are basically the same as those used thousands of years ago. I'd seen identical four-thousand-year-old pottery at the Göeldi museum in Belém and stared at dioramas depicting villagers going through this same process.

There exist two species of manioc, one sweet and one poisonous, and that's the hitch. Both are used but the poisonous one must be detoxified first. Beneath the tough bark, sacs of milk-filled latex ooze when the tuber is cut. The acid milk is extracted by cutting the root into smaller and smaller pieces and continual rinsing. Once the toxins are released, the manioc is safe to eat. When dried, the manioc is converted to meal, flour, and starch. To make tapioca, the Indians put the grated damp manioc in water, stir it, and allow the starch to settle. The damp starch is removed and toasted, forming tapioca balls. For nontropical people like ourselves, this is the only form of manioc we know. Most of the tapioca available at our markets is the instant variety. But pearl tapioca is truly more delicious. It must be soaked in twice its volume of water for an hour or more until the water is absorbed. Then it is converted into luscious puddings made with sugar, eggs, cream, coconut milk, vanilla, and cinnamon.

Lastly, like all other starchy roots and grains, manioc can be fermented. Amazonian women and children chew the fresh manioc mush, mixing it with saliva to quicken the fermentation. Shanty bars add spoonfuls to tropical fruit juices to create heady cocktails.

Heading back, by the time we reach the dock the river is high enough for us just to step aboard Caito's boat. We slip down the river, watching the trees slide by. "Tucano!" Caito whispers, pointing ahead. I grab his binoculars and I see huddling above on the bow of a tree this glorious bird with its absurd bill, bobbing its head from side to side. The black feathers glisten and the black point of the bill appears like a brushstroke on the vibrant orange-yellow, with its red stripe arching back over the beak to meet a thin black muzzle. The brilliant white of his throat and chest match his tail feathers. In an instant he notices us, and with a few quick flaps he is off over the river, moving like a missile and diving into the foliage on the other side.

minas gerais

DATELINE: OURO PRETO, MARCH 12

By the first decade of the eighteenth century, Brazilians began making expeditions from São Paulo to the hills of Minas Gerais on a quest for gold. The travelers called themselves *bandeirantes*—not bandits, as the sound of the word implies, but banner-carriers in the name of the Portuguese royal court.

Saturday street market in Ouro Preto

Minas Gerais (General Mines) is hemmed in by the surrounding states of São Paulo, Rio de Janeiro, Goiás, Bahia, and Espírito Santo. The state owes its name to what once seemed an inexhaustible reserve of gold, iron ore, manganese, nickel, diamonds, emeralds, semiprecious stones, crystalline masses, and quartz. The mineral-rich center is Ouro Preto, once the seat of Minas government.

At 10:00 P.M. I land at the Belo Horizonte airport, a two-hour drive from Ouro Preto. My driver, José, and I speed up linear hills and roller-coaster down, driving across cantilevered chasms with long stretches of missing guardrails due to the various vehicles that have careened into the abyss. Stars sparkle overhead like chips of ice, rods of lightning bounce beyond the black hills, illuminating for an instant the black horizon with its silhouettes of pine trees.

Signs for Ouro Preto become more frequent, and soon we're weaving down narrow stone-paved roads and crossing stone bridges, arriving in the main square. Its monumental column honoring the local revolutionary hero Tiradentes is surrounded by the illuminated facades of splendid baroque and rococo buildings. Up a narrow, winding road, José parks against the stuccoed wall of the Solar das Lajes, my hotel for the next ten days. Somewhere nearby the sound of gurgling water and the scent of jasmine add to the tranquillity of the night. José deposits the luggage in the hallway of the hotel and wishes me a happy stay. Out from the dark steps an owl-faced man, with round horn-rimmed spectacles, a shock of white hair, and a puffy white beard, who bids me good evening and introduces himself as Pedro. He arranges to have the baggage and me sent to my room and invites me to come down and have a drink with him after I freshen up.

Up in my room, I lean through the open window, breathe in the cold mountain air, and stare out, dazzled by this sweeping postcard view—the town spills before me, and the luminescence that bathes the multiple churches, chapels, and public buildings creates iridescent blue and green reflections. Little whitewashed houses seem to cascade down from the hills, and their windows catch the light like diamond dust. The sound of bells comes from all over the place. Up here it's chilly enough to feel like a crisp fall night, though we are in the height of a scorching Brazilian summer.

Pedro is busy pouring a dark, heavy purple liquor into little stemmed glasses and passing around a plate of sugar cookies. The taste of the liquor, made from the jabuticaba berry, is like sweet huckleberries and black grapes. Clusters of these small cherry-sized berries cling to the barks of huge deciduous trees that grow from Minas on down, and into the state and city parks of São Paulo. The fruit is so beloved by the

Brazilians that when it is in season public parks rent out the trees by the day. The berries are made into this rich liquor and into jams.

OVERLEAF:
A still life of flowers and eggs is very familiar to me.

Naturally our conversation turns to food. Pedro talks of his orchards of plum, apricot, peach, and apple trees and his garden of herbs, tomatoes, eggplants, and zucchini. And he tells me that cilantro has no place in the cooking pots of Minas, but is used only along the coast. Here they use parsley instead. He asks if I ever tasted the cachaça from Minas. It's the best in Brazil, and one in particular, Milagre de Minas, made here in Ouro Preto, is flavored with fifteen herbs. It is served and drunk like rare wine.

"The taste of the local food," he says, with eyes getting larger and friendlier, "is the energy in the food. There is energy in our ground. You eat the energy! The flavors and preparations hold on to more European traditions; foods we have been preparing in the same manner since the arrival of the bandeirantes. There is little African influence here. We use the malagueta pepper, of course, to season and some manioc flour, but we make our polenta with cornmeal, not from manioc. And we like the brown beans, not the black ones, what we call *mulatinha* [mulatto]."

When the taste of the liquor becomes cloying Pedro uncaps icy bottles of beer. During my visit, this habit of treating guests generously with libations will be frequent. Before I say good night, he points out the window at a big illuminated church. "That church is São Francisco de Assis. Very beautiful church," he says. "You meet me in front at seven-thirty after you take breakfast. It's market day—I'll take you around."

I'm awakened by shafts of sunlight and the sounds of ancient bells pealing out from all directions. I lie in bed picking out the varying tones, like notes from different instruments in an orchestra. The day is as dazzling as the night. Puffs of clouds float below a brilliant blue sky, and Pedro's orchard clings to the hillside in terraced steps punctuated by trees glistening with lacy sprays of blossoms.

Breakfast in the cozy dining room offers the same sweeping view, and I enjoy the simple fare—fruit, coffee with steamy milk, and a basket of warm, sweet corn bread served with butter and satiny rich orange and lime marmalade that Pedro puts up himself.

On my walk to the church little vignettes of local life play out—men and women leave their houses, locking them with large skeleton latchkeys; parents accompany small children dressed in pinafores or short pants, who clutch schoolbooks in their little arms; by the side of the road groups of women scrub laundry in a stone trough that overflows with water shooting from the mouth of a stone lion's head. Stooped old men in leather britches and boots lead their mules over cobblestone streets, *(continued on page 178)*

Frango com Quiabo
CHICKEN WITH OKRA

2 3- to 3½-pound chickens, cut into 8 pieces each, backs and wing tips removed (reserve for another use)
4 garlic cloves, chopped
Salt and freshly ground pepper to taste
4 tablespoons (½ stick) unsalted butter
4 medium onions, chopped
¼ cup vegetable oil
¼ cup extra-virgin olive oil
2 cups homemade or canned low-sodium chicken stock
1½ pounds okra, trimmed and cut into ½-inch rounds (about 4 cups)
½ teaspoon preserved malagueta pepper oil or hot pepper sauce

Polenta with Fresh Corn (recipe follows), for serving

Wash and dry the chicken pieces. Pull the skin away from the flesh, but do not detach it. In a large bowl, toss the chicken with the garlic, salt, and pepper and refrigerate for 1 hour.

In a large skillet, heat the butter over medium heat and sauté the onions until they are light gold, about 5 minutes. Set the cooked onions aside.

In the same skillet, heat the vegetable and olive oils over medium heat. When the oils are hot, add the chicken pieces and sauté them until the skin curls up crisp and golden. Drain on paper towels and reserve.

Drain the oil from the pan, add the stock, and bring to a boil, scraping up the brown parts that adhere to the bottom of the pan. Reduce the heat and continue to cook at a low simmer.

Meanwhile, generously coat a cast-iron skillet with vegetable oil and heat over medium-high heat for about 5 minutes. Add the okra and stir constantly with a wooden spoon for about 12 minutes. The gum will stick to the sides of the pan. Remove the okra from the heat.

Cut away the curled fried skin from the chicken pieces and reserve.

Add the chicken pieces and onions to the simmering sauce and cook for 10 minutes, until the pieces are cooked through. Add the okra and season with salt and pepper. Add the malagueta oil or hot pepper sauce and cook for another minute. Serve with the fried chicken curls and polenta.

SERVES 6

Polenta com Milho Cozido
POLENTA WITH FRESH CORN

6½ cups water
1 teaspoon salt
2 cups polenta
1 cup cooked fresh corn kernels
6 tablespoons unsalted butter, cut into pieces
½ cup freshly grated Parmesan cheese

In a large saucepan, bring the water to a boil over high heat. Add the salt and reduce the heat to a simmer. Slowly add the polenta, stirring constantly with a wooden spoon. Cook, stirring, for 20 minutes. Add the kernels and cook another 5 minutes, or until the polenta is smooth and slightly stiff. Remove from the heat and stir in the butter and cheese. Serve immediately.

SERVES 6

Tutu à Mineira
MASHED BEANS

Tutu à Mineira is a very basic dish of unseasoned cooked beans to which salt is added. Manioc flour is blended with the juice of the beans, then added back into the beans and topped with lots of chopped scallions and hard-boiled eggs. It is served with all varieties of pig, which might include roast pork, grilled or fried pork chops, fried pork cracklings, or sausages. Always accompanied by boiled rice and kale, it is Minas Gerais's variation of feijoada. There are many tutu variations that go beyond the rudimentary recipe. The following recipe is more flavorful than the standard one. When the beans are served whole, thus eliminating the pureeing, the dish is called feijão de tropeiro. Both are legitimate regional dishes.

1 pound mulatinha beans, brown beans, such as cranberry beans, or white beans, such as navy, or great northern beans, washed and picked clean

3 cups beer or water

1½ tablespoons extra-virgin olive oil

1 medium onion, chopped

2 garlic cloves, chopped

1 large tomato, peeled, seeded, and chopped

1 green bell pepper, cored, seeded, ribs removed, and chopped

½ cup manioc flour

½ teaspoon chopped fresh oregano or ¼ teaspoon dried oregano

¼ cup chopped fresh parsley
Salt and freshly ground pepper to taste

½ cup chopped scallions, green part only (reserve the white bulbs for another use)

Pork Roast and Sausages (see page 181), Simple Boiled White Rice (see page 12), Kale (see page 13), and Malagueta Pepper Sauce (see page 96), for serving

Soak the beans overnight with water to cover by several inches. Drain the beans and place them in a large soup kettle with water to cover by 3 inches. Bring to a boil and skim off any foam or impurities. Add the beer or additional water and bring to a boil again. Reduce the heat to a simmer and cook for 45 minutes, stirring from time to time so the beans do not stick to the kettle.

In a sauté pan, add the olive oil and place over medium heat. Add the onion and garlic and sauté for about 5 minutes, or until the onion is translucent. Add the tomato and green pepper and cook another 4 minutes, or until the pepper is limp and almost tender.

Add the manioc flour, toss, and cook another minute. Add about 3 cups of bean liquid, a little at a time, until the mixture forms a light, wet paste. Fold in the oregano and parsley and set aside.

When the beans are soft and tender, season them with salt and pepper, turn off the heat, and set aside for 10 minutes. Drain the beans, reserving the cooking liquid.

In a food processor, pulse the beans on and off in batches until smooth, adding a little bean liquid as needed to keep the mixture loose. Continue to process until all the beans are pureed. All the bean liquid may not be required. The consistency should be smooth, soft, and not heavy.

Place the bean puree in a clean kettle and fold in the manioc flour mixture. Keep warm over a pan of simmering water until ready to serve.

When ready to serve, sprinkle with the scallion greens. Serve with pork roast, rice, kale, and Malagueta Pepper Sauce.

SERVES 12 OR MORE

ABOVE:
Frango com Quiabo (chicken with okra and polenta) is prepared in heavy black stone vessels used throughout the valley.

OPPOSITE:
A pot of okra ready for the fire

the beasts delicately balancing pickaxes, saddlebags, and gold-sifting pans. Other than the chirping of birds, the only sound is the chinking of the mules' hooves, and even that is softened by the grass that grows between the cobblestones.

I follow the steep narrow streets into the Praça Tiradentes and drink in the beauty of this timeless square. Born Silva Xavier, Tiradentes was a full-time dentist christened by his rebel followers with this name, which translates as the "Tooth Puller."

I arrive at the church of Saint Francis, nestled in a smaller square. Tented stands house tables and bins chock-full of onions, potatoes, pumpkins, peppers, turnips, cauliflowers, tomatoes, garlic, beans of all colors, peas, okra, kale, barrels of fruits, and baskets of figs, cherries, and grapes. Tin pails are full of just-picked zinnias, cosmos, daisies, bachelor's buttons, roses, and wild field flowers. I meet Pedro, who is securing a basket filled with celery, cabbage, onions, live chickens, and eggs to his motorcycle.

We have a fast chat and coffee at a nearby café, and he tells me what churches I must visit and gives me the name of a restaurant where I can eat the best Minas food. Pedro is a bit disparaging about the local restaurant fare. "Naturally you will eat better at home, and tonight I will make a nice Minas soup for supper for you and some friends."

For the rest of the morning I meander about the town, impressed by this transplant of European sensibilities and architectural *(continued on page 182)*

Molho Apimentado
HOT PEPPER SALSA

Molhos made with vinegar or fresh lime juice are a typical and piquant accompaniment to grilled meat and bean dishes.

1 medium onion, finely chopped
1 large garlic clove, finely chopped
1 medium firm ripe tomato, seeded and chopped
¼ cup chopped fresh parsley
¼ cup vegetable oil

½ cup red wine vinegar
4 or more drops of malagueta pepper oil or hot pepper sauce
Salt and freshly ground pepper to taste

In a small bowl, combine all the ingredients. Cover and chill at least 1 hour before serving.

MAKES ABOUT 1½ CUPS

Conjiquinha con Lingüiça
DRIED CORN WITH SAUSAGES

The Brazilian Indian method of drying corn is called conjiquinha. The same method is called samp among the American Indians of the Northeast. The corn is mixed with a lye and water mixture, the outer skins removed, and the kernels dried and stored for winter use. Conjiquinha is available at Brazilian markets.

2 cups conjiquinha or milled dried corn
2 medium onions, grated
1 whole head garlic, peeled and chopped
1 green bell pepper, cored, seeded, and grated
2 pounds excellent quality, mildly spicy thin pork, chicken, or lamb sausages

Salt to taste
Boiled White Rice (page 12) and Sautéed mustard greens (see page 36), to serve

Bring 4 cups of lightly salted water to a boil over medium-high heat, then add the corn. Reduce the heat and simmer, stirring from time to time, and add more boiling water as it evaporates. When the corn is almost tender (about 1 hour to 1 hour and 15 minutes), add the onions, garlic, and pepper. Add the sausages and salt, cover, and cook another 15 minutes. Stir from time to time, making sure the corn does not stick to the bottom of the pan. Remove the sausages from the pan. Place a skillet over medium-high heat and briefly sauté the sausages to give them color.

Serve the corn and sausages together with white rice and sautéed mustard greens.

SERVES 6

Lombo e Lingüiça Assado

PORK ROAST AND SAUSAGES

1 5-pound loin of pork, trimmed, with a little fat left intact, rolled and tied
4 garlic cloves, peeled and thinly sliced
1 quart milk
1 tablespoon extra-virgin olive oil
1 tablespoon chopped fresh marjoram, oregano, or thyme
Salt and freshly ground pepper to taste

2 medium onions, trimmed and quartered
2 tablespoons all-purpose flour
1½ cups homemade or canned low-sodium chicken stock or water

LINGÜIÇA
¾ pound sweet lingüiça sausage (or sweet Italian-type pork sausage)

Place the pork loin in a pan, add the garlic and milk, turn to coat, and cover. Refrigerate for 5 hours or overnight, turning once or twice.

Preheat the oven to 375° F.

Remove the loin from the liquid and discard the liquid. Pat the loin dry and place it in a roasting pan. Rub the meat with the olive oil and marjoram, oregano, or thyme, and season generously with salt and pepper.

Scatter the onions around the pan and roast for 1 hour and 45 minutes, until the internal temperature reaches 160° to 165° F. Place the roast on a warm platter, cover, and let it rest for 15 minutes before slicing.

Meanwhile, skim off most of the excess fat from the pan. Set the pan over medium heat, sprinkle with the flour, and stir briskly with a large fork or wooden spoon. Add the stock or water and scrape up the brown bits adhering to the bottom of the pan. Bring to a boil, season with salt and pepper, and continue to cook until the gravy has thickened. Strain into a warm gravy boat, pressing down on the caramelized onions, which should be discarded.

Lightly prick the sausage with a kitchen fork from top to bottom. In a large skillet, add the sausage and about an inch of water. Brown on all sides over medium heat, adding more water as it evaporates (see Note). The addition of water reduces spattering grease and crisps up the skins faster. Cook until browned, about 12 minutes.

SERVES 6

NOTE: Quite often the Mineira cook will brown the sausage, then finish cooking it in the beans before pureeing the beans.

Turkey roasted in a wrapping of banana and lime leaves

BELOW:
Heads of garlic and onions are halved to be roasted for the stuffing.

ideas plunked in the middle of Brazil. The narrow streets are lined with old colonial houses that are almost childishly fashioned with their cutout cobalt-blue painted doors and framed windows. But the second-story windows of the bigger houses are more elaborate, sporting balconies enclosed with lacy wood screens.

The streams, brooks, and little rivers that zigzag through the town pass under small stone bridges, one of which leads me to the Tavernna do Chafariz, Pedro's recommendation. In the sun-drenched dining room a huge wooden table is set with bowls of lettuces and salads of tomato and marjoram, sliced beets and onion, eggplant, cucumbers, cabbage slaws, and tabouli. The last is a culinary influence from the Lebanese, who began to settle in Brazil around fifty years ago. Generally, Brazilians are not great salad eaters, and this display of simply prepared salads is a nice surprise. A black clay bowl is filled with *feijão de tropeiro,* named for the muleteers who drove their mule packs into the hills, carrying a canteen of aromatic brown beans cooked with peppers, onions, scallions, tomatoes, garlic, and herbs. Another bowl holds velvety pureed

brown beans called *tutu à Mineira* (page 177), which is sometimes mixed with shredded pork or chicken. Both dishes are prepared and seasoned in the same manner, save that one is pureed and the other not. Perhaps the muleteers didn't mind the fact that their wives missed the last step. The table groans with familiar parts of the pig—roasted sucklings, tender white loins, chops, *conjiquinha,* dried corn with sausages, juicy rendered lardoons, and chunks of fried pork fat, as crisp as chips. Other bowls are filled with strips of fried river fish, stewed chicken and okra, shredded kale, rice, roasted potatoes, and grilled corn polenta. These homey dishes remind me of good country cooking anywhere. I leisurely eat my way through everything and find the roasts are perhaps the most flavorful, moist, and delicious pork I've tasted anywhere. I save a little room for the doce table, which gleams with bowls of crystallized fruits and fruit pastes. The sweet they call *ambrosia* is a mixture of fat stewed prunes mixed with clotted cream. There is also banana puree as thick and dark as molasses; slices of green transparent citron swim in syrup; translucent strips of green mango that have been rolled into little rosettes and strung on thread are stewed in sugar syrup and clove (page 192); and dense, rich guava paste sits next to a big round white Minas cheese—a coupling called Romeo and Juliet. Minas cheese, or *queijo de Minas,* is slightly tart, moister and denser than our farmer cheese. Brazilians love dessert, and *(continued on page 186)*

Every region has its own version of feijoada. Here it's made with crushed beans, roasted pork, and sausages and called Tutu à Mineira.

Peru à Brasileira

MARINATED TURKEY ROASTED IN BANANA LEAVES

Though the turkey can be steamed, split and barbecued, or roasted, I prefer the roasted version.

1 10- to 12-pound turkey or capon, wing tips removed and giblets reserved

STOCK

1 onion, quartered
2 garlic cloves, crushed
2 celery ribs, chopped
1 carrot, peeled and chopped
1 bay leaf
6 whole peppercorns
1 sprig thyme
3 sprigs parsley

STUFFING

4 medium onions, halved
3 garlic heads, halved
1 cup extra-virgin olive oil

1 bottle dry white wine
1 cup cachaça or white rum

PEPPER PUREE

3 malagueta peppers or 3 small hot red chili peppers, cored, seeded, ribs removed, and chopped

3 red bell peppers, cored, seeded, ribs removed, and chopped
½ cup white wine vinegar
4 medium onions, chopped
10 garlic cloves, chopped
2 tablespoons chopped fresh oregano
Salt to taste
⅛ teaspoon ground nutmeg
½ cup extra-virgin olive oil

About 3 banana leaves or corn husks from 12 ears corn
18 pesticide-free lime or lemon leaves, washed (optional)
1 cup beer

Polenta with Fresh Corn (see page 176), Mashed Beans (see page 177), Simple Boiled White Rice (see page 12), and Malagueta Pepper Sauce (see page 96), for serving

Wash the turkey and pat it dry with paper towels. Place it in a large pan, breast side down, cover with a clean kitchen towel, and refrigerate for 1 hour or more.

To make the stock, in a medium saucepan, add the wing tips, neck, and all the giblets except the liver. Add the onion, garlic, celery, carrot, bay leaf, peppercorns, thyme, and parsley. Cover with water and bring to a boil. Skim off the impurities, reduce the heat, and simmer for 1 hour, adding a little boiling water as it reduces and skimming occasionally. Strain and cool the stock, then refrigerate, covered tightly, until ready to use.

While the stock is simmering, make the stuffing. Preheat the oven to 400° F. Place the onions and garlic in a medium ovenproof dish and pour the oil over. Roast for 40 minutes, or until the onions and garlic are caramelized and lightly charred. Do not allow the mixture to burn. Remove from the oven and cool.

Stuff the turkey cavity with the onions and garlic and truss. Place the bird, breast side down, in a roasting pan and pour over the wine, reserving ⅛ cup, and cachaça or rum. Cover tightly and refrigerate for at least 8 hours or overnight, turning the bird 2 or 3 times during the marination.

To make the pepper puree, in a medium bowl, soak the malagueta or chili peppers and bell peppers in the vinegar for 30 minutes. Drain and reserve the liquid. Puree the peppers in a food processor, pulsing on and off. Fold the puree back into the vinegar and set aside.

In the food processor, add the chopped onions, garlic, and oregano and puree with the reserved ⅛ cup white wine. Fold the onion puree into the pepper puree mixture and stir in the salt and nutmeg.

Heat the ½ cup olive oil in a medium saucepan over medium heat. Add the puree mixture and 1 cup of the turkey stock and simmer for 1 hour, stirring from time to time. Cool the pepper sauce.

Remove the turkey from the refrigerator and carefully lift the skin around the breast and neck area and rub a little pepper sauce between the flesh and skin. Set aside the turkey and the remaining pepper sauce.

Cut the banana leaves, if using, in 18-inch sheets. Hold each sheet firmly and carefully run the leaf over a gas-stove flame to release the oils in the leaf and make it flexible. Set aside.

Preheat the oven to 500° F. Using a large, deep ovenproof casserole, line the bottom with 3 or 4 prepared banana leaves or half the corn husks. Liberally salt the bird and place the turkey over the leaves or husks, breast side up. Brush some of the pepper sauce over the bird and tuck the lime or lemon leaves, if using, around the turkey. Roast for 10 minutes. Reduce the temperature to 325° F., cover with 2 or 3 sheets of banana leaves or the remaining corn husks, and continue to roast for 2 hours, basting once or twice with some of the remaining pepper puree. When the thigh is pierced with a knife and the juices run clear, remove the turkey from the oven and cool for 15 minutes before carving.

While the turkey is cooling, bring the remaining pepper puree and beer to a boil, reduce the heat, and simmer for 10 minutes. Carve the bird and arrange it on a platter over fresh banana leaves and spoon over the heated pepper sauce–beer mixture.

Serve with polenta, beans, boiled rice, and Malagueta Pepper Sauce.

Serves 10 or more

CLOCKWISE
FROM TOP
LEFT:
*Doce de Leite,
sweet clotted
cream, Doce de
Figuinho, pre-
served figs, and
Doce de Manga,
sweet mango curls
crystallized in
sugar syrup*

they love it sweet. My Brazilian friends are always amused by our typical response to their confections: "Oh, it's so sweet!" Well, that's exactly what they think dessert should be.

Pedro's kitchen seems to float in the late-afternoon light and the sweet aroma of chicken soup. This dish ranks high with the Mineiros and is considered as much a comfort food as a plate of beans. We all sit down for supper, and Pedro ladles out big portions into warm, immense soup plates. Pedro serves up a nice green salad and a plum tart for dessert.

For an inn that, according to its owner, is only a congenial place to sleep and have an amiable breakfast, Pedro's kitchen turns out to be the hub of hospitality. Meals are always being prepared for guests invited on a whim. The morning after the dinner party, I'm in the kitchen working alongside Pedro while he prepares a dish of sautéed chicken with okra (page 176). Clay pots are heating on the wood-burning stove while he cuts the chicken in small pieces, partially pulls back the skin, and marinates the meat in a little garlic and seasonings. When the chicken is sautéed, the skin curls up crisp and crunchy and is served rather like the *chicerones* so popular in Latin American and Caribbean cookery. The preparation of the okra is something quite different. Pedro lightly oils a large clay pot and warms it on the stove. He adds the sliced okra, stirs slowly, and little by little the vegetable releases its sticky gum. The gum sticks to the sides of the pot, and the okra remains crunchy as it cooks, not gooey. He whips up a creamy corn polenta punctuated with fresh corn kernels as well and considers the meal just enough to sustain us the afternoon as we cook dinner. "We'll have tutu with pork loin and sausages [page 181] for supper," says Pedro.

When it's time to make the tutu, the beans are already simmering in a good amount of stock and beer. Pedro adds small amounts of sautéed onion, garlic, tomato, and green bell pepper and a little fresh oregano and parsley for seasoning. He purees the beans in a beat-up *liquidificador,* a coy word they use for "blender." The creamy puree is lighter than I anticipated, and a delicious foil to the meats, rice, and kale (page 13) that will

be served that night. The concept is rather like that of a feijoada, but one in which all the elements have been individually and separately prepared, rather than cooked in the bean pot. The evening is to be festive, and Pedro, in typical Brazilian fashion, thinks the menu should be enlarged. "Not everyone eats red meat"—he laughs—"and so I'm going to make a turkey in banana leaves" (page 184). The turkey is a small, plump bird, and he carves it into pieces, then slathers it with a paste of peppers, garlic, and oil and sets it aside to marinate. When it's time to steam the bird, he shrouds the pieces in banana leaves and places them in a steamer, filling the bottom with water. A coin is thrown in the bottom of the kettle before fitting in the basket, and when the coin begins to rattle the cook knows it's time to add more liquid. This trick is even more impressive considering the fact that Brazilian currency is *(continued on page 196)*

Costelinha à Mineira

LITTLE RIBS AND FIDDLEHEADS

In the forests and along the multitudes of streams and rivers throughout the state of Minas Gerais, folks forage for wild mushrooms, herbs, and fiddlehead ferns. This pork dish often appears with the addition of fiddlehead ferns in the spring.

3 pounds pork back ribs
1 sprig thyme
1 sprig rosemary
1 sprig marjoram
⅓ cup cachaça (optional)
3 tablespoons vegetable oil or bacon fat
1 large onion, chopped
3 garlic cloves, chopped
1 tablespoon tomato paste
   Salt and freshly ground pepper to taste
1 teaspoon urucum (tasteless red coloring) or 1 teaspoon mild paprika dissolved in ¼ teaspoon vegetable oil
1 bay leaf
1 cup homemade or canned low-sodium chicken stock

BEAN PUREE

2 cups cooked pinto or cranberry beans or prepared Tutu Peri Peri without the addition of manioc flour (farinha de mandioca) (see page 53)

10 scallions, including some of the green, chopped
1½ cups fiddleheads or asparagus tips
2 tablespoons fresh lime juice

   Malagueta pepper oil or hot pepper sauce, for serving

In a large soup kettle, add the ribs, thyme, rosemary, marjoram, cachaça, and enough cold water to cover and bring to a boil. Boil for 5 to 10 minutes, depending on the fattiness of the ribs. Cool in the liquid.

Remove the ribs from the liquid and cut them in single lengths.

In a large, deep, heavy skillet, heat the oil or bacon fat over medium-high heat. Add the ribs, in batches if necessary, and brown on all sides. Remove the ribs and reserve. Pour off most of the fat and sauté the onion for 5 minutes, or until wilted. Add the garlic and cook for another minute or two. Add the tomato paste, season with salt, pepper, and urucum or paprika and oil, and cook another minute.

Add the bay leaf and stock and bring to a simmer. Return the ribs to the skillet and continue to cook until the ribs are fork tender, about 25 minutes.

While the ribs are cooking, warm the beans in a saucepan over low heat with enough bean liquor to make them wet but not soupy. When they are hot, puree the beans in a food processor or blender with some of the liquor. Add a tablespoon or two of the puree to the rib mixture and mix thoroughly to thicken the sauce. Add half of the chopped scallions to the bean mixture, season with salt and pepper, and keep warm over a double boiler.

Bring a saucepan of lightly salted water to a boil, add the fiddleheads or asparagus tips, and blanch for 3 minutes, or until almost tender, then drain under cold running water.

Fold the fiddleheads or asparagus and remaining scallions into the rib mixture, add the lime juice, and cook another 2 or 3 minutes, or until the fiddleheads or asparagus tips are hot.

Serve the ribs with the bean puree and malagueta pepper oil or hot pepper sauce on the side.

SERVES 4 TO 6

Doce de Figuinho
PRESERVED LITTLE FIGS

A long and tedious recipe, but worth it.

24 small green figs, firm and underripe
4 cups sugar
12 cups cold water
1 cinnamon stick

1 teaspoon lime powder (available at hardware stores and plant nurseries)

Minas cheese or farmer cheese, for serving

OVERLEAF, LEFT: *Guabiroba, cajá mango, mixirica (small tanger-ines), and tange-rina—all freshly picked and ready to be made into jelly and doces*

RIGHT: *Copa de leite ("cup of milk") are known as calla lilies to us.*

Wash the figs and with a sharp paring knife, make a very small X in the center of the bottom side of each fig.

Place the figs in a large nonreactive bowl and cover with cold water. To remove the impurities, place a clean white cotton kitchen cloth over the bowl so that the cloth just touches the water. Replace the cloth with a clean one twice a day for 3 days. The cloth will first turn dark, then lighten as the process is repeated. When the cloth remains almost white, the figs are ready to cook.

Place the figs in a copper (for best heat distribution) or heavy-bottomed nonreactive saucepan. Add the sugar and cover with the water. Add the cinnamon stick, bring to a simmer, and cook for 40 minutes. The figs will be a deep, dark translucent green. If the figs should discolor or turn brownish during the cooking time, add the lime powder tied in a cheesecloth bag, which should be removed and discarded after cooking.

Cool and store covered in the refrigerator.

Serve with soft Minas cheese or farmer cheese.

These keep for 2 months or more.

MAKES 24 PRESERVED FIGS

Doce de Abóbara
PRESERVED PUMPKIN

We consider the pumpkin a holiday squash. In Brazilian cooking it has no limits and is used in both savory and sweet dishes.

3 pounds West Indian pumpkin meat, without skin, or hubbard squash or regular pumpkin meat, cut into small cubes

2 cups sugar
1 star anise
2 tablespoons grated, peeled fresh ginger, or more to taste

Place the pumpkin cubes, sugar, and star anise in a copper or heavy-bottomed non-reactive saucepan. Add 5 tablespoons cold water and bring to a simmer over low heat. Stir often, making sure the mixture does not stick to the pan. Add a little more water if the mixture is too thick and starts to stick. When the mixture begins to sim-mer add the ginger and cook for 40 minutes, or until the pumpkin fibers collapse and become a puree (see Note).

Cool and store covered in the refrigerator for up to two weeks.

MAKES ABOUT 5 CUPS

NOTE: West Indian pumpkin and hubbard squash cook faster than regular pumpkin. Allow a little more cooking time for regular pumpkin.

Doce de Manga
PRESERVED MANGO CURLS

2 cups sugar	**2 green mangoes (see Note)**
2 cups water	

Combine the sugar and water in a nonreactive medium saucepan over medium-high heat. Stir with a wooden spoon until the sugar dissolves, then simmer for 5 minutes. Set the syrup aside and keep it warm.

Peel the mangoes with a sharp paring knife. Starting at the stem end, slice the mangoes in very thin strips, cutting against the large pit, and set aside.

Return the syrup to the heat and bring to the soft ball stage, about 234° F.

Working in batches, add about 10 mango slices to the syrup and poach until they are almost translucent, about 5 to 8 minutes. Using a long surgical tweezers or narrow tongs, lift each mango slice from the syrup, one by one, and carefully curl it around the tweezers or tongs, using a spoon so you don't burn yourself. Place the curls on wax paper and continue cooking the remaining slices. If the syrup begins to thicken, add a little more hot water.

When all the slices are cooked, cool the syrup in a bowl and return the cooled mango curls to the syrup. Serve at room temperature.

To store, cover tightly and refrigerate. Preserved mango curls will keep for 4 weeks.

MAKES ABOUT 1 QUART

NOTE: Mangoes vary in size from small to large. The green variety is most readily available at Latin American markets. Do not use the ripe stringy variety. Unripened papaya can be substituted for the mango.

Doce de Carambola
PRESERVED STAR FRUIT

When purchasing fresh carambola be sure they are a sunny golden color tinged with green with brown-tinted edges. If the edges are very brown the fruit is beginning to rot and the edges will have to be cut off, thus sacrificing the star shape.

24 large carambola	**2½ cups water**
4 cups sugar	**4 whole cloves**

Wash the carambola and drain. Slice the fruit into ¼-inch star-shaped slices and set aside.

In a medium saucepan combine the sugar and water and bring to a simmer, stirring until the sugar is dissolved. Add the cloves and sliced carambola. Bring to a boil, skim away the impurities, then reduce the heat and simmer for 45 minutes to 1 hour, or until the fruits are translucent and a rich amber color.

Pour the contents of the saucepan into a bowl and cool in the liquid. When cool the fruits can be jarred with the liquid and refrigerated. This keeps for 3 weeks. Serve with cinnamon ice cream or other fruit doces.

MAKES ABOUT 8 CUPS

Doce de Abacate
SWEET AVOCADO

The Brazilian cook is more likely to serve avocado as a sweet than a savory.

2 small ripe but firm avocados	**⅓ cup superfine sugar, or more to taste**
1 tablespoon fresh lime juice	**About ¾ cup milk**

Peel and pit the avocados and place them in the bowl of a food processor or blender. Add the lime juice and sugar and puree. Gradually add the milk. The consistency should be the thickness of yogurt.

Cover and chill. This keeps 1 or 2 days.

SERVES 6 OR MORE

OVERLEAF:
Fresh mountain water fountains are everywhere. Local ladies sell vegetables and flowers from their gardens in the heart of Ouro Preto.

Doce de Leite do Maria dos Dores Paiva
SWEET CLOTTED CREAM

Doce de Leite is a staple on the dessert tables of Minas Gerais. It is served as an accompaniment to the array of sweets that appear on the sideboard. In the fazendas, it is always made fresh, along with the cheese. It's available in cans and used as a filling for *rocambole*—sponge cake rolled with the cream like a jelly roll or roulade. Street vendors use buckets of the stuff to fill hot hollow tubelike doughnuts in the streets of small towns.

4 cups milk	**2 cups sugar**

Place the milk and sugar in a medium copper pot and set over a pan of simmering water. Stir the mixture with a wooden spoon until the sugar dissolves, about 10 minutes.

Continue cooking for 1½ hours, stirring from time to time. Keep the water bath filled with enough hot water so it does not evaporate and scorch the milk. Then stir frequently for an additional half hour, or until the cream becomes a rich, light caramel color, thickens, and forms small curds.

Cool and refrigerate. Doce de Leite will keep covered and refrigerated for 10 days.

MAKES ABOUT 4 CUPS

all paper. The coin is actually a U.S. penny that Pedro guards like gold.

Pedro has arranged a lunch for me with Dona Anna Maria, a friend who is just concluding a lecture series on the local rococo architecture for a group of visiting students. Our fast and furious lunch is at one of the unpretentious restaurants near the college. You can find these popular buffet-style restaurants near colleges and in the downtown business areas of most large towns and cities. They offer a variety of hot dishes and salads at popular prices in a clean, pleasant atmosphere, and your plate is priced according to weight. Our two lunches of various salads, rice, beans, and sautéed trout cost just over five dollars and are surprisingly good.

Just as we finish lunch, the rains begin. Dona Anna is disappointed. "The light in the church will be poor. It will be difficult to see the full beauty of the ornate decoration."

As I trail behind her to the nearby church of Nossa Senhora do Pilar, the overhanging balconies are protection enough to prevent us from getting soaked. The altar drips with silver and gilt, and trumpeting plaster angels burst out in relief from the painted wooden ceiling in high baroque exuberance. Despite the poor light, the overall effect is splendid. The gold and silver splashed on walls, fittings, and objects were a brilliant statement and a direct reaction to the Portuguese monarchy. The local citizens, overtaxed, dealt with a foreign administration that owned the mines, distributed the concessions, and dictated taxes. The church was the only safe haven to keep the gold. Artists, sculptors, builders, artisans, and musicians flocked to Ouro Preto, and what they accomplished in a short time is remarkable. But in a mere eighty years, the gold was exhausted, and Tiradentes became the new republic's hero.

Dona Anna Maria asks an old custodian to light the crystal chandeliers that hang about the altar so I can see the surrounding painted paneling. The scenes include a man hunched over a little fire in a field, roasting chestnuts in a brazier; women harvesting wheat in the fields, fruits being gathered from the trees, and wild greens nipped by a stream complete the naïf allegory of these four seasons. I want to know if these scenes are a memory of a distant homeland, or whether they depict seventeenth-century life here in Ouro Preto. "Chestnuts," she says, "are very much a part of the winter diet in Minas, though they are usually just roasted or saved to be candied for holidays." She knows of no particular recipes that make use of them. "And we use wheat flour for our cakes and breads more than we do manioc flour. But the herbs," she says, "were most likely little ferns, fiddleheads, used in a popular Minas casserole with baby back ribs" (page 188). She explains that local cooks depend on wild things to augment their dishes and suggests, in fact insists, that I spend a weekend at her inn at Tiradentes to try some of the local specialties. "My town is a microcosm of Ouro Preto, a place you must see before leaving Brazil. There are but two churches and only five chapels, so it won't exhaust you."

DATELINE: TIRADENTES, MARCH 21

The trip to Tiradentes is a pretty two-hour drive through quiet open countryside and drifts of pine forests. Aside from occasional fruit orchards, what is most remarkable are the earthen-red peaks of anthills towering four feet high above the fields. From a distance they look like habitable huts. If the landscape appears more ordinary than the rest of Brazil, these mountainous mounds of dirt are a reminder that I am still in a very foreign place.

As we enter the town of Lagoa Dourada, Anna Maria points to the only billboard we've seen on the drive. In big blue letters the word "Rocambole" advertises a bakery that sells this indigenous Minas dessert. "You must try it," she says, "and I'll buy some *queijadinha* for tea."

The little white painted bakery smells of sweet butter and sugar, and the glass cases are filled with dozens of *ramcamboles,* jelly-roll logs rolled around a thick butterscotch filling and sprinkled with sugar crystals. A queue of customers waits at the cash register while the logs are boxed and tied with string. I'm introduced to Senhora do Libano, the owner, whose family has been making this Minas specialty at this same location for more than eighty years. She cuts two slices and hands one to each of us in waxy paper napkins. The golden sponge cake is moist and light, and the filling creamy with a hint of caramel and cocoa. I also sample the queijadinha—little cupcakes like a puff of light sponge made of eggs, sugar syrup, a bit of flour, and the delicious flavor of crumbled Minas cheese. It is one of the lightest and most delicious little tea cakes I've ever eaten. We buy a dozen for tea later on.

We approach the village of Tiradentes, situated alongside the old gold-mining route next to the gentle Rio dos Mortes. The dirt road narrows as we approach Tiradentes, the hero's birthplace. A stunted pillory dominates a large angled square, and the entire town is visible from here. Beige stones pave the streets, worn down and polished with age and use, and the grassy cracks, matted and vibrant green, wind up streets lined with white houses trimmed with cobalt blue. Churches, chapels, and belfries pop out above the houses and glow in the afternoon sun. Across the square and across a stone footbridge the largest house in this small town is the Solar da Ponte, the grand manor house Anna Maria and her husband, John Parsons, have converted into an inn. A couple of honks on the horn and the barn-red wooden doors open into a stone courtyard surrounded by gardens.

The house is pristine white inside and out, appointed with luxurious furnishings from the colonial period. It's a sumptuous welcome after six weeks on the road. Dona Anna Maria suggests I settle in, take a swim in the pool, and join her and John for tea at their house across the village.

After tea Anna Maria introduces me to her cook, who is preparing doces for dinner that evening. Marie dos Dores, a large smiling woman, stands nunlike in her white dress and apron, stirring a large pot of *doce de leite* (page 193). The glazed-tile kitchen floor and white plaster walls are conventlike in their purity and cleanliness. A half-dozen freshly made Minas cheeses rest under a covering of gauze on an old scrubbed white-pine table, and bowls of preserved lime shells and sweet pureed pumpkin are cooling on a sill. "All the sweets," she tells me, "are simple to prepare; it only takes time." I don't think she would have left that spot if the world came to an end, so engrossed is she with her watchful eye and her professional hand that guides the wooden spoon in steady turns around the pot. I return to the inn for a nap just as the shops are closing.

When I return to the Parsons' house for dinner later that evening, I stroll through the village past a group of old men sitting at a table in front of the one bar. A few young men quietly play billiards in the back. The stone streets reflect the glow of candlelight coming from dining room windows facing the street. Shadowy figures are setting tables, and I can even hear the conversation from behind the lace curtains of the open windows. It all seems so unhurried and delightful, knowing that everyone is performing the same domestic tasks at the same time.

Anna Maria's table gleams with silver, crystal, and candlelight, and after our plates of creamy cauliflower soup, we help ourselves at the buffet to the hearty stew *costelinha à Mineira*—the little pork ribs cooked in a sauce of onions, garlic, tomato, stock, cachaça, lime juice, and generous amounts of fiddleheads. Like the best "peasant fare" all over the world, this cuisine is art.

traveler's guide & sources

The tourist infrastructure of Brazil is sketchy, especially once you leave the big cities. Here are a few helpful hints and remarks on hotels, restaurants, and other places I like. As everywhere, places change—restaurants get better, some get worse, and others disappear. Portions are large and a plate of food in a Brazilian restaurant is more often than not enough for two. You should call ahead to check hours, prices, and so forth.

São Paulo

The city of São Paulo reminds me of New York City—both the good and the bad—only with twice the population of New York. It is advisable not to walk around with expensive watches or jewelry, and to watch your camera and video cameras, too.

■ Airports and Transportation

GUARULOHOS
Nineteen miles from the center of the city, serving international and domestic flights. On arrival, limit dollar exchange to one hundred dollars; better rates are made at tourist and local banks. Before going through customs, shop the duty free. Duty on all imports to Brazil is very steep, and this is your last chance to buy film, batteries, liquor, and so on, at reasonable prices. Special taxi service is available at fixed prices.

CONGONHAS
In the southern part of the city. This airport serves the regional airlines, including Varig, Vasp, Transbrasil, and charters, offering frequent flights to the various cities within the state, as well as the Rio shuttle.

CITY BUS SERVICE
Frequent and reliable, and a good way to get around the city. Don't drive unless familiar with the city. Avoid rush hours at 8:00 A.M., noon, and 6:00 P.M., when the buses are overcrowded.

TAXIS
Regular taxis are hailed in the street. Service is reliable, prices vary, and call services are best for long distance.

ALO TAXI
Tel. (011) 229.7688
Twenty-four-hour service with an extra charge for personal pickups.

TRAINS

LUZ STATION
Paca da Luz 1 (Luz section)
Tel. (011) 991.3039
Offers service to the interior of the state. Built in the late nineteenth century, this Victorian structure was brought over from England and is worth a visit.

TOURIST BUSES
Luxury buses connect throughout the entire country. Costs are almost 80 percent less than air travel, but distances are enormous. Contact a recommended travel agency or phone bus terminal information. Tel. (011) 235.0322

TRAVEL AGENCY
RABE VIAGENS E TURISMO LTDA.
Rua Barao do Triumfo 464 (Brooklin section)
Tel. (011) 543.7200; fax 241.6566
National and international travel arrangements.

■ Inns and Hotels

CAESAR PARK
Rua Augusta 1508 (Bela Vista section)
Tel. (011) 258.0011
Luxurious and well located.

MAKSOUD PLAZA
Alameda Campinas 150 (Bela Vista section)
Tel. (011) 251.2233
Deluxe accommodations, good restaurants in the hotel, great nightclub featuring international singers and musicians, swimming pool. The North American businessman's hotel of choice.

GRAND HOTEL CA'D'ORO
Rua Augusta 129 (Bela Vista section)
Tel. (011) 256.8011
One of the city's charming European-style hotels. This Northern Italian standby also serves a very good cozido (a boiled-meat-and-vegetable meal similar to bollito misto) on Sunday.

■ Motels

These are fairly luxurious and designed to accommodate lovers on the run.

■ Restaurants

ANTIQUARIUS
Alameda Lorena 1884 (Jardins section)
Tel. (011) 64.8686 / 282.3015
Dine on refined Portuguese dishes, especially the cod, served in a charming atmosphere with a lavish display of old paintings and antiques. Everything is for sale.

ARABIA
Rua Haddock Lobo 1397 (Jardins section)
Tel. (011) 64.4776
Serving tasty light Middle Eastern dishes; express meals available next door. Young, zesty art director, film, and newspaper crowd at lunch.

BABY-BEEF RUBAIYAT
Alameda Santos 86 (downtown)
Tel. (011) 289.6366
A Paulista favorite off the Avenida. One of the great places in São Paulo to sample churrasco.

DA FIORELLA RISTORANTE
**Bernardino de Campos 294
(Brooklin section)**
Tel. (011) 240.6722
Quaint and homey with good Italian dishes.

FELZI
Rua Manoel Dutra 536
(Bela Vista section)
Tel. (011) 35.4677
Sophisticated Italian food in a charming old house in one of the few old parts of the city.

MASSIMO
Alameda Santos 18826 (off Avenida Paulista, upper Jardins section)
Tel. (011) 284.0311
One of Brazil's truly great restaurants, offering excellent, sophisticated pasta, fish, and meat dishes with Italian flair and a Saturday feijoada that is the best in the state. Great wine list.

O PROFETA
Alameda dos Aicas 40 (Moema section)
Tel. (011) 549.5311
A place to experience the dishes from Minas Gerais, but only if you can't get to Minas itself.

RODEIO
Rua Haddock Lobo 1468 (Jardins section)
Tel. (011) 282.1355
Best meat in the city. Start with an energy rush of beef tea, then the sliced picanha (cap of the rump) grilled over coals within view of your table. The soccer player rice and chopped salad are a must. American presidents and celebrities dine here.

FASANO
Rua Haddock Lobo 1644 (Jardins section)
Tel. (011) 852.4000
A mausoleum of varnished woods, glass, mirrors, and brass serving top-of-the-line nouvelle Italian and French cuisine at exorbitant prices.

SÃO PAULO GRILL
Rua Joaquim Floriano 72 (Ibirapuera section)
Tel. (011) 820.6306
Great meats, touristy chic.

SUSHI-YASSU
Rua Tomas Gonzaga 110
(Liberdade section, Japan Town)
Tel. (011) 279.6030
Serves some of the best sushi in the city, despite the videos.

JULIO
Rua Paula Souza and rua 25 Marco (downtown, 5 blocks from Mercado Central)
No phone
About a ten-minute walk from the Mercado Central in the rua Paula Souza downtown. Unpretentious white-tablecloth restaurant serving good fish, grilled chicken, rice, and beans. Go for lunch.

TRUTA ROSA
Avenida Vereador Joe Diniz 318
(Brooklin section)
Tel. (011) 247.8629
Good fish and farm-raised trout.

■ Bars and Cafés

SUPREMO BAR
Rua da Consolacão 3473 (Jardins section)
Tel. (011) 282.6142 / 282.9837
American-type bar. Meeting place and hangout for artists, literary types, and the well-heeled. Great drinks, good snacks, and steak with batatas frittas.

PANDORO EUROPEAN BAR
Avenida Cidade Jardim 60
(Jardins section)
Tel. (011) 881.9208
Cosmopolitan café, afternoon and early evening hangout for the older set, serving good drinks and pasteis.

CACHAÇARIA PAULISTA
Rua Mourato Coeho 593
(Pinheiros section)
Tel. (011) 815.4756
More than two hundred brands of cachaça served late into the night.

BOURBON STREET MUSIC CLUB
(AND RESTAURANT)
Rua dos Chanes 127
(Moema section, direction Santo Amaro)
Tel. (011) 61.1643 for reservations / 816.0829
for music programs
Good jazz and Monday night jam sessions—any of Brazil's great musicians may show up. Real bar atmosphere serving good, light Brazilian fare.

■ Museums and Galleries

MASP—MUSEU DE ARTE DE SÃO PAULO
Avenida Paulista 1578 (Bela Vista section)
Tel. (011) 251.5644
Largest collection of Western art in South America. Exhibits include retrospectives of Brazilian artists. On Sunday mornings visit the flea market on the plaza level of this landmark building, offering all sorts of bibelots, treasures, and junk.

GALERIA DE ARTE DO SESI
Avenida Paulista 1313 and rua Pamploma
Tel. (011) 284.5877
Important scheduled art exhibits across from MASP.

MUSEU DE ARTE SACRA
Avenida Tiradentes 676 (Luz section)
Tel. (011) 227.7694
Religious and liturgical art dating from the seventeenth century. The museum is installed in a monastery built in 1774.

GALLERY LUIZA STRINA
Rua Pare João Maneo 974-A
Tel. (011) 280.2471
Contemporary Brazilian artists.

■ Books and Newspapers

BANCA EUROPA NATIONAL
Avenida Europa at Groenlandia
(Jardins section)
No phone
National and international newspapers and magazines. Open twenty-four hours.

CARIOCA
Rua Oscar Freire at Bela Cintra
(Jardins section)
Tel. (011) 280.8632
International magazines and books.

LIVRARIA CORREA DO LAGO
Rua João Cachoeira 267 (Itaim section)
Tel. (011) 282.0066
Rare and out-of-print editions, art books, and old prints.

■ Soccer

ESTADIO MUNICIPAL PAULO MACHADO DE CARVALHO
Praça Charles Miller (Pacaembu section)
Major matches are held here. Most clubs have their own stadiums.

South of São Paulo
Santos

The major port city and home of the Coffee Exchange is a two-hour drive from São Paulo. From there Highway 5 will take you north past some of Brazil's most beautiful beaches—the coastline is called the Litoral. Villages north of Santos are weekend and holiday destinations for Paulistas.

DALMO BARBARO (RESTAURANT)
Estrada da Bertioga
Tel. (124) 53.3188
Fourteen kilometers from Guaruja outside the town of Estrada da Bertioga is a good place to lunch on simply prepared fish dishes before continuing by ferry north in the direction of Camburi.

Camburi

One of the many "primitive" fishing villages, Camburi lies along the Litoral where chic Paulistas have weekend homes. Pousadas (country inns) and camping sites are available, most of them in the sierra just above the beach.

MANACA (RESTAURANT)
Rua do Manacá 102
Tel. (124) 65.1566 / 65.1560
A bamboo house in a seductive jungle setting just off Camburi's main dirt street is the place to lunch and dine. Host Edhino offers a variety of delectable fish dishes. Start with the superb marinated and grilled squid appetizer.

Rio de Janeiro
■ Airports

GALEÃO INTERNATIONAL
Forty-five minutes from Rio's coast where most of the hotels are located. Most major airlines service the airport.

SANTOS DUMONT
Located just outside downtown Rio, this airport serves the Rio–São Paulo shuttle and a few air-taxi firms. It is a twenty-minute drive from the beaches and walking distance from downtown.

■ Inns and Hotels

COPACABANA PALACE
Avenida Atlântica 1702 (Copacabana)
Tel. (021) 255.7070
All the romance and luxury you expect from a very discerning hotel.

OURO VERDE
Avenida Atlântica 1456 (Copacabana)
Tel. (021) 542.1887
Quiet, international hotel and restaurant on Copacabana Beach.

■ Restaurants

PENAFEIL
Rua Sanhor dos Passos 121 (Proximo Avenida Passos, downtown)
Tel. (021) 224.6870
Simple white-tablecloth restaurant serving typical Carioca fare. Go for lunch.

BAR DO ARNAUDO
Rua Almirante Alexandrino 316 (Santa Teresa section)
Tel. (021) 252.7246
Take the cable car from Flamengo over the aqueduct and up to this delightful old part of the city. Lunch or dine at this small taverna on typical Carioca dishes, including cabrito, a delicious stew of goat, tomato, onions, and herbs served with a creamy moist pirão. Try to get a table overlooking the lush ravine and old houses.

SENTA AI
Rua Barão de São Felix 75 (downtown, next to Central Terminal Railroad)
Tel. (021) 233.8358
Service is dreadful, the prices high, the atmosphere chaotic, the ceiling low, and the fish and lobster are great. Dicey area at night.

MONTE CARLO
Rua Duvivier 21 (Copacabana)
Tel. (021) 541.4147 / 541.4097
Crisp and low-key in the Continental style of yesteryear, this restaurant caters to executives and seriously well-heeled locals. Banquettes and chairs covered in fabric designed by Miró is all there is to the decoration. Excellent and authentically prepared dishes include picadinho with okra and oxtail stew with polenta and watercress. Discreet good service.

SIRI MOLE & CIA
Rua Francisco Otaviano 50 (Copacabana)
Tel. (021) 267.0894
Sophisticated Bahian food behind the rocks between Copacabana and Ipanema.

ANTIQUARIUS
Rua Aristides Espinola 19 (Leblon)
Tel. (021) 294.1049
Excellent Portuguese fare with pricey antiques and paintings for sale. Another branch of this fine restaurant is located in São Paulo.

PLATAFORMA
Rua Adalberto Ferreira 32 (Leblon)
Tel. (021) 74.4022
Good moderately priced churrasco. Open everyday till late.

VILLA RISO
Estrada da Gavea 728 (São Conrado)
Tel. (021) 322.1444; fax 322.5196
One of the still-existing great plantation houses with beautiful gardens of imperial palms and breathtaking views of the mountains São Conrado and the Two Brothers. This cultural center includes an art gallery showing mostly up-and-coming Brazilian artists. Available for private parties. Open to the public on Sunday for one of Rio's best feijoada, a choice buffet, and typical local desserts.

■ Bars and Cafés

COLOMBO
Rua Gonçalves Dis 32 (Center)
Tel. (021) 232.3200
Don't take a wrong door and walk into the stand-up bar near the kitchen, offering light snacks and sandwiches. Enter the center door to this Belle Epoque dream world, every vitrine, mirror, panel, and chair made in Paris at the turn of the century. Drink sucos, enjoy an empada, a pasteis, or a sandwich, soak up the atmosphere, and enjoy the crowd. Forget the menu, which isn't worth it.

MIL FRUTAS (IN RIO AND BARRA)
Rio: Rua Jardim Botânico 585
Tel. (021) 511.2550
Barra: Up from the ocean at rua Olegario Maciel 440, Loja D
Tel. (021) 494.3522
For a delicious sampling of Amazonian and tropical-fruit ice creams and sorbets.

ARATACA
Rua Domingos Ferreira 41 (off the Avenida Atlantica in Copacabana)
Tel. (021) 255.7593
Food stuffs and health remedies from the Amazon are sold at this small stand-up bar where you can sample a good tacacá.

PEOPLE
Avenida Bartolomeu Mitre 297-C (Leblon)
Tel. (021) 294.0547
A big, chic blue-velvet boîte. Go late for the jazz, but check the schedule first.

MISTURA FINA
Avenida Borges de Medeiros 3.207 (Lagoa)
Tel. (021) 286.0195
Local hot spot offering good food and jazz on the ground floor. Jazz greats appear upstairs, and reservations are a must. Entry and cover charge upstairs. Drinks and nibbles available.

BACALHAU DO REI
Rua Marquês de São Vincente 11 (Gavea)
Tel. (021) 239.8945 / 274.1395
Best codfish croquettes in the city. This stand-up bar serves the cognoscenti and local workers.

ACADEMIA DE CACHAÇA
Rua Conde Bernadotte 26, Loja G (Leblon)
Tel. (021) 239.1542
A great place to sample all kinds of aguardente from around the country and taste a bit of the food from the northeast (Minas Gerais).

BOOKMAKERS
Rua Marquês de São Vicente 7 (Gavea)
Tel. (021) 274.4441
A good bookstore selling Brazilian and English titles with a little bar and terrace in the back. An art gallery upstairs exhibits good and bad contemporary painters. Jazz is hot on Monday nights—check for the schedule.

GUIMAS
Shopping São Conrado Fashion Mall
Tel. (021) 32.5791
Good food and drink in a shopping mall. Late-night hangout for jazz musicians, with an occasional session when they feel like it. Fortunately this pleasant place is installed on the side of the building and gives no indication that you are in a mall. However, if you miss mall life, this is one of the best in the city, including cinemas offering current American films with Portuguese subtitles.

■ Markets

The feira, or street market, is a wonderful way to come in contact with the Cariocas. The Ipanema feira on Monday and Friday and the Thursday Leblon feira on the Humberto Compos are especially recommended from 9:00 to 11:00 A.M.

South of Rio
■ Restaurants

QUINTA
Rua Luciano Galet 150 (Vargem Grande)
Tel. (021) 437.8395 / 437.7272
Luis Correa de Aranujo is the proprietor of this exquisitely appointed country house. Excellent fish, grilled langoustine, and a great duck. Open weekends only. Go early enough to walk through the sumptuous gardens. It's located one hour from the city by car. Reservations are necessary.

CÂNDIDO'S
Rua Barros de Aarcão 532
(Pedra de Gauaratiba)
Tel. (021) 395.1630 / 395.2007
The charming owner and hostess, Carmen Sampai, serves some of the coast's best seafood, shellfish, and a few Bahian specialties, overlooking the sea in the old fishing village of Pedra de Gauaratiba. One hour's drive south of the city.

LOKAU
Avenida Sernambetiba 13500
(Barra da Tijuca)
Tel. (021) 399.0279
A view, a park, and a mini-zoo accommodate fauna, flora, and surfers and swimmers from across the road. Grilled fish and seafood in a casual atmosphere.

Paraty

A three-hour drive south of Rio, this eighteenth-century colonial village is cut off from time and traffic. In 1703 the Gold Register House was founded, and this cobblestoned walking town was linked by trails to Rio and the gold mines of Minas Gerais. Hours can be spent wandering this lovely town. The region is famous for its cachaça, which can be sampled at little bars, and local distilleries are open to the public.

There are sixty islands, big and small, outside the harbor, almost all undeveloped. The area is known for some of the best sailing along Brazil's Atlantic coast, and tour boats leave the quay throughout the day. Beaches and coves are reached by schooners taking large groups, and you can always cajole a fisherman to give up a day of fishing to visit hidden coves and beach-side restaurants. Cars are left outside the village or garaged at recommended pousadas (country inns).

PARATY TOURS
Tourismo Ecológico
Avenida Roberto Silveira 11
Tel. and fax (0243) 71.1327
For information and hotel reservations and other activities, including schooners, sailing, biking, diving, hiking, and guides.

■ Inns and Hotels

POUSADA DO OURO
Rua Dr. Pereira 145
Tel. (0243) 71.1378; fax 71.1311
A charming colonial house with delightful service, a swimming pool, a bar, a good restaurant, and comfortable rooms. Located within the old town.

POUSADA DO SANDI
Largo do Rosario, No. 1
Tel. (0243) 71.2100; fax 71.1236
Luxurious setting, with rooms, apartments, and suites. All the amenities of the Ouro but fancier. Located in the center of the old town.

POUSADA DO PRINCIPE
Avenida Roberto Sileira 289
Tel. (0243) 71.2266; fax 71.210
Attractive and pleasant, just outside the old town.

■ Restaurants

RESTAURANTE DE HILTINHO
Rua Marechal Deodora 233
Tel. (0243) 71.1432
Try the camarão casadinho (married shrimp), two very large prawns joined together with a stuffing of farofa, shrimp, and spices, and the baked fish, served with a light pirão and sautéed bananas.

DONA ONDINA
Rua Tenente Francisco Antonio 2
Tel. (0243) 71.1584
Known for its many wonderful shrimp dishes. Both Dona Ondina and Restaurante de Hiltinho's use of farofa is based on the cooking of the once-local Caiçara Indians.

BAR DO CARIOCA
Paria dos Ranchos Trindade
No phone
A near impossible forty-five-minute drive down narrow ravines or an easy boat ride from Paraty. Simple fried fish, squid, caiparinhas, and beer. Nothing fancy—just a good place to have freshly caught fish if you are in the neighborhood. Go to the south end of the beach and ask for the proprietor, Carlos Alberto.

North of Rio
Buzios

Two and a half hours north of Rio by car or thirty minutes by plane, this fishing town evolved into a chic weekend retreat back in the sixties for Cariocas and the international set. Villas and hotels are spread about the myriad coves and beaches, and the main town is a hub of delightful pousadas, fine restaurants, boutiques, handicraft and antique shops, nightclubs, and bars. Be prepared to swim all day and dance all night.

■ Inns and Hotels

A ESTAGLAGEM
Rua Pedras 156 (Armacão de Buzios)
Tel. (0246) 3.1243
Seven charming rooms surrounding a quiet patio in the heart of the old town, located within walking and hiking distance of the many beaches. They serve a delightful breakfast of tropical fruit and juices, bread, and cake. No lunch, but a great light supper served in the tiny snug bar, which is the animated center of Buzios nightlife. Weekends attract international jazz musicians who come from Rio to play, and the patrons include locals, the yachting set, and jazz enthusiasts.

POUSADA DO SOL
Rua Pedras 199
Tel. (0246) 23.1249
Across the street from Estaglagem. This charming place overlooking the beach and the fishing boats is situated next door to one of the hottest discos in town.

■ Bars and Cafés

FIGARO
Praça Santos Dumont 56 (Centro)
No phone
A French café serving coffee, homemade breads and jams, and sandwiches.

CAPTAIN'S BAR
Praia da Armacao
No phone
Offers good drink and food and a waterside sunset right on the harbor (a ten-minute walk from Estaglagem). Fishermen pass by, and Nicholas the chef and owner will recommend one to take you to the many beaches (inaccessible from the land itself because of the rough coastline) for a day of swimming, snorkeling, and lunch at the remote beach restaurants and barraquinhas serving the freshest food in the area.

FERNANDO'S POINT
Avenida J.B. Ribeiro Dantas
(Vila Caranga area)
Go for the excellent lobster.

BAR DO PESCADOR
Barada 3
No phone.
On Praia da Tartaruga (Turtle Beach), only accessible by boat. Excellent fish are served with fried manioc, vegetables, and salads. Or buy a lobster or fish hawked by a local fisherman and the kitchen will prepare it for a price. All good food and drink here, and delightful help.

Bahia

Porto Seguro and Trancoso

The Portuguese first landed in the fishing village of Porto Seguro in 1500. The town still retains its colonial charm, but the sight of fishermen mending nets and raking piles of drying shrimp is quickly being replaced by hordes of Brazil's all-pervasive youthful beach culture. The town teems with vacationers during their summer months.

If you have the stamina, take the ten-minute ferry ride from Porto Seguro, followed by a rickety bus ride, to Trancoso, a seaside colonial town.

Not to be missed is an underwater national park some twenty miles out to sea, where one can snorkel in crystalline blue waters and see incredible varieties of small tropical fish or walk at ankle depth and hunt for sea urchins near the reefs. There are no tour boats going to this area, but local fishermen will take you for the day for a fee.

■ Inns and Hotels

HOTEL DE PRAÇA
CX. Postal 21
Trancoso, Porto Seguro CEP 45820
Tel. (073) 868.1177
You may encounter Sonia Braga, the Brazilian actress and owner of this charming little place, during the high season. Breakfast is the only meal served.

■ Restaurants

CAPIM SANTO
Tel. (073) 868.1122
This small restaurant tucked off the entrance to the square offers lunch and dinner in a garden setting. Excellent fish dishes and Bahian specialties are prepared with a modern and healthy twist. Baked fish fillet with yogurt, roasted with lemon grass (capim santo) and wrapped in banana leaf, gratin of lobster baked in pineapple, and shrimp catupiry are some of the specialties.

Arraial D'Ajuda

Situated between Porto Seguro and Trancoso, and a bus ride away from either. Once there, walk along the beach and across a few shallow rivers for spectacular views of cliffs, sea, and sierra. D'Ajuda is a lively, noisy town and police comb the beach frequently, arresting drug pushers on the spot.

MUCUGE HOTEL VILLAGE
Tel. (073) 288.2332
D'Ajuda's most sophisticated and pleasant inn, offering comfortable rooms, small bungalows, and a fun bar serving good food.

Salvador

The Pelourinho, literally "the pillory," where slaves were punished, is the historical center of Salvador. More than three hundred buildings surrounding this square and three rococo churches of monumental beauty have been restored to their former brilliance. The area has been designated a national monument, and the city is lively and safe. Some of the best food is made and served in the streets by the famed Baianas, who sit at pristine tables in white lace dresses, colorful turbans, and masses of silver jewelry, cooking up shrimp fritters called

acarajé. Sweet vendors proliferate.

The Elevador Lacerda (pedestrian elevator) takes you down the cliff from the old city to the harbor. At the base is the Mercado Modelo—a series of tourist shops worth wandering through, with two restaurants upstairs. Eat at the one on the right as you enter the room. Though geared for tourists, there are many Bahian specialties served by waitresses in native dress. The Terminal Touristico is nearby, and you can take the ferry to Itaparica, a large island of inns, restaurants, and beaches.

Many major luxury hotel chains are represented in Salvador.

■ Inns and Hotels

HOTEL PELOURINHO
Rua Alfredo Brito 20
Tel. (071) 321.9022
Well situated in the center of the old city, this hotel is a grand old place, if perhaps a little seedy around the edges. Service is casual, but the rooms are clean and affordable and the views of the city and the Bay of All Saints are spectacular. Nearby is the House of Benin, where *afoxes* (groups that parade during Carnival singing in African tongues) and Olodum drum groups congregate.

PITUBA PLAZA HOTEL
Avenida Manoel Dias da Silva 2495 (Amaralina)
Tel. (071) 248.1022; fax 240.2493
A reasonable and pleasant place to stay, and a ten-minute taxi drive from the center of town.

ENSEADA DAS LAJES
Avenida Ocianica 511
(Rio Vermilho)
Tel. (071) 336.1027
Set on a rocky cliff overlooking the Atlantic. Charming rooms, a luxurious breakfast, and a swimming pool are among its amenities. The drawback is the management's lackadaisical attitude toward its guests.

■ Restaurants

CASA DA GAMBOA
Rua Newton Prado 51
(Pelourinho)
Tel. (071) 321.6776
One of Salvador's oldest restaurants in the Pelourinho district, overlooking the bay. A lovely colonial atmosphere and the best place to sample the true Bahian kitchen.

BARGACO
Rua P, S/N Lotes 18/19
Quadra 43 (Centro de Convencoes)
Tel. (071) 231.5141 / 231.2390
Casual, popular, airy place serving great fish,
fried squid, and excellent moquecas.

CASA DO BENIN
Rua Padre Agostinho 17 (Pelourinho)
Tel. (071) 243.2994
Excellently prepared West African fish dishes
and filet mignon with fresh ginger sauce,
bananas, and sweet peppers.

Itaparica

A frequent ferry makes the twenty-
minute trip from the Salvador ferry slip
at the Terminal Touristico to the island
of Itaparica across the bay. It is a refreshing change from the bustle of Salvador;
one can tour the city by day and return
to the "country" for the night. Bicycles
can be rented by the day.

ARCO-IRIS
Estrada da Gamboa, 102—Mar Grande
Vera Cruz CEP 44 470
Tel. (071) 833.1130
This homey, reasonably priced inn offers private
rooms and small cottages set within a mango
orchard. The owners make great efforts to please
all their guests. They serve excellent Bahian food
in an outdoor setting.

The Amazon
Belém

The gateway to the Amazon, 160 kilometers south of the equator, Belém is a
nineteenth-century Beaux Arts city,
chockablock with parks, villas, an opera
house, churches, the main cathedral, and
the Bishop's Palace. Visit the elaborately
decorated villa of the major city planner
and influential architect, Francisco
Bolonha. Another treasure is the Belle
Epoque duplicate of the Paris Gallerie
Lafayette, with its grand gilded double
staircase. This once-chic department
store called Paris N Belém now sells
remnants and inexpensive material. The
streets are enclosed by tunnels of mango
trees, some more than a hundred years
old. When in bloom they perfume the
city, and when they bear fruit, the
streets are fragrant with sweet mangoes
that fall heavily to the pavement.

■ Inns and Hotels

EQUATORIAL PALACE HOTEL
Avenida Braz de Aguiar 612
Tel. (091) 241.2000; fax 223.5222
Modest, accommodating, with a helpful staff.
Offers a delicious breakfast of tropical fruits and
juices, manioc cereals, and tapioca crepes.

■ Restaurants

LA EM CASA
Avenida Gov. Jose Malcher 247
Tel. (091) 223.1212
Pleasant outdoor dining in the center of the city.
The place for Amazonian specialties, including
pato no tucupi, caranguejo, and tropical fruits.

RESTAURANTE DO CIRCULO MILITAR
Praça Frei Caetano Brandão
(across from the Cathedral Se)
Tel. (091) 223.4374
Tour the battlements of the old Forte do Castelo,
taking in a pretty view of the city, and dine by the
river's edge on Amazonian fish. Be sure to sample the local tropical juices.

CANTINA ITALIANA
Trav. Benjamin Constant 1401 (between Braz de
Agular and Avenlda Nazare)
Tel. (091) 225.2033
When you hunger for something familiar, try this
wacky place, run by a delightful mad hatter.
Stick to the delicious antipasti, pizza, and the
pool room upstairs.

■ Bars and Cafés

TIP TOP
Tip Top (pronounced "tchipy-topy") serves
Amazonian tropical-fruit ice creams and sorbets.
One block south of the Batista Campos Praça.

AÇAÍ MINERAL
The best açaí made with mineral water in the rua
Piedade, located one block east of the Praça
República. Try the tapioca crepes too.

■ Museums

MUSEU EMILIO GOELDI
Avenida Magalhaes Barata 376 and Avenida
Nazare
Tel. (091) 224.9233
A jewel of a zoo with botanical gardens featuring
spectacular flora and fauna and a museum featuring arts, crafts, pottery, archaeological find-
ings, and dioramas depicting the life of the
native Indian.

■ Markets

VER-O-PESO MARKET
On the quai from Rua Castilho Franca to Avenida Marechal Hermes

From 3:00 A.M. boats arrive at this major market-place filled with exotic fruits and Amazonian fish. By 9:00 A.M. the excitement lulls; most of the produce has been sold. First, visit the area closest to Guajara Bay selling baskets of açaí and Amazonian fruits, then the stalls selling shrimp, jambu, medicinal and magical herbs and potions, and varieties of farinha de mandioca. Sip hot, sweetened cereals of tapioca, manioc, and corn from gourd bowls. Visit the meat market across the way and return to the eating stalls and ask for Carmen's loja, for the best tacacá at the market. Watch for pickpockets.

Behind the stalls and close to the river's edge a large bar attracts locals and tourists at sunset.

Minas Gerais

One could spend weeks visiting the many historical colonial towns throughout this state. The distances between them are vast. Here are two beauties.

Ouro Preto

This town preserves its early eighteenth-century appearance with sumptuous palaces, houses, fountains, bridges, and the miniature opera house, the oldest in the Americas. Winding, steep streets lead up and down to thirteen churches and seven chapels built in the colonial baroque and rococo styles. Boutiques are filled with local handicrafts, soapstone carvings, semiprecious and precious stones, and crystal. Though the highways are excellent, hiring a taxi at the airport dispatch is the best bet. Inns, hotels, and restaurants abound.

■ Inns and Hotels

HOTEL SOLAR DAS LAJES
Rua Conselheiro Quintinho 605
Tel. (031) 551.3388

A relaxed bed-and-breakfast overlooking the city. Proprietor Pedro Corea de Araujo will direct you to the best restaurants, churches, and markets in town. A shuttle bus that circles the town frequently passes the inn; otherwise it's a ten-minute walk to the center of town. Worth a visit is the nearby colonial town of Marina, which can be reached by bus. Bring sneakers.

POUSADA DO MONDEO
Largo de Coimbra, 38
Tel. (031) 551.2040

This historic house in the center of the city caters to international visitors, offering choice rooms and suites.

■ Restaurants

RESTAURANTE TAVERNA DO CHAFARIZ
Rua São José 167
Tel. (031) 551.2828

A picturesque dining room overlooking a small ravine and cascading brook. Lunch is a buffet of regional dishes. Sample them all, including the famous tutu à Mineira and fruit doce.

CASA DO OUVIDOR
Rua Diretia 42
Tel. (031) 551.2141

Charming, candlelit second-story restaurant specializing in local dishes and steak au poivre.

Tiradentes

Situated 274 kilometers south of Ouro Preto is the microcosm town of Tiradentes. Brazilians refer to it as the Paraty of the mountains, though a tenth its size. The town is worth the drive through lush countryside; one can rent a car or hire a taxi, then continue on to Rio or return to Belo Horizonte for air connections. Another nearby colonial town is São João del Rei. One really does not need a car while visiting these towns; bus service to nearby towns is regular and inexpensive.

■ Inns and Hotels

SOLAR DA PONTE
Praça das Merces
Tel. (032) 355.1201

For the fatigued traveler Anna Maria and John Parsons' sumptuous antique-filled villa is the place to stay. It boasts beautifully appointed rooms and a large swimming pool, and an excellent breakfast and light lunch are served.

A NOTE ON THE WATER: It is best to ask the advice of the concierge or hotelier regarding the safety of the water. Some areas have decent potable water. However, for the tourist it is advisable to drink bottled water, called agua mineral—with or without gas (carbonation).

For the diet conscious, spend a few days at the beach and drink only coconut water. This regimen will help you lose weight and feel terrific.

Sources

The following list of shops offers a variety of Brazilian ingredients, such as manioc flours, polvilho flours, dendê oil, rice flour, tapioca, malagueta peppers, carne sêca, and canned hearts of palm. Some canned tropical-fruit concentrates are available, but for the purposes of this book, frozen tropical-fruit pulp is preferred and more readily available at fancy food shops and Brazilian or Latin American markets that import from the Caribbean. Of course, markets and mail-order sources come and go, so be sure to check with each location before ordering.

Boston area

INTERNATIONAL MARKET
365 Somerville Ave.
Somerville, MA 02143
(617) 776-1880
Brazilian groceries, flours, beans, carne sêca, fruit concentrates

USA AND BRASIL MARKET
77 Bow St.
Somerville, MA 02134
(617) 776-5000
Brazilian groceries, flours, beans, carne sêca, fruit concentrates

AQUI BRASIL MARKET
139 Brighton Ave.
Suite 5
Allston, MA 02134
(617) 787-0758
Brazilian groceries, flours, beans, carne sêca, fruit concentrates

WAYSIDE MARKET
2742 S. Main St.
Waterbury, CT 06770
(203) 753-2380
Brazilian groceries, flours, beans, carne sêca, fruit concentrates

California

VIA BRAZIL
1770-A Lombard St.
San Francisco, CA 94123
(415) 673-7744
Brazilian groceries, flours, beans, carne sêca, fruit concentrates

CANT AND ASSOCIATES
10826 Venice Boulevard
Suite 105B
Culver City, CA 90232
(310) 827-9136
Brazilian groceries, flours, beans, carne sêca, fruit concentrates

Chicago

EL MERCADO MEAT MARKET
3767 N. Southport Ave.
Chicago, IL 60613
(312) 477-5020
Lingüiça, paio, carne sêca

LA UNICA FOODMART
1515 W. Devon Ave.
Chicago, IL 60660
(312) 274-7788
Complete line of Brazilian groceries and frozen fruit pulps

Florida

FRUIT AND SPICE PARK
24801 S.W. 187th Ave.
Homestead, FL 33031
(305) 247-5727
500 varieties of exotic fruits, herbs, and spices; some can be sampled, and some seedlings for sale

VIA BRASIL
6640 Collins Ave.
Miami Beach, FL 33141
(305) 866-7718
Brazilian groceries, flours, beans, carne sêca, fruit concentrates

SABOR BRASIL
6996 Indian Creek Dr.
Miami Beach, FL 33141
(305) 861-5949
Brazilian groceries, flours, carne sêca, fruit concentrates

MAMA'S BRAZILIAN PRODUCTS
827 E. Oakland Park Blvd.
Store #70
Fort Lauderdale, FL 33334
(305) 565-7777
Complete line of Brazilian groceries, fruit concentrates and doces, empadas, pasteis

RICE AND BEANS
1930 E. Sunrise Blvd.
Fort Lauderdale, FL 33304
(305) 764-5960
Complete line of Brazilian groceries and take-out Brazilian dishes

PADARIA BRASILEIRA BAKERY
3110 N. Federal Hwy., Loja 3118
Pompano, FL 33064
(305) 782-3391
Cakes, doces, pão de queijo

LUV'N PIECES BAKERY
3190 Commodore Plaza
Coconut Grove, FL 33133
(305) 461-2110
Cakes, mousse, empadas, croquettes

LORENZO'S FRUIT AND VEGETABLE
16445 W. Dixie Hwy.
North Miami, FL 33160
(305) 944-5052
Fresh tropical fruits, roots, vegetables

Minnesota

DISCOVER BRAZIL
844 Grand Ave.
St. Paul, MN 55105
(612) 222-4504
Complete line of Brazilian groceries, including
flours, beans, carne sêca, fruit concentrates

New Jersey

SEABRA'S
60 Lafayette St.
Newark, NJ 07105
(201) 589-8606
Complete line of groceries, fresh fruit, vegetables, and frozen fruit pulp

COISA NOSSA
70 Adams St.
Newark, NJ 07105
(201) 578-2675
Brazilian groceries, flours, beans, carne sêca,
fruit concentrates

New York

EMPORIUM BRASIL
15 W. 46th St.
New York, NY 10036
(212) 764-4646
Brazilian groceries, flours, beans, carne sêca,
empadas, pasteis, fruit concentrates

SALUMERIA BIELLESE
378 8th Ave.
New York, NY 10001
(212) 736-7376
Lingüiça sausages and other varieties

AMAZONIA
3306 31st Ave.
Long Island City, NY 11106
(718) 204-1521
Brazilian groceries, flours, beans, carne sêca,
fruit concentrates

EMPORIUM
3188 30th St.
Astoria, NY 11102
(718) 204-8181
Brazilian groceries, flours, beans, carne sêca,
fruit concentrates

Ohio

KAPOK INTERNATIONAL, INC.
23 Bell St.
Suite 3
Chagrin Falls, OH 44022
(216) 247-9700
Wholesale distributor of Amazonian fish and
tropical-fruit concentrates

United Kingdom

NOTE ON UK SOURCES: Many of the
ingredients used in Brazilian cooking
are available in Indian, Afro-Caribbean,
West African, and Portuguese food
shops, supermarkets, and street markets.
Londoners are especially well served,
and there are too many such establishments in the capital to list individually
here. For fresh produce try Brixton and
Shepherds Bush markets. Also recommended are:

Food shops

LISBOA DELICATESSEN
54 Golborne Road
London W10
0181 969 1052

DORADO
280 Battersea Park Road
London SW11
0171 924 3985

LA TIENDA
81 Praed Street
London W2
0171 706 4695

Restaurants

PAOLO'S
30 Greyhound Road
London W6
0171 385 9264

SABOR DO BRASIL
36 Highgate Hill
London N19
0171 263 9066

Index

Conversion Chart
EQUIVALENT IMPERIAL AND METRIC MEASUREMENTS

American cooks use standard containers, the 8-ounce cup and a tablespoon that takes exactly 16 level fillings to fill that cup level. Measuring by cup makes it very difficult to give weight equivalents, as a cup of densely packed butter will weigh considerably more than a cup of flour. The easiest way therefore to deal with cup measurements in recipes is to take the amount by volume rather than by weight. Thus the equation reads:

1 cup = 240 ml = 8 fl. oz. $\frac{1}{2}$ cup = 120 ml = 4 fl. oz.

It is possible to buy a set of American cup measures in major stores around the world.

In the States, butter is often measured in sticks. One stick is the equivalent of 8 tablespoons. One tablespoon of butter is therefore the equivalent to $\frac{1}{2}$ ounce/15 grams.

LIQUID MEASURES

Fluid ounces	U.S.	Imperial	Milliliters
	1 teaspoon	1 teaspoon	5
$\frac{1}{4}$	2 teaspoons	1 dessertspoon	10
$\frac{1}{2}$	1 tablespoon	1 tablespoon	14
1	2 tablespoons	2 tablespoons	28
2	$\frac{1}{4}$ cup	4 tablespoons	56
4	$\frac{1}{2}$ cup		110
5		$\frac{1}{4}$ pint or 1 gill	140
6	$\frac{3}{4}$ cup		170
8	1 cup		225
9			250, $\frac{1}{4}$ liter
10	$1\frac{1}{4}$ cups	$\frac{1}{2}$ pint	280
12	$1\frac{1}{2}$ cups		340
16	2 cups		450
18	$2\frac{1}{4}$ cups		500, $\frac{1}{2}$ liter
20	$2\frac{1}{2}$ cups	1 pint	560
24	3 cups		675
25		$1\frac{1}{4}$ pints	700
30	$3\frac{3}{4}$ cups	$1\frac{1}{2}$ pints	840
32	4 cups or 1 quart		900
36	$4\frac{1}{2}$ cups		1000, 1 liter
40	5 cups	2 pints or 1 quart	1120
48	6 cups		1350
50		$2\frac{1}{2}$ pints	1400
64	8 cups or 2 quarts		1800

SOLID MEASURES

U.S. and Imperial Measures		Metric Measures	
ounces	pounds	grams	kilos
1		28	
2		56	
$3\frac{1}{2}$		100	
4	$\frac{1}{4}$	112	
5		140	
6		168	
8	$\frac{1}{2}$	225	
9		250	$\frac{1}{4}$
12	$\frac{3}{4}$	340	
16	1	450	
18		500	$\frac{1}{2}$
20	$1\frac{1}{4}$	560	
24	$1\frac{1}{2}$	675	
27		750	$\frac{3}{4}$
32	2	900	
36	$2\frac{1}{4}$	1000	1
40	$2\frac{1}{2}$	1100	
48	3	1350	
64	4	1800	
72	$4\frac{1}{2}$	2000	2
80	5	2250	$2\frac{1}{4}$
100	6	2800	$2\frac{3}{4}$

OVEN TEMPERATURE EQUIVALENTS

Fahrenheit	Celsius	Gas Mark	Description
225	110	$\frac{1}{4}$	Cool
250	130	$\frac{1}{2}$	
275	140	1	Very Slow
300	150	2	
325	170	3	Slow
350	180	4	Moderate
375	190	5	
400	200	6	Moderately Hot
425	220	7	Fairly Hot
450	230	8	Hot
475	240	9	Very Hot
500	250	10	Extremely Hot

EQUIVALENTS FOR INGREDIENTS

all-purpose flour—plain flour
baking sheet—oven tray
cheesecloth—muslin
coarse salt—kitchen salt
confectioners' sugar—icing sugar
cornstarch—cornflour
eggplant—aubergine

granulated sugar—caster sugar
half and half—12% fat milk
heavy cream—double cream
light cream—single cream
parchment paper—greaseproof paper
plastic wrap—cling film
scallion—spring onion

shortening—white fat
squash, zucchini—courgettes or marrow
unbleached flour—strong, white flour
vanilla bean—vanilla pod
zest—rind